# Business Administration for NVQ 1 a

## Book 2
## Level 2 Units 10-20

his book is to be returned on or be

Rachel Murphy, BA (Hons)
Christine Gentleman, MA

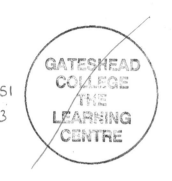

Withdrawn

Stanley Thornes (Publishers) Ltd

First published in 1993 by:
Stanley Thornes (Publishers) Ltd
Ellenborough House
Wellington Street
CHELTENHAM
GL50 1YD
England

£11.50

A catalogue record for this book is available from the British Library.
ISBN 0 7487 1512 6

Typeset by GCS, Leighton Buzzard, Beds.
Printed and bound in Great Britain by Hillman Printers (Frome), Ltd., Frome, Somerset

# Contents

# How to use this book

This book contains all the underpinning information and practical activities that you need to achieve Units 10–20 for an NVQ or SVQ in Business Administration at Level 2.

Each unit contains:

- the **underpinning knowledge**
- practical **tasks**
- **assessment activities** (one at the end of each).

If you work through the units and complete all the tasks, you will be ready to be assessed. Keep the work you prepare in your portfolio. It will provide evidence of achievement towards your NVQ. Once you feel ready to be assessed on a unit, you can tackle the **assessment activities.** Alternatively you can use some other assessment route and keep the **activities** in this book for practice. The tasks and activities in this book are based round a company called **Microplus Ltd** to give you a feeling for the organisation and activities of a real company.

You can use this book in the classroom or in the workplace on your own, and use the chapters in any order.

**Business Administration Book 1** contains all the material for Level 1 Units 1–9.

# Welcome to Microplus Ltd

Microplus was set up in 1979 by Alan Brown who established himself as a sole proprietor. Initially the company dealt with providing a stationery supplies service to local companies. Alan purchased premises in Bristol, employed two people – a typist and a clerk – and dealt in buying and selling all types of office goods including furniture and equipment.

By 1985 the business had flourished to such an extent that 20 people were now employed and Alan began to feel under pressure with the responsibility of running the organisation on his own.

After lengthy consultations with his bank manager, Alan decided to look for a partner to help with the day-to-day running of the business and who would bring more money into the company. He wanted someone with a specialist skill which the business needed. The person appointed was Roger Taylor, an accountant, who was capable of dealing with the increased volume of paperwork in the form of orders, bills, accounting records and so on.

By 1989 the business had grown to such proportions it was decided to convert it to a private limited company.

Alan became the Managing Director and Roger his Chief Accountant. In addition, there were six other directors, each responsible for a specific area of the business. One of these was Rachel Bywaters, the Company Secretary.

In early 1990, with the rapid evolution of new technology, the company decided to diversify and move into the highly competitive computer market. As well as the supply of hardware and software, the company expanded to meet the needs of customers and provided a training service, which proved to be a great success. In 1991 a Small Business Agency was introduced to provide a secretarial, information processing and photocopying service to members of the public. By this stage the office in Bristol was the head office and two new branches were opened in Newcastle and Manchester.

With the flotation of the shares on the Stock Market in 1991 a further four branches were opened, allowing the company to cover the whole of the UK in six regions (see map overleaf). The regions and office locations are as shown.

1 MIDLANDS — Nottingham office
2 NORTH EAST REGION — Newcastle office
3 SCOTTISH REGION — Glasgow office
4 SOUTHERN REGION — Bristol head office
5 WEST REGION — Manchester office
6 YORKSHIRE AND HUMBERSIDE REGION — Leeds office

The company has also opened offices in Spain, France and Germany to take advantage of the European Single Market initiative.

The administrative structure consists of eight departments and various sections within the departmental structure. For example, under the control of the accounts department is the payroll section. The company organisation chart shows the structure of Microplus Ltd.

The **Managing Director**, Alan Brown, has overall charge of the company procedures and personnel. He is accountable to the board of directors and shareholders of the company.

The Managing Director's Personal Assistant will filter any calls and requests and will represent him in his absence.

The **Company Secretary**, Rachel Bywaters, deals with insurance, passing information to shareholders, legal matters, office systems and personnel. She is in overall charge of the general office and oversees the work of some departments and sections.

The **Chief Accountant**, Roger Taylor, has control over anything to do with financial transactions, financial information for management and producing company accounts. He oversees the work of other departments and sections.

## Departments under the Company Secretary

| Department | Responsibilities |
|---|---|
| General office | Word processing, data processing and computer programming. Filing, typing, reprographics, reception and petty cash. |
| Mailroom (section) | Mail in and mail out, parcels, internal mail, special deliveries, recorded letters and registered post. |
| Switchboard (section) | Processing incoming and outgoing telephone calls. Receiving instructions from internal telephone callers. Making calls on behalf of employees of the company to other organisations. Taking calls from clients, customers and members of the public. Dealing with calls left on the ansaphone and passing messages on. |

# Microplus Ltd – organisation chart

MANAGING DIRECTOR
(PA to Managing Director)

## COMPANY SECRETARY
(PA to Company Secretary)

## CHIEF ACCOUNTANT
(PA to Chief Accountant)

### GENERAL OFFICE

- Office Manager
- Computing/WP Supervisor
- Typing Supervisor
- Mail Room Supervisor
- Cashier
- Customer Services Assistant
- Computing/WP Operators (4)
- Mail Room Assistant
- Receptionist
- Switchboard Operator
- Clerk/Typists (3)

### PERSONNEL & TRAINING

- Personnel Manager – PA
- Training and Recruitment Manager – PA
- Training Officer
- Personnel Clerk

### MAINTENANCE & SECURITY

- Maintenance Manager – PA
- Head of Security
- Security Guard
- Maintenance Labourer

### MARKETING

- Marketing Manager – PA
- Marketing Assistant

### TRANSPORT

- Transport Manager – PA
- Drivers (2)

### ACCOUNTS

- Accounts Manager
- Payroll Supervisor
- Payroll Operator
- Accounts Clerks (4)
- Payroll Clerk

### PURCHASING

- Purchasing Manager – PA
- Stock Supervisor
- Stock Clerks (3)
- Purchasing Clerks (2)

### SALES

- Sales Manager – PA
- Assitant Sales Manager
- Shop Manager
- Sales Clerk
- Shop Assistant

## Business Centre
Centre Manager
(PA to Centre Manager)

- DTP Manager
- Computer Programmer
- WP Operator
- Print Room Manager
- Consultants (Accounts, Computing, Business Start-up)

| | |
|---|---|
| Maintenance and security | Safety and security of premises, dealing with unauthorised visitors, maintaining the buildings and dealing with emergency procedures. |
| Marketing | Advertising, publicity, market research and public relations. |
| Personnel and training | Recruitment, training, staff welfare, resignations, dismissals, job grading, staff records, trade union negotiations, the transfer and promotion of employees and some social events. |
| Transport | Ensuring company vehicles are serviced, insured and taxed on time. Arranging repairs, etc. Organising deliveries and stores administration. Arranging for the transportation of goods throughout the UK and overseas. |

## Departments under the Chief Accountant

| Department | Responsibilities |
|---|---|
| Accounts | Invoicing, credit notes, debit notes, statements, financial records and management accounts. |
| Payroll (section) | Calculating and processing weekly pay and monthly salaries, Statutory Sick Pay, Maternity Pay, holiday pay, expenses claims, etc. Monthly returns and payments to Inspector of Taxes, BACS returns to the banks, cash handling for weekly pays. Issues Forms P45 and P60 and deals with various salary queries and form filling for government departments. |
| Purchasing | Locating suppliers, costing and placing orders. |
| Sales | Processing orders, sending quotations, pricing orders, allocating discounts and searching for new customers. |
| Stock room (section) | Receiving and recording stock coming in from suppliers or goods going out to customers. |

# UNIT 10
# Creating and maintaining business relationships

---

## Create and maintain professional relationships with other members of staff

---

Unit 8 of Book 1 dealt with maintaining working relationships. This unit takes the subject further and looks at the creation of those relationships and attitudes to work.

### Enjoying the work you do

Most people enjoy their work, find it stimulating and develop friendly relationships with colleagues. Work can provide job satisfaction – a feeling of self-worth.

At work, everyone employed by the organisation has common aims. You want your organisation to prosper and give you job security. You also aspire to be successful in your chosen career. Finally, work is one of the places where you can learn a lot about life in general.

#### Job satisfaction

People prefer to work in pleasant surroundings doing a job which gives satisfaction. How would you define job satisfaction? Could it be any (or all) of these?

● Having good bosses

● having friendly colleagues

● having interesting and responsible duties

● having security of employment

● earning a good salary.

1

Almost half of your life is spent at work so you should aim for employment which is not dull or tedious. Your job as a **whole** needs to be challenging and interesting, otherwise you will become bored and frustrated. There are various positions within an office environment and each of us have preferences about areas of work we **enjoy** doing. People who work as secretaries or in administration may not like working in accounts or finance and vice versa.

At college, school or work, as a trainee, you are given the chance to decide which area of office work suits **you**. When you have gained sufficient experience in various departments you will be able to assess which role you would prefer (if any) in an office.

Your choice at this stage is an important one – take time to consider it. Look at the comments below. They are made by two people, one who enjoys work and one who does not. Put them into two groups. Then decide if you would like to work with the person who is obviously unhappy at work.

## Looking for a job

**Task 1 ➤**     Look at the situations vacant columns in a national newspaper. Choose five jobs you would apply for if you were looking for work just now. Which of these benefits would entice you to apply? Place them in order of importance to you.

a)  Responsible and interesting work.

b)  Good prospects for promotion.

c) Status.

d) Further training provided.

e) Salary.

e) Security of employment.

f) Organisation has a reputation of caring for its employees.

k) The people who work there are very friendly.

### Preparing for interviews

Prepare yourself well for an interview by:

- Researching the organisation's background and the goods or services it provides. This shows you are interested in the organisation and displays initiative.

- Making notes on questions you would like to ask the interviewer(s). Try to remember them at the interview.

When you are being interviewed take these steps to **climb** the ladder to success:

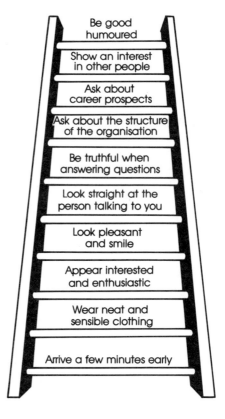

Be good humoured

Show an interest in other people

Ask about career prospects

Ask about the structure of the organisation

Be truthful when answering questions

Look straight at the person talking to you

Look pleasant and smile

Appear interested and enthusiastic

Wear neat and sensible clothing

Arrive a few minutes early

The ladder to success

**Task 2 ➤**

1 Choose a well-known organisation, such as British Airways, British Telecom, Amstrad or GEC, which interests you.

2 Write to the Customer Services Department and explain you are

**2** Write to the Customer Services Department and explain you are carrying out a project in the course of your studies.

**3** Ask if it will help you by sending as much literature as possible about the organisation, for example, what they produce, how many people they employ, and so on.

**4** When you receive the information read it through, taking notes as you go along.

**5** Write a brief report on the items you found interesting. Would you like to be employed by the organisation and if so why?

**6** If you were invited for an interview with your chosen organisation what sort of questions would you ask the interviewer(s)?

**7** Have a group discussion on the finished project and ask your tutor to look over your report.

**Note:** Some organisation details may be found in your library.

When you successfully find employment you need to try to repay the interviewer's confidence in selecting you. You may have been offered the job because of qualifications and experience but your personality would also have been a decisive factor. The interviewer must have believed that you would **fit in** with the existing personnel.

## Creating professional relationships

When you start a new job it can be a daunting experience – especially for someone who has not worked before. Don't worry! Every one of your new colleagues has been in the same situation – **and survived.**

Make sure you have a job description and that you **understand** it. A job description should tell you:

- What your **responsibilities** are.

- **Who** you are responsible to.

- What is **expected** of you.

- What your **position** in the team is.

In the modern office **teamwork is essential**. It is very much an 'all hands on deck' situation where employees pull together. Teams are made up of groups of staff of varying skills, grades and expertise. You will be expected to undertake all sorts of jobs from making the coffee to making decisions. Teamwork is demanding but rewarding; it is certainly not boring as no two days are the same.

You can learn to enjoy being part of a team by creating friendly relationships with other staff. How do you do this? Think of how you like to be treated – with **RESPECT:**

| R | **respond** to requests from colleagues |
|---|---|
| E | be **eager** to become involved in the organisation |
| S | **support** other colleagues |
| P | always be **polite** |
| E | **establish** a rapport with colleagues |
| C | **co-operate** with others |
| T | **think** before you speak. |

## Relationships with colleagues

New employees need to **create** pleasant relationships with people they come into contact with regularly. Good working relationships need to be established from the start. You may need help to learn the different aspects of the job. Take advice from other colleagues who may be able to give you useful tips.

How do you **maintain** good working relationships with others?

- Never **use** people

- be prepared to listen to criticism

- maintain a keen **INTEREST** in your organisation.

| I | show an **interest** in the job others do |
|---|---|
| N | **negotiate** with colleagues |
| T | **trust** the advice of more experienced colleagues |
| E | **expect** to have to change your routine at times |
| R | **realise** you will sometimes be criticised |
| E | be **eager** to learn new tasks |
| S | look for job **satisfaction** |
| T | always **try** your best. |

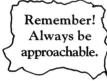

Remember! Always be approachable.

Try to offer assistance when it is needed. However, do not become the office doormat and always think you have to oblige. If you are really busy or if someone is trying to play on your good nature then refuse, but politely.

## Menial tasks

People employed in an office often have to carry out tasks that they find boring (or beneath them). Jobs like filing, opening the mail, photocopying, etc. are not very stimulating. However, they are an essential and important part of the office routine and have to be done.

**Never** leave these tasks to the junior members of staff. They need training in **all** aspects of office work. Always take your turn.

**Task 3 ➤**

In which of these situations would you offer to help? Say why. Discuss your answers with other members of your group.

Your head of department says:

a)  Can you make some coffee for my guests?

b)  Could you get me Mr Matthews on the phone?

c)  Will you find Smartcar's file?

d)  Could you stop what you are doing and type this for me? It's urgent.

e)  Will you take over reception for an hour to let Mandy away for lunch?

f)  Can you phone round the hotels and try to book a double room for Mr and Mrs Maxwell?

A sales representative in another department says:

g)  Do me a favour and pick up a bunch of flowers for my wife when you are out at lunch.

h)  Go to the post office at lunch time and find out if the parcel of books from Germany has arrived yet.

i)  On the way home from work pop these papers into the lawyer

j)  Make me a cup of coffee, I'm too busy to make it myself.

k)  Photocopy 12 copies of this booklet – I need them within the hour.

l)  Help me find a missing file – the MD is looking for it.

## Coping with problems at work

You may have to deal with awkward situations in the course of your work. Organisations now encourage positive communication and assist employees and supervisors to resolve any issues relating to employment. Obviously, the procedure to follow will depend upon how serious the problem is, whether it is a personal problem or one with a colleague.

Grievance procedures may follow these stages:

Stage 1    Raise the issue with your **immediate** supervisor who will record the problem and usually give advice on how to resolve it.

Stage 2    If you are unhappy with the reply from your supervisor you will need to supply written details of the complaint to your departmental manager. If the problem is still unresolved at this stage proceed to the next stage.

Stage 3    Refer to the General Manager or a member of the senior management team. The problem could then be discussed by an elected committee.

This kind of procedure is designed to help and encourage all employees to achieve and maintain good standards of conduct. The aim is to ensure consistent and fair treatment for all personnel. However, individual employees can do a lot to stop a tense situation getting out of control.

**TIPS ➤ ➤**

### Keeping control in situations

- If a colleague is acting strangely, for example, a person becomes moody when she/he is usually good natured, do not patronise but ask if there is anything you can do to help.

- If you are unsure of how to handle a situation do not be afraid to confide in your supervisor, but never tell tales as this will not gain you friends and could cause a great deal of friction.

- If you receive conflicting instructions from senior staff members ask your immediate supervisor for guidance.

- **Never** take on the role of **boss**. If there is a conflict of interests with a colleague speak to your supervisor.

- Avoid heated exchanges with other members of staff. If someone says something which upsets you, walk away and take time to calm down.

### Office gossip

Never become involved in office gossip – it strains relationships and has a nasty habit of backfiring. This is a summary of a report given by a student who was employed in a large office:

'I began working in the accounts department when I was 18. I enjoyed my work and had a nice boss and very friendly colleagues. Everybody mixed well and pulled together as a team, helping one another when necessary. However, after five years of doing the same job I applied for a transfer to the general office as Office Supervisor. I felt a move would be good for my career and it was promotion. I was delighted when I learned I had been successful in my application.

'My joy soon turned to despair. I never imagined there would be such a difference in atmosphere and working relations from one department to another. How wrong I was. There was so much gossiping and backbiting among staff members. I was appalled at the open display of **office politics**

> **Warning! Office gossip harms relationships and can damage your career.**

and the unwillingness of people to help others who were busy. The situation had got so out of hand that the office wasn't functioning properly. It was very inefficient and lacked co-ordination. Sadly, it seemed beyond repair. I felt totally out of control and handed in my resignation.'

As you will no doubt realise, office gossip not only causes friction, it is also **dangerous.** It can, and does, affect people's lives in a wider sense. The student who related this story was so shaken by her experience she thought of changing her whole career. If you do aim for a career in office work heed this warning.

**TIPS ➤ ➤**

### Avoiding office gossip/politics

- If a colleague tries to discuss another member of staff with you tell him/her politely, but firmly, that you are not interested and walk away. The message will soon be received that you do not condone such behaviour.

- If you hear others gossiping try to discourage them by pointing out that they could in turn be the subject of gossip – not something they will enjoy.

- Be on guard – some colleagues may try to trick you into divulging personal information about another member of staff.

- **Never** breach a confidence.

**Task 4 ➤**

Write down brief notes on how you would deal with each of these situations. When you have finished get together with other members in your group and discuss your solutions to the problems.

a) A new Personal Assistant has been appointed by the company to work for the Business Centre. The Manager there can be quite brusque at times but is really very nice. The new assistant does not always understand the instructions she is given by her boss. Instead of seeking clarification from the Manager she stumbles through the work relying on your advice. How could you improve this situation?

b) You are working as a word processor operator in the General Office. A new employee started a few months ago doing the same job. At first she was very friendly and accommodating. Recently she has become more noticeably withdrawn. She is coming in late in the morning and not pulling her weight with the workload. Today you have been pushed to the limit and she returns after a long lunch break of nearly two hours. When she comes back to the office you give her a piece of your mind in front of everyone. She rushes out of the office in tears and the supervisor asks you to go to her office. There you are told, in no uncertain terms, that your behaviour was outrageous. It is then explained to you that the girl's mother is terminally ill. You feel shocked and guilty at the way you spoke to her.

   i)    Was your supervisor wrong in not making other staff aware of the situation? If not, why?

ii)    Did you have any right to speak to another employee in this manner? What steps would you take in a similar situation?

iii)   What would you do to try to repair the relationship with your colleague?

iv)    How would you explain your behaviour to others? (Bear in mind that the employee probably wants her home situation kept confidential for now.)

c)  You are working in the personnel department. It is extremely busy today as Terence McManus and Theresa McPherson are both holding interview sessions. The Receptionist lets your office know when each candidate arrives for interview. Someone has to escort interviewees from reception to the waiting room. You have been running back and forth all day, without even a coffee break, and no other staff member has offered to take over. What will you do?

d)  The company has installed a payphone in the foyer to try to stop staff making personal calls from office phones. Memos have been displayed warning employees that the new telephone system provides a printout of all calls made from each extension. Personal calls can only be made from extension phones in cases of emergency. This is the second time you have witnessed one of the security guards using the Sales Manager's telephone for personal calls. You know he has a sister in Canada and from the conversation you overheard you think this is who he is ringing. What will you do?

## Know your organisation

To perform your own role efficiently and effectively you need to:

- develop an insight into how the organisation works
- establish an identity with your organisation
- know the products or services provided
- familiarise yourself with procedures
- get to know the people employed in different departments
- understand the work carried out by each department.

Study your internal telephone directory which will be similar to the one used in Microplus, shown overleaf.

**Task 5 ➤**    Using the internal directory shown overleaf decide who would deal with these situations:

a)  A customer with a complaint.

b)  A legal letter.

c)  A new business enquiry.

d)  An enquiry from HM Inspector of Taxes.

| Department | Position | Extension |
|---|---|---|
| **Accounts** | | |
| Black, David | Accounts Clerk | 316 |
| Black, Helen | Accounts Clerk | 317 |
| Burton, Michael | Accounts Clerk | 318 |
| McMillan, Jane | Accounts Manager | 314 |
| Taylor, Roger | Chief Accountant | 311 |
| Watson, James | Accounts Clerk | 315 |
| White, Roz | PA to Chief Accountant | 312 |
| **Business Centre** | | |
| Dunlop, Jim | Centre Manager | 400 |
| Freeman, Angela | PA to Manager | 401 |
| Indira Gopal | WP Operator | 403 |
| Gilmour, Tracy | Print Room Manager | 407 |
| Keenan, Carly | Computer Programmer | 402 |
| Little, Denise | Desk Top Publishing Manager | 406 |
| McColm, Peter | Accounts Consultant | 404 |
| Newall, Karine | Computing Consultant | 405 |
| Todd, Gavin | Business Start-Up Consultant | 408 |
| **Computing/word processing** | | |
| Bell, Pauline | WP Operator | 322 |
| Brown, Joyce | WP Operator | 321 |
| Fisher, James | WP Operator | 323 |
| Pearson, Lorraine | Computer/WP Operator | 320 |
| Wagstaff, Stephen | Computer Supervisor | 319 |
| **General office** | | |
| Anderson, Rita | Customer Services Assistant | 371 |
| Armour, John | Clerk/Typist | 328 |
| Cowlie, Gail | Receptionist | 326 |
| Grant, Gina | Typing Supervisor | 325 |
| McDonald, Joanne | Clerk/Typist | 327 |
| Thomas, Michelle | Office Manager | 324 |
| Welsh, Sarah | Cashier | 329 |
| Wilson, Jean | Clerk/Typist | 330 |
| **Legal** | | |
| Bywaters, Rachel | Company Secretary | 303 |
| Shearer, Karen | PA to Company Secretary | 304 |
| **Mailroom** | | |
| Kennedy, Robert | Mail Room Assistant | 359 |
| Wells, James | Mail Room Supervisor | 358 |
| **Maintenance and security** | | |
| Ingram, Paul | Security Guard | 334 |
| Jamieson, James | Head of Security | 331 |
| Robert, Keith | Maintenance Manager | 332 |
| Smith, James | Maintenance Labourer | 333 |

*continued*

| Department | Position | Extension |
|---|---|---|
| **Managing Director's suite** | | |
| Brown, Alan | Managing Director | 300 |
| Gibb, Fiona | PA to Managing Director | 301 |
| **Marketing department** | | |
| Allen, John | Marketing Manager | 335 |
| McKenzie, Peter | Marketing Assistant | 337 |
| Murphy, Margaret | PA to Manager | 336 |
| **Payroll** | | |
| Beretti, June | Payroll Clerk | 357 |
| Clark, Isobel | Payroll Supervisor | 355 |
| Reid, Annabel | Computerised Payroll Operator | 356 |
| **Personnel and training** | | |
| Barbour, Barry | Personnel Clerk | 310 |
| Gilmour, Carol | PA to Training/Recruitment Manager | 308 |
| McClune, Thomas | Training Officer | 309 |
| McManus, Terence | Personnel Manager | 305 |
| McPherson, Theresa | Training and Recruitment Manager | 306 |
| Santos, Linda | PA to Personnel Manager | 307 |
| **Purchasing** | | |
| Gibson, Maureen | Purchasing Clerk | 341 |
| Karson, Sean | Purchasing Clerk | 340 |
| Morrison, Catherine | PA to Purchasing Manager | 339 |
| Oliver, June | Purchasing Manager | 338 |
| **Sales** | | |
| Cameron, Marion | Shop Assistant | 372 |
| Goodwin, Dorothy | Sales Manager | 342 |
| Hendry, George | Assistant Sales Manager | 344 |
| Holden, Paul | Shop Manager | 343 |
| Kenny, Michael | Sales Clerk | 345 |
| Lowe, Richard | PA to Sales Manager | 346 |
| **Stock room** | | |
| Cook, Rose | Stock Supervisor | 347 |
| Cummings, Carol | Stock Clerk (Sales) | 349 |
| Dempsey, Jane | Stock Clerk (Purchasing) | 350 |
| Dott, Elizabeth | Stock Control Clerk | 348 |
| **Switchboard** | | |
| Cairns, Paula | Telephonist | 0 |
| **Transport** | | |
| Edmunds, Petra | PA to Transport Manager | 352 |
| Gauld, Peter | Transport Manager | 351 |
| Logan, David | Driver | 353 |
| Mackle, Hugh | Driver | 354 |

e)  A customer who needs brochures printed.

f)   Information received about new telephone systems.

g)  Copyright licences.

h)  Orders coming in from customers.

## Understanding your role

It is **up to you** to develop your role and make an effective contribution to the teamwork in the office. Office work consists mainly of clerical and secretarial activities relating to the handling of information. Information needs to be:

- processed efficiently to reach the **right person**

- be produced in an **appropriate form**

- provided at the  **correct time**.

Each member of staff is a link in a chain. If the chain is broken then production can grind to a halt. Make sure you know which link you are and aim to relate to others.

To be **effective** in your role try to develop these skills:

| Skill | What you need to do |
|---|---|
| • Communicate effectively with people | • Be brief and clear as well as discreet and tactful |
| • Anticipate people's needs | • Adopt a co-operative attitude |
| • Find out information when required | • Be flexible |
| • Produce accurate and presentable work | • Appear neat and tidy |
| • Organise your working day | • Establish  priorities |
| • Deal with temperamental people | • Develop a sense of humour and keep calm |
| • Handle telephone calls correctly | • Be pleasant to callers – internal and external |

## Organising your work to meet deadlines

To develop harmonious working relations you need to be able to plan and organise your work and see a job through to its completion on schedule. This instils confidence in others regarding your abilities.

Planning ahead is an essential part of any job. Some of the tasks you undertake in the course of your work will follow a set pattern, for example the daily opening of mail, weekly balancing of cash books or sending out monthly accounts. Other work will arrive irregularly on your desk. Try to spread your workload as evenly as possible.

**TIPS ➤ ➤**

**Organising your workload**

Try to identify:

- what needs to be completed by a **specific time**;

- what can be left aside to be dealt with at a **slack period**;

- what needs to be completed quickly to enable other staff members to carry out **related tasks**;

- what tasks have to be given your **uninterrupted** attention;

- what tasks can be set aside **temporarily** if an urgent job needs to be done **immediately**.

If others are dependent on you to complete work or provide information that they need to do their jobs then it is vital that you inform them **immediately** of any delays.

**Planning aids**

To plan ahead you need to be able to identify **what is to be done** and **by when**. If you do this your efforts will be co-ordinated effectively with others in the team. You may use planning aids to assist in recording information in an organised form. There are many planning aids such as the one shown here.

| Date: 12/2/9- | DAY PLAN |
|---|---|

| APPOINTMENTS | |
|---|---|
| 9.00 | 2.00 |
| 9.30 | 2.30 |
| 10.00 Mr Spencer | 3.00 |
| 10.30 | 3.30 |
| 11.00 | 4.00 Departmental meeting |
| 11.30 | 4.30 |
| 12.00 | 5.00 |
| 1.00 | EVENING In-house training |

**THINGS TO DO**
1. Open mail and distribute
2. Check boss's diary and tickler files
3. Supervise Angela taking messages from ansaphone
4. Prepare report for Mr Brown on health and safety
5. Write memo to departmental staff reminding them of meeting
6. Draw up list of interviewees for receptionist
7. Draw up health and safety check-list for new employees
8. Prepare notes and agenda for monthly shareholders' meeting

**NOTES**
Inform switchboard that Mr Brown should not be disturbed this afternoon as he is hosting the meeting of the Training Enterprise Council in the conference room.

**Task 6 ➤**    Think about your timetable at college or school. Do you have any assessments which have to be completed by a certain date? If you are already employed in an office could you list the tasks which need to be carried out each day?

Photocopy the day plan on page 255 for each day of the week and enter **your own details** in the order you would carry out tasks. Compare your finished plans with those of other students in your group.

### Tickler files

Your tutor may let you know in January of certain assignments which have to be completed by March or April. How would you remember the dates? Would you record them in a diary? This form of recording may be sufficient for your needs now. However, in a busy office prior information may be received at various times, long before tasks need attending to. A system has to be adopted which will ensure that work is completed at the appropriate time.

In an office, tickler files are used as **reminder systems** which help to ensure you **bring forward** items which need attention at the right time.

**Task 7 ➤**    Today is Monday 25 October. You work as a Personal Assistant to the Training and Recruitment Manager of Microplus. Theresa has just informed you that she is chairing the next local meeting of the Institute of Training and Development, scheduled for Thursday 9 December. Theresa needs the minutes of the last meeting in typescript form along with an agenda for the forthcoming meeting. In all, 35 copies have to be distributed to institute members by Monday 22 November.

What problems might you come across if these details were recorded in an ordinary diary? Discuss them with other members of your group.

If you use an ordinary card index as a **tickler** system you could divide the box into the 12 months of the year. At the end of each month **bring forward** any items which need attending to the following month. The months can also be divided into separate weeks within the system, allowing for easy transfer to a daily planner.

**Task 8 ➤**    1 Taking the situation in Task 7 as an example, insert a note of the relevant details in the November section of the tickler system.

2 At the end of October transfer details of November's work to the 'current' section.

3 On Monday 15 November transfer the details to the daily planner for the following week. (Use a copy of the day plan on page 256.)

This procedure will help to ensure that each member receives a copy of the minutes and agenda on time.

### Electronic diary

Many computer packages offer diary facilities which incorporate reminder functions. Each day, when you log on, you will be prompted on screen with **things to do today**. If your computer has this facility, **use it** – it is quick, efficient and can save a lot of wasted energy.

### Desk diary

As a double-check and in case there are problems with the other reminder systems, for example, computer failure, brief details of tasks which have to be carried out some time in the future should always be recorded in a desk diary.

**Task 9 ➤**

Today is Monday 5 April 1993. Below are listed jobs which have to be carried out over a two-month period from April to May. Produce your own tickler system for dealing with them and draw up daily planners for the third week in May.
(For the purpose of this task we will assume that the year is 1993.)

**Routine tasks which are carried out every working day:**

**8.50**  Open mail, sort and distribute.

**9.15**  Check diary and tickler system.

**9.30**  Fill in day planner with 'things to do today'.

**9.45**  Check stationery stock.

**15.00**  Ask boss to sign today's correspondence.

**15.30**  Take outgoing mail to mailroom.

**16.00**  Check diary for following day, taking note of things to do for tomorrow, and sort tickler system.

**Things to do in April:**

12th    Provide Receptionist with a list of interviewees who will be attending on the 14th.

16th    Circulate minutes of meeting and agenda to shareholders.

23rd    Prepare a memo and circulate to staff of Personnel Department reminding them of departmental monthly meeting being held in conference room 1 on 28th.

30th    Road tax due for renewal on van registration number G426 NJS.

**Things to do in May:**

10th    Check with caterers the arrangements for luncheon in conference room 3 on Friday this week. Regional managers' monthly meeting is scheduled for then and 15 will be attending.

18th    Issue all employees with new literature on health and safety at work.

20th    Renew subscription to *Business Education* journal.

21st    Give Mr Brown final draft of employee holiday rota.

Planning your work will lead to conducive working relationships. If other colleagues note that you are systematic in your approach and well-organised then you will be regarded as a professional. This can only help in the maintenance of a harmonious working environment and lead to greater job satisfaction and prospects.

## Standards of appearance

Employers are not the only ones who expect their employees to take care with their appearance. Staff themselves look unfavourably on colleagues who appear scruffy, untidy or dress in outrageous or unsuitable fashion.

When you are employed in the business world appearances **do matter**. If you like to dress casually try to keep that style for leisure time.

Although many employers are quite modern in their approach to dress and appearance there are still conventions which are obeyed.

**TIPS ➤ ➤**

Remember!
You are a representative not only for your organisation but also for the other people you work with.

**Looking good**

- Always look bright and cheerful as a person and in your general appearance.

- Wear appropriate items of clothing to **fit in** with the job you do.

- Women should avoid wearing trousers in those organisations which frown on this practice. If you have to wear trousers (and your organisation allows this), avoid jeans.

- Follow your organisation's code on dress and appearance.

- Men look more effective in a shirt and tie, with suit or smart trousers, although some modern offices do allow casual dress wear (again no jeans).

- Make sure that your hair is clean, neat and styled.

- Check that your nails are kept clean and well-shaped.

- Check your clothes are clean and fresh looking – if any item looks creased then iron it.

- Wear clean underwear and hosiery every day.

- Check your footwear and make sure shoes are polished – do not wear them until they are falling apart.

- Women can use light make-up but do not overdo this – none at all is better than too much.

## Appraisal procedures

Job appraisal systems are quite common in business. These involve discussions between individual members of staff and their managers on their individual performances. Appraisals may be carried out monthly, quarterly or annually.

What is recorded, assessed in an appraisal and discussed with you? Generally, records are kept of:

- progress – your job performance since the previous appraisal; new skills you have learned; improvements made; any decline in your efficiency or work quality.

- personality – changes observed in your character or manner; how you cope under pressure; your telephone manner; your general attitude.

- relations – relationships with colleagues and clients; your work as part of a team; any friction between you and others.

- attendance – recurring absences or prolonged leave, especially those which are unexplained; reasons for any personality or attitude change.

- time-keeping – reasons for bad time-keeping; how time-keeping could be improved to take account of travel arrangements; alternatives (for example, flexitime) which may suit your personal circumstances better.

Appraisals are helpful, not only to management but also to the individual employee. You get the opportunity to clarify your position within the organisation and ask questions on any aspects of the job of which you are unsure. Appraisals also help you to judge whether you have a good future with the organisation.

> Remember!
> **Objective criticisms may also come out of appraisals. Do not get upset if your mistakes are pointed out to you - learn by these and you will become more efficient.**

## Health and Safety at Work Act 1974

The aim of this Act is to prevent accidents in the workplace. The main responsibilities of the **employer** and the **employee** are as shown in the table overleaf.

An additional six regulations were introduced through the European Commission in 1993. These place further responsibilities on employers. Not all regulations are new, many clarify or make more explicit what is current law.

All employers must now:

- assess the health and safety risk of their work activities regarding staff and anyone else who may be affected in the work environment;

- make arrangements for putting into practice any preventative and protective measures which follow the assessment;

- carry out health surveillance of all employees where appropriate;
- appoint competent staff to devise and apply any protective steps shown to be necessary;
- set up emergency procedures;
- give employees information about health and safety matters;
- co-operate with other employers who may share the workplace;
- make sure that employees have adequate health and safety training and are capable of doing their jobs without risk;
- supply temporary workers with adequate health and safety information which meets their needs.

| Employer | Employee |
|---|---|
| Provide and maintain plant and systems of work without risk to health – including a safe and healthy working environment | Take reasonable care for own health and safety, and other people who may be affected by her/his acts or omissions at work |
| Arrange for ensuring, so far as is reasonably practicable, safety and absence of risks to health in connection with use, handling, storage and transport of materials | Co-operate with employer so far as is necessary to perform any duty under the Act |
| Provide information, instruction, training and supervision necessary to ensure the health and safety of employees at work | Not intentionally or recklessly interfere with or misuse any equipment, safety device, etc., provided to keep up with the Act's requirements |
| Ensure that entry and exit from the workplace is safe and without risk | |
| Notify employees, by a written statement, of the general policy with respect to health and safety and arrangements for carrying out that policy | |

## Assessment activity 10.1

> Remember! Keep your work from this activity for reference and assessment.

Describe how you would deal with these situations. Discuss your answers with other group members.

a) An advert is being run for a temporary Personal Assistant (to cover maternity leave). You have been asked to draw up a brief note detailing the personal qualities the person appointed will need to possess. List these qualities in the order of importance.

b) Your boss is always finding fault with the work of the new junior who started last month. The junior tries his best and you have found him quite able to carry out tasks efficiently. It seems as if your boss has taken an instant dislike to the juinior. As a result he has become very nervous. Every time your boss comes into the office the junior panics and goes to pieces. What would you do to try to improve the situation?

c) A new trainee has just started work in the marketing department. You have been asked to show her the ropes for the first week. She is progressing well and is coping with any tasks you give her. On the Thursday of the first week you find her in tears. When you ask what is wrong she tells you that some colleagues in the office are continually making fun of her in your absence. They think she is trying to show them up by being so efficient and are taking her shyness as a sign of being superior. How would you deal with this situation while ensuring your intervention will not be seen as a sign of favouritism? What tips would you give the trainee on developing relations with her new colleques? Would you ask anyone else to intervene? If so, who and why?

d) You have recently started work in the general office as a clerk/typist. Jean Wilson is the most senior clerk/typist and has been with the company for years. She seems a pleasant enough person to the other members of staff but you think she dislikes you. When you were interviewed for the job you wore sensible clothing and your hair was neat and tidy. However, you feel more comfortable in your casual clothing (which could be termed as a bit way-out) and you have had your hair spiked. You think this is at the root of the problem. How could you resolve it? Would you compromise about your dress code? If not, why not?

# Create and maintain professional relationships with customers and clients

## Customer care

To create a pleasant atmosphere for clients of your organisation make them feel **WELCOME**:

- **W** **Wish** customers/clients a 'good morning/afternoon'
- **E** **Enquire** about their needs
- **L** **Listen** attentively
- **C** **Communicate** effectively
- **O** **Offer** assistance
- **M** **Make** polite conversation
- **E** **Enjoy** meeting people

Always try to make clients feel relaxed. Give a high quality of service by being warm, friendly and enthusiastic. Think about how you like to be treated when you visit a strange organisation. Put yourself in the client's shoes and you will find that it is much easier to be courteous and helpful.

Many clients will be regular visitors – try to use the personal touch with these people and address them by name.

## TIPS ➤ ➤    Customer/client care

| Always | Never |
|---|---|
| Welcome clients warmly – if possible stop what you are doing to greet someone | Show indifference to clients |
| Address the client by name (if you know it) | Say 'take a seat and I'll be with you in a minute' |
| Treat every client as an individual | Forget the waiting visitor |
| Treat every client with courtesy at all times | Argue with a client or be disrespectful |
| Be professional and keep your voice calm and unhurried | Be rude or impatient or become flustered |
| Look at people when talking to them. Give them your complete attention | Carry on writing things down while speaking to a client or keep your head bowed |
| Keep clients informed at all times about any delay in meeting their requirements | Assume that the client has been received by his/her host. |

## Task 10 ➤

1 Look at this conversation between a client and member of staff. Get together with two others in your group and try to role-play the situation **exactly as it is written here**. Have someone time the exercise.

```
Client:     Excuse me – can you help?
Employee:   What with?
Client:     I would like to speak to Jane McMillan from
            the accounts department please.
Employee:   What about?
Client:     It's a personal matter.
Employee:   Oh! Have a seat and I'll see if she's about.
Jane:       Jane McMillan, accounts department.
Employee:   There's someone in reception asking for you.
Jane:       Who?
Employee:   I don't know, wait and I'll ask.
Employee:   (Shouts across the room to the client)
            'What's your name?'
```

```
Client:        Barry Ascot from Generic Software.
Employee:      Barry Ascot.
Jane:          What company is he with?
Employee:      Something software or another.
Jane:          It's Generic Software. Have Barry brought
               to my office by the Receptionist. When
               Barry leaves come to my office straight
               away - I need to speak to you!
Employee:      Wait a minute.
Receptionist:  Good morning Barry - would you like to come
               this way and I will show you through to
               Jane's office.
Client:        Morning Gail, thank you.
Employee:      Bye.
```

**2** What has gone wrong in this situation? What is your opinion of the employee?

**3** Now carry out another role-play. This time act the situation exactly as you would handle it in real life. Use your own initiative to play the parts in the correct manner. Again have the exercise timed.

**4** Which role-play lasted longer?

**5** Which did you prefer?

**6** Why do you think Jane wanted to speak to the employee?

## Identifying with your organisation

> **Remember!**
> Your next
> visitor may
> be a new
> customer/
> client.

Knowing what is happening in your organisation helps you to:

● give people the kind of assistance they appreciate;

● get more satisfaction from your job.

Alway keep an internal telephone directory next to you – it can be the most useful source of information.

## Developing skills to create professional working relationships with customers/clients

Members of staff provide vital links between an organisation and its various contacts. You may be an excellent typist but you will never be a successful secretary or PA unless you develop good working relations with clients.

**TIPS ➤ ➤**    **Maintaining customer/client relationships**

■ Make clients feel **special**.

■ **Listen** to people when they are talking to you.

- Develop a technique of asking **open-ended questions** which cannot be answered by a simple yes or no, for example 'How long have you been in business for yourself Mr.....?' This will allow a conversation to begin.

- **Never discuss** a client's business with anyone else – even other members of staff (except on a professional basis). Respect confidentiality.

- Always make **eye contact** with people you are talking to.

- **Smile** now and again (but do not display a permanent grin) during the conversation. Clients will find it difficult not to smile back.

**Task 11 ➤**    How would you deal with these customers?

a)   An angry customer with a complaint which you think is petty.

b)   A customer who has left her briefcase in the reception area. When she remembers it she goes back and finds it has disappeared. It has not been handed in to customer services.

c)   A female customer who complains about the state of the WC. She threatens to report the organisation to the Environmental Health Officer.

d)   A male customer, who appears to have had a bit too much to drink. He is becoming rather loud and offensive towards other customers.

e)   A customer who has fallen on the stairs. You think his leg may be broken.

f)   A client who has an appointment with a colleague. The colleague has been held up at another appointment and telephones to let you know. She asks you to convey her apologies and arrange another meeting. The client is not happy and threatens to take her business elsewhere.

## Customer enquiries

Employers prefer staff who have the technical skills, qualities and attitude to deal with customers and clients. These attributes can only come with experience but all employees should make every effort to develop them. Try to cultivate these qualities and attitudes:

| Qualities | Attitudes |
| --- | --- |
| Efficiency | Enthusiastic |
| Flexibility | Tactful |
| Well-organised | Diplomatic |
| Good memory retention | Loyalty to company and clients |
| Uses own initiative | Employs good human relations |
| Willing to undertake new tasks | Has a sense of humour |

**Task 12**  ➤    Picture this scenario:

Write down every point you consider to be wrong in the situation. Consider how this predicament has arisen? Do you think that the person leaving the desk is a **lost sale**? Why?

## The benefits of staff training

The 1990s have witnessed an upsurge in the number of employers who have discovered the benefits of staff training. If employees are provided with training in customer services and company product ranges they will be **better equipped to deal with every aspect of their jobs**. Clients will be happier with the quality of services and staff members feel qualified in their roles.

You must be able to deal with oral and written enquiries and to provide correct, up-to-date information by telephone or in writing.

Refer to Units 2 and 8 of Book 1 and review your skills in these areas.

**Task 13**  ➤    What further training would you like to receive at school, college or work? Summarise the benefits of this training a) to yourself and b) to your employer/future employer. Put the main points in writing.

## Dealing with telephone enquiries

Prospective customers telephone various companies to find the one which offers:

- **quality** at an affordable price
- **fast and efficient** service
- **staff** who can give accurate details and prices as quickly as possible.

If you receive a telephone enquiry and cannot provide the information immediately **do not make a guess**. Ask for the caller's telephone number and say you will ring back shortly with details.

As soon as you put the telephone down find the requested information. People find it infuriating when they are told that someone will call them back in a few minutes – then do not. If there is a delay in gaining access to the information, ring the caller back and explain the situation.

Explaining the situation

**Never** leave finding any requested information until later as the prospective customer will probably, by that time, have found another company which will gladly and promptly provide the goods or service required.

Few of us talk to friends and business associates about the excellent service we receive from organisations. However, if an organisation is inefficient and found to be lacking in customer relations, the news will spread like wildfire.

**TIPS ➤ ➤** **Keeping well-informed**

| Always | Never |
|---|---|
| Keep a folder on your desk which contains details of goods and services provided | Assume that goods or services which are not listed cannot be provided |
| Keep up-to-date with new products or services | Tell a customer/client that you do not know if your organisation provides an item or service |
| Ask a colleague for advice when in doubt | Guess the answer to a client's question |
| Inform your boss of any item or service which you are asked for often (but which you definitely do not provide) | Order an item from a supplier without the prior consent of an authorised member of staff |

| **Always** | **Never** |
|---|---|
| Discard old catalogues and price lists as soon as you receive updates | Quote details from the first catalogue you find lying around – always check it is the most recent |
| Keep leaflets of special offers and new products in a plastic wallet inside your folder for easy access | Put current leaflets and advertising material away in a drawer – you may have trouble finding them again |

**Task 14 ➤**  Use this task as a role-play exercise. One person in the group is working at customer enquiries and the others are customers. Photocopy the Business Centre Services and Price Guide on pages 37–43 for this. (File this in your folder after use – you will need it again for later tasks.)

**Customer 1**
You are Vincent Welsh from Caterplus. You are telephoning Microplus enquiring if the company can print 200 business cards for you. You want to know what styles are offered and how much it will cost.

**Customer 2**
You are Jean Symons. You are thinking of starting a new business – working from home providing knitted garments for sale. You wish to enquire about a consultation with the Small Business Advisor. When can you have an initial talk? You would like it arranged as soon as possible.

**Customer 3**
You are Amy White from Smartsec Recruitment. You telephone Microplus to have a repeat of the order you received last month of 200 letterheads. You need them as soon as possible as you are down to your last ream.

**Customer 4**
You are Stephanie Dunsmore of Bolan Opticians. Mr Bolan wants some posters printed offering free eye tests. What sizes are available and what are the costs? He also needs some leaflets produced to be sent out to employers informing them of recent EC regulations concerning VDU operators.

## Dealing with difficult customers

Now and again you will come across a dissatisfied client. Some complaints will be genuine, while others come from people who will complain no matter how hard you try to please them.

Try to pacify discontented clients. You need to use effective questioning techniques or interviewing skills to find the root of the problem.

**TIPS ➤ ➤**     ## Dealing effectively with difficult customers

- Remember the old saying – the customer is always right!
- Try your utmost to please.
- Ask the date of the purchase or service.
- Ask the full nature of the complaint.
- Assure the customer that any faulty goods will be replaced. (The Trade Descriptions Act states that all goods must be worthy of the purpose for which they are sold.)
- Keep calm when dealing with an abusive caller. Let her/him talk out the problem and then offer solutions.
- Remain pleasant and never try to outwit a complainant.
- Even if the customer is at fault – never suggest this. Be diplomatic and offer sensible solutions.

## Meeting clients' needs

You may be asked for items or services which your organisation can provide but are not listed. In this case you should use your initiative. Unusual requests can nearly always be accommodated.

Do you think the situation portrayed in the picture could really arise? The shopkeeper will usually open the box and sell you one.

This is only one example of meeting the needs of the customer. Most organisations have a policy of providing goods and services in the quantities customers may require and at prices they can afford.

# Privacy to conduct business

Some enquiries from customers and clients need to be dealt with in private. These can be from people needing advice on:

**Personal matters** If, for example, you are working in a solicitor's office you could be dealing with clients who are having marital difficulties, trouble with the law or court proceedings.

**Finance** Banks, building societies and financial institutions deal with mortgages, personal loans, hire purchase, etc. Some people may have difficulties in meeting their payments; others may wish to invest more money. Accountants will have clients who are faced with difficulties regarding taxation or whose businesses are experiencing difficulties.

**Medical conditions** Medical records are highly confidential and conversations regarding health problems are best dealt with on a one-to-one basis.

All the above situations require discretion.

If you sell goods or provide services you will have personal callers, who for one reason or another, do not wish to conduct their business in an open office. Every client must be offered privacy in business matters. Many organisations now provide access to interview rooms where clients can carry out their negotiations in privacy. Smaller organisation should have an office which can be vacated if the need arises.

**Task 15 ➤** Form a group and discuss which of these consultations you think should be carried out in private. Give reasons for your answers.

a) A businessman's consultation with his accountant.

b) A travel agent discussing a Caribbean cruise with a young couple planning their honeymoon.

c) An insurance agent's conversation with a client whose claim for compensation for burglary has been declined due to her home being insecure.

d) A college principal's discussion with a student about the reasons for the decline in the quality of his work.

e) An employer's discussion with a member of staff over her relationship with one of the personal assistants.

f) A financial representative's consultation with a client regarding remortgaging a property.

# Using effective questioning techniques

Customers and clients may come to you for advice about a product or service. You will need to use effective questioning techniques to explore every aspect of the client's requirements. How do you do this?

**TIPS ➤ ➤**       **Effective questioning and interviewing skills**

- Try to make the client comfortable by extending a warm greeting.

- Ask the client to take a seat.

- Ask the client to explain the nature of her/his business with you.

- Enquire as to what areas you may be able to help with.

- Ask what price range the client can comfortably afford (if purchasing goods or services).

- If you think the client is in the process of making the wrong decision offer alternatives and try to put across your ideas in a constructive and positive way.

- Do not tell a client that you know better – offer your advice and give some different options if possible.

- Leave the final decision to the client.

- Ask the client how and when payment will be made – there may be special discounts or offers available.

- Ensure the client of complete confidentiality.

**Task 16 ➤**       Carry out this role-play exercise which deals with personal enquiries. (You will need to consult your copy of the Business Centre Services and Price Guide for this task.)

**Customer 1** You are Petra Bonfanti. You have recently opened a boutique in town and need some advice on book-keeping, etc. An appointment has been arranged for you with Karine Newall, the Computing Consultant of Microplus. You have arrived 20 minutes early for the interview as you are extremely nervous. Ask the person meeting you for some information on the various services which the Business Centre provides.

**Customer 2** You are Edward Devine of Premier Wines. You have a promotion of Australian wines lined up for next month. In conjunction with a major supplier you are running a competition for customers with the prize of a free four-week holiday to anywhere in Australia plus £500 cash. This is an important promotion and you need to advertise it well. You wish to speak to someone who can advise you about leaflets and posters; these have to be effective but relatively cheap.

**Customer 3** You are Joan Pasanda, Chairwoman of the local community council. You are organising a fund-raising dance for the last Friday of next month. Expectations on numbers attending are high but you do not want to throw money away by having more tickets printed than necessary. Ask if it is possible to have 100 printed now and maybe another 50 or so produced quickly next week, if necessary.

# Consumer rights

Customers and clients who buy goods or services are protected in law. This is a safeguard against faulty or unreliable provision. When dealing with members of the public, employees need to be aware of the relevant laws which apply to their business. Consumer confidence is enforced by these Acts of Parliament:

> The Trade Descriptions Act 1968
> The Consumer Credit Act 1974
> The Unfair Contract Terms Act 1977
> The Sale of Goods Act 1979
> The Supply of Goods and Services Act 1982
> The Financial Services Act 1986
> The Consumer Protection Act 1987.

### The Trade Descriptions Act 1968

This Act was introduced to protect the consumer from suppliers who give false descriptions of goods or services. The Act is breached if a supplier:

- gives a false impression of the goods or services;

- sells goods or services which are wrongly described by the manufacturer;

- falsifies descriptions of quantity, size or content.

### The Consumer Credit Act 1974

This Act controls the practices of supplying goods or services on credit. People buying goods or services using extended payment terms must be given a **written contract** which clearly states:

- the cash price, deposit paid and total credit price;

- the names and addresses of supplier and purchaser;

- the total amount payable under the agreement;

- the APR (Annual Percentage Rate);

- the repayment terms;

- action which will be taken in the event of default of payment;

- the rights of consumer and supplier.

Consumers who enter into a credit agreement have the right to change their minds and cancel agreements unless they have signed the agreement at the supplier's business address.

The consumer usually has a few weeks after the initial agreement (called the cooling off period) in which to cancel it. Cancellation must be in writing direct to the supplier.

### The Unfair Contract Terms Act 1977

This Act aims to outlaw the display of **disclaimer notices** which are used by organisations who try to shun their responsibilities. For example, if you attend a nightclub or a disco and leave your jacket in the cloakroom you normally pay for this service and are supplied with a ticket. This you produce for the return of your property. There is often a notice displayed at the cloakroom which says 'The organisation cannot be held responsible for the loss or damage of any property left with the attendant'. If the attendant has mistakenly given your jacket to someone else the organisation will, however, have to compensate you for the loss unless the terms of the disclaimer can be proven to be **fair and reasonable**. A notice cannot be used to avoid paying compensation.

Disclaimer notices may be placed in full view of customers but the majority of them count for nothing.

### The Sale of Goods Act 1979

This Act basically states that **goods sold must be fit for the purpose for which they are bought**. All goods must:

- be as described and in working order;

- carry out the task for which they are intended.

If the goods fail:

- the buyer is entitled to a **full refund**;

- the buyer may accept a replacement or repair if she/he wishes to do so – this is not necessary so do not be coerced;

- the buyer need not accept a **credit note**.

The buyer is **not** entitled to a refund or credit note if:

- an article does not fit

- she/he causes damage to the item

- she/he no longer likes the article or item

- she/he had the fault pointed out at time of purchase

- she/he should have noticed the fault before buying

- she/he was not the original purchaser of the item.

### The Supply of Goods and Services Act 1982

**Part 1** of the Act deals with the supply of goods and updates the Sale of Goods Act 1979 to take the following into account:

- goods supplied as part of a service

- part-exchange items

- goods or items on hire.

These must also be as described and **fit for the purpose intended**.

**Part 2** deals with standards of services provided by:

- garages

- construction trades

- service companies, and

- hairdressers amongst others.

This part attempts to protect consumers against delays in repairs or construction, services, overcharging and unsatisfactory work.

### The Financial Services Act 1986

This Act is for the protection of investors whether they are investing in stocks and shares, buying insurance or pension benefits. The SIB (Securities and Investments Board) oversees the work of five Self-Regulatory Organisations (SROs) which authorise investment institutions to carry out business. Investors who lose money entrusted to an authorised financial institution will be compensated by the SIB scheme.

### The Consumer Protection Act 1987

This Act assists the consumer further by making it an offence for a supplier to:

- give misleading information on prices, for example, goods marked as being on **sale** at reduced prices must have previously been sold at a higher price;

- offer goods for sale which are not reasonably safe.

# Public liability

Owners of properties used by members of the public have to ensure their premises and fittings are safe and secure. They need to take out insurance to cover themselves against claims for compensation if customers or clients suffer injury:

- through negligence of an employee of the organisation;

- in unsafe premises they own or control;

- by unsecured fittings;

- by the use of faulty products;

- through faulty work or professional negligence.

**Task 17 ➤**    Which consumer protection act is being breached when:

a) A customer purchased goods or services which were wrongly described by the manufacturer.

b) Workmen installing double glazing in a customer's home have not carried out the work properly.

c) A customer who has signed a credit agreement at home and subsequently cancelled the contract in writing two days later does not have the cancellation accepted by the supplier who pressurises the customer to remain tied to the contract.

d) A client leaves his briefcase in the care of the Receptionist at a hotel he is visiting for lunch. When he returns to collect his case it cannot be found. The manager points to a notice which states that any items left in the reception area are left at the **owner's risk**.

e) A customer has bought a car on credit terms. She signs the paperwork to enter the contract. A few weeks later she receives a copy of a new agreement for her signature. The accompanying letter states that she was undercharged on the initial sale.

f) An accountant offers to carry out work for a small business. He is charging excessive prices for everyday services such as sending letters to the Inland Revenue, etc.

g) A young man is admitted to hospital with serious burns after working with a hired power tool which was faulty.

h) A customer purchased a dining room suite in the sale. The salesman assured her she was 'getting a real bargain' as the same item would have cost her £200 more the previous week. A friend calls round to visit the next day. She informs the customer that the dining room suite is identical to that purchased by her brother and his wife a few weeks ago at the same shop. They paid £50 less than the so-called **sale** price.

# Assessment activity 10.2

**Remember! Keep your work from this activity for reference and assessment.**

Use your copy of the Business Centre Services and Price Guide for this activity. It will deal with personal, telephone and written enquiries from customers and clients. Role-play the personal and telephone enquiry situations, draft replies to written enquiries and write a report on any serious complaints for your supervisor.

**Written enquiry 1**
From Mr Brian Gardener of Executive Estates, 212 High Street, (your town):

> I have recently started up in business in this area and urgently require some printing. Could you please supply me with a quotation for the following:
>
> 500 A5 leaflets
> 100 laminated lightweight two-coloured business cards
> 400 letterheads on top-quality paper.
>
> I would be grateful if you would also send me a current catalogue of your services along with details of discounts allowed.

**Telephone caller 1**
'Hello, this is Emma Porteous of Signwrite. Our secretary is absent from work and we have some urgent letters which have to be sent out today. If I send the office junior in with an audio cassette could you manage to have the letters ready for the last post? There are five one-page letters of medium length. What will it cost?'

**Personal caller 1**

'Hi! I'm Ian Brown from the Language School. Could you photocopy this 12 page correspondence course and have it bound? Black and white copying will be sufficient. When will it be ready?'

**Personal caller 2 (with a complaint)**

'I am Aileen Freeman from Freeman-Smith Solicitors in the town. I called into Microplus's office last Monday and placed an order for a new ansaphone machine with George Hendry. George promised that he would have the machine delivered to my premises on Saturday morning. My business normally closes on Saturdays, therefore, I made a special visit to the office for 10 a.m. (when I was told to expect delivery). I waited for over two hours. During this time I telephoned George's office five times – only to be told he was not there. I had the distinct feeling that he was there and was avoiding having to speak to me. This is now Wednesday – I have had no apology, not even a phone call. I have left a message for George every day – he never replies. I wish to close my account with your organisation as I believe I can receive a better service elsewhere.'

(You are really angry and won't be fobbed off – be as realistic as possible.)

**Telephone caller 2**

'Hello, this is Carl Whitaker from Wilmslow Communications. Could I speak to the person who deals with publicity for your organisation. I would like to know if your company would be willing to buy advertising space in the programme of a charity fun day. The proceeds from the fun day are to be sent to charities for relief in Somalia.'

**Written enquiry 2**

From the headmaster at the local Senior Secondary School:

```
I wish to enquire if it would be possible for a group
of 10 of my students to visit your premises as part of
a work-experience project.

The ten students are interested in forming careers in
the business world. I think that a visit to your
company would provide a valuable insight into the
workings of the modern office.

If you can accommodate us I will be quite happy to
leave the dates and times open to your choice.
```

**Telephone caller 3**

'Claire Baldwin calling from Prudential Insurance. I have to send a quotation to your Company Secretary and I have mislaid the details of her name. How do you spell the second name please?'

**Personal caller 3**

'Hello, I'm Wayne Byres, a friend of Tracy Gilmour's. I want to make a

surprise visit to Tracy this evening but I can't seem to find her address. We were at university together and I have not met up with her for four years so we have a lot to catch up on. I don't wish to disturb her at work, and as I said I want to surprise her tonight. Could you give me a note of her address please.'
(Persist with asking for this and don't take no for an answer – soft soap the person at the enquiry desk as much as possible.)

### Telephone caller 4
'Hello, Suzy from Executive Travel here. I would like to confirm Mr Brown's travel arrangements for his trip to Lisbon next week. Who should I speak to?'

### Personal caller 4
'I need to speak to your Purchasing Manager right away! I have been trying to arrange an appointment with her for three weeks now and I think she is avoiding me. Well I am not taking no for an answer this time. I will sit here until she agrees to see me. I am Rhys Williams from 21st Century Software.'

# UNIT 11 Providing information to customers/clients

---

## Respond to customer/clients specific requests for information on products/services offered by the organisation

---

### Customer enquiries

People may contact your organisation for a variety of reasons:

- to ask for information on goods or services;
- to place an order;
- to ask about the processing of an order;
- to complain about faults or bad service;
- to query invoices, statements or accounts.

> ### Remember!
> The tips given in the previous unit for enhancing customer relations. When dealing with customers and clients always make them feel welcome.

### Customer relations

Customer relations are built upon the service provided to people. If you offer a warm, friendly, efficient and helpful service the majority of customers will come back again. You cannot hope to learn how to handle customer enquiries or deal with difficult customers until you are actually faced with each type of situation. No amount of theory can replace actual **contact time** with customers.

**Be prepared!**

From your folder take out, and keep to hand, the Microplus organisation chart, telephone directory and **Business Centre Services and Price Guide** (given on pages 37–43).

Before you can answer enquiries and deal with customers and clients you need to know:

- who deals with what in your organisation;

- details of the products and services supplied, for example:
  - if you sell goods you need to familiarise yourself with the items you stock, their uses, the range available and those which must be ordered direct from a supplier;
  - if your organisation provides a service, such as estate agency, insurance, financial or legal, you need to know the full range of services provided;
  - if your organisation manufactures items for supply to a trade you need a good knowledge of the products and their functions;

- who to contact when further information is required;

- the legal requirements concerning the sale of goods or provision of services;

- your own organisation's procedures.

**Task 1 ➤**

1 A new employee is starting work with your organisation on Monday. You are asked to write down some brief guidelines which will help her to cope with customer relations. What do you think are the most important points to be considered and why? Write or produce in text form the guidelines you would issue.

2 Form a group and discuss your individual guidelines then, working as a group, produce a final copy.

3 Are there any other tips you would give to a new employee about customer care? If so, what are they? (Think about your own experiences as a customer.)

This unit is a **practical** rather than theoretical session on customer relations. The best way to achieve success in providing information and building customer relations is to practise realistic tasks. Role-playing will bring together the need for good customer relations and the necessary knowledge of company products and services.

Tasks will be centred on the Business Centre services provided by Microplus. Try to familiarise yourself with these services and always refer to the Services and Price Guide when undertaking tasks. Use your own initiative when dealing with the situations which are involved. Many of the tasks will be of greater benefit to you if you form a group of four or five students and deal with them as role-play activities.

## What is a business centre?

A **business centre** provides an extensive service to new and small businesses and members of the public. Start-up costs for new businesses can be prohibitive. By providing a service which deals with office and secretarial functions business centres can save small firms a great deal of money and lost custom. The service is reliable and cost-effective. Microplus's Business Centre also offers staff training and development courses in new technology.

On this and the following pages you will find details of the important facilities provided by the Business Centre.

## THE BUSINESS CENTRE SERVICES AND PRICE GUIDE

**Business management consultancy**   £20.00 per hour
(Initial consultation free of charge)

Gives expert management advice on how to start a business and keep it operating successfully; how to run a business professionally; how to present ideas in the form of a business plan to financial institutions; corporate strategy; company development and budget forecasting.

### A professional communication service

Telephone answering   £15.00 per month

Answering the telephone, taking messages, contacting clients and booking appointments.

Mail processing   £10.00 per month

Providing clients with a business address which avoids having to use a home address or a PO box number.

Fax transmission incoming/outgoing   50p per page

Adds extra prestige to the client's business. The fax number may be added to letterheads and business cards. There is no charge for the rental of the number.

All three communication services for £25.00 per month.

### A professional secretarial service
Word processing   £2.95 per A4 page
£12.50 per hour

All businesses require writing or typing. Often business people, students and the general public would like to be able to sit down, have a coffee and relax with an independent secretarial advisor, to discuss the appropriate approach to a specific letter, report or curriculum vitae. The Business Centre can assist in composing letters, estimates, reports, theses, dissertations, press releases, etc. We also provide proof-reading, copy-editing and re-writing services which are fast, reliable and cost-effective.

Mail shots    30p each
(Including letter, laser printing, label and data entry.)

We provide a personalised mail shot service. This involves putting each name and address into a database, setting a standard letter and then merging the two together. The database is also used to print individual labels which not only saves time, but money. If, at a later date, a follow-up letter needs to be sent to the same contacts, the original database can be used again but with a different standard letter, without the cost of re-keying the data.

### Book-keeping and computerised accounts

Book-keeping services    Between £10/£20 per hour

We offer a professional book-keeping and computerised accounts service. It is a simple process for the business person to post to us, each week, receipts, invoices, bank statements and anything else associated with the financial operation of the business. We guarantee to keep the book-keeping records up-to-date.

### Database and spreadsheets
Initial set-up charge £25.00
Input and upkeep £12.50 per hour

A fundamental spreadsheet or database, holding related factual information on associates, clients, contractors, staff, suppliers, stock, etc. can be a godsend to any business. The information can be used time and time again for management, statistics, sales figures, listings, financial analyses, accounting, project control, bar charts, flow charts, graphs, presentations, forms, etc.

Our staff will build affordable spreadsheets and customised databases for businesses enabling them to update perpetually and retain statistical working information.

A single letter, leaflet or mailshot for target customers could promote any special offers. We would input the information into the spreadsheet or database to produce bespoke letters, leaflets or mailshots with the customers' names and addresses, and labels for the envelopes.

### Design, typesetting, artwork and printing

We use Apple Macintosh computers, an image scanner and laser printers to run the design, artwork, illustrations, graphics, typesetting and printing departments. Clients need some form of business stationery, whether it is business cards, letterheads, compliment slips, brochures, leaflets, etc. At this point decisions have to be made on a business logo. We can have it designed and typeset to create the artwork ready print.

If a client wants only 20 business cards and 50 letterheads – that's fine – that's all we'll print. If a client orders printing in the morning it can probably be delivered by late afternoon, providing it's black ink on white or coloured card/paper.

**We can supply these items:**

| | | | |
|---|---|---|---|
| Booklets | Brochures | Bulletins | Business cards |
| Calendars | Circulars | Cards | Compliment slips |
| Delivery notes | Envelopes | Forms | Handbills |
| Invoices | Invitations | Labels | Leaflets |
| Letterheads | Logos | Mailings | Memo pads |
| Menus | Message forms | Newsletters | Pamphlets |
| Posters | Price lists | Receipts | Reports |

**Artwork and typesetting**   £10.00

Business cards (prices do not include artwork)

| Quantity | White | Coloured |
|---|---|---|
| 100 | 15.20 | 16.20 |
| 200 | 19.40 | 20.40 |
| 300 | 23.00 | 24.00 |
| 400 | 26.50 | 28.50 |
| 500 | 30.60 | 32.50 |
| 600 | 34.00 | 37.00 |
| 700 | 38.00 | 44.00 |
| 800 | 41.20 | 48.80 |
| 900 | 44.80 | 52.70 |
| 1000 | 47.70 | 56.90 |

Laminated/coloured business cards

Lightweight black ink   From £15 per 100
Lightweight two-colour   From £25 per 100
Middleweight black ink   From £18 per 100
Middleweight two-colour   From £28 per 100

**Compliment slips** (coloured and white)

In black ink on 100gsm paper. (Prices do not include artwork.)

| Quantity | White | Coloured |
|---|---|---|
| 100 | 5.00 | 5.10 |
| 200 | 9.50 | 9.80 |
| 300 | 14.00 | 14.40 |
| 400 | 18.00 | 18.50 |
| 500 | 22.50 | 27.00 |
| 600 | 27.00 | 30.60 |
| 700 | 31.50 | 34.20 |
| 800 | 36.00 | 37.80 |
| 900 | 41.50 | 42.50 |
| 1000 | 45.00 | 47.00 |

**Leaflets**

| Quantity | A5 | A4 |
|---|---|---|
| 100 | 3.50 | 5.00 |
| 1000 | 13.00 | 20.00 |

A4 printing (standard paper)
In black ink on 80gsm paper (Prices do not include artwork.)

| Quantity | White | Coloured |
|---|---|---|
| 100 | 10.60 | 12.30 |
| 200 | 14.20 | 16.00 |
| 300 | 17.80 | 19.80 |
| 400 | 21.40 | 23.60 |
| 500 | 25.00 | 27.40 |
| 600 | 28.60 | 31.20 |
| 700 | 32.20 | 35.00 |
| 800 | 35.80 | 38.70 |
| 900 | 39.40 | 42.50 |
| 1000 | 43.00 | 46.30 |

A4 one-colour printing (top-quality paper)
(Prices do not include artwork.)

| Quantity | White | Coloured |
|---|---|---|
| 100 | 15.20 | 15.10 |
| 200 | 23.10 | 21.80 |
| 300 | 31.00 | 28.50 |
| 400 | 38.80 | 35.30 |
| 500 | 46.70 | 42.10 |
| 600 | 54.60 | 48.80 |
| 700 | 62.40 | 55.60 |
| 800 | 70.30 | 62.40 |
| 900 | 78.20 | 69.10 |
| 1000 | 86.10 | 76.00 |

A4 two-colour printing

| | | |
|---|---|---|
| 100 | 25.20 | 25.10 |
| 200 | 43.00 | 41.80 |
| 300 | 61.00 | 58.50 |
| 400 | 78.80 | 75.30 |
| 500 | 84.60 | 82.20 |

**Photocopying services**

Colour copying

| Quantity | A4 | A3 |
|---|---|---|
| 1 – 50 | 0.90 | 1.80 |
| 51 – 100 | 0.85 | 1.70 |
| 100+ | 0.80 | 1.60 |
| Sepia colour | 1.40 | 2.40 |
| Slide copying | 1.40 | 2.80 |
| Enlargements extra | 0.20 | 0.40 |

Laminate finishes (each)

| | | |
|---|---|---|
| Polishing | 0.25 | 0.50 |
| High gloss film | 0.50 | 1.00 |
| Satin film | 0.50 | 1.00 |
| Matt film | 0.50 | 1.00 |
| Linen textured | 0.60 | 1.20 |
| Sand textured | 0.60 | 1.20 |

Black and white photocopying
(reduced and enlarged copies 10p extra for first copy)

| Quantity | A4 | A3 |
|---|---|---|
| 1 – 50 | 0.05 | 0.10 |
| 51 – 100 | 0.04 | 0.08 |
| 101 – 1000 | 0.03 | 0.06 |
| 1000 – 5000 | 0.02 | 0.04 |

**A 15% discount is given to these groups:**

| | | |
|---|---|---|
| Students | – | Must produce a current student card |
| Charities | – | Must produce a Registered Charity Number |
| Unemployed | – | Must produce a UB40 |

Local clubs, churches and schools.

**General services**

| | | | |
|---|---|---|---|
| Collating | – | per 100 sheets | 1.20 |
| Stapling | – | per 100 staples | 2.80 |
| Folding | – | per 100 | 12.00 |
| Perforating | – | per 500 | 10.00 |

## TRAINING AND DEVELOPMENT COURSE DESCRIPTORS

| | |
|---|---|
| COURSE TITLE: | Instructional Skills |
| Points covered: | Motivation and the learning process |
| | Task and faults analysis |
| | Learning methods |
| | On and off the job training |
| | Course design |
| | Planning and preparation of training sessions |
| | Use of visual aids |
| Suitable for: | Job experts who are required to develop, prepare and present instructor-driven training sessions |
| Duration: | Five days (course starts on the first Monday of each month) |
| Cost: | £1277 + VAT |
| Entry requirements: | None |

| COURSE TITLE: | Time Management |
|---|---|
| Content: | Time analysis |
| | Key time |
| | Delegating tasks |
| | Identifying time wasters for yourself and others |
| Suitable for: | Those requiring to use time management techniques to achieve more during a working day |
| Entry requirements: | None |
| Duration: | Two days (Monday and Tuesday) every week |
| Cost: | £591 + VAT |

| COURSE TITLE: | Basic Autocad |
|---|---|
| Content: | Autocad Environment and Drawing Editor |
| | Basic edit commands |
| | Use of display and manipulation commands |
| | Dimensioning and text |
| | Plotting |
| Entry requirements: | None |
| Duration: | Four days (Tuesday – Friday, beginning second Tuesday of every month) |
| Cost: | £335 + VAT |

| COURSE TITLE: | Autocad Advanced |
|---|---|
| Content: | Sectional views and hatching |
| | Layers and arrays |
| | The use of blocks and W blocks |
| | Inquiry commands and attributes |
| | Isometric projection and 3D views |
| Entry requirements: | Attendance at basic Autocad Course or equivalent |
| Duration: | Four days (beginning third Tuesday of every month) |
| Cost: | £335 + VAT |

| COURSE TITLE | VDU Safety Awareness |
|---|---|
| Content: | Health and safety law |
| | The VDU operator |
| | The environment |
| | Lighting |
| | Workstation design and ergonomics |
| | Upper limb disorders |
| | European Directives |
| Entry requirements: | None |
| Suitable for: | Those requiring to make decisions with regard to VDUs or those who use VDUs during their working day. |
| Duration: | One day (every Monday) |
| Cost: | £100 + VAT |

| | |
|---|---|
| COURSE TITLE: | Industrial First Aid |
| Content: | Aids to diagnosis |
| | Action at an emergency |
| | Recovery position |
| | Resuscitation techniques |
| | Dealing with wounds |
| | Shock |
| | Sprains and strains |
| Entry requirements: | None |
| Duration: | Two days (second Wednesday and Thursday of the month) |
| Cost: | £250 + VAT |
| | |
| COURSE TITLE: | Introducing WordPerfect |
| Content: | Document creation |
| | Saving and printing |
| | Block functions |
| | Formatting text |
| | Tabulation |
| Entry requirements: | Keyboarding skills (25 wpm minimum) |
| Duration: | Two days (every Thursday and Friday) |
| Cost: | £250 + VAT |
| | |
| COURSE TITLE: | Extending WordPerfect |
| Content: | Multi-page documents |
| | Headers and footers |
| | Search and replace |
| | Standard paragraphs |
| | Columns |
| | Tables |
| | Mail-merge |
| | Macros |
| Entry requirements: | Introducing WordPerfect Course or equivalent |
| Duration: | Two days (every Monday and Tuesday) |
| Cost: | £250 + VAT |

**Task 2 ➤**    Form a role-play group to carry out this task. Use the Services and Price Guide to provide the answers to these customer enquiries. Personal callers are shown as **customers** and telephone callers shown as **callers**. For written enquiries prepare typed replies.

**Customer 1**
'What will it cost to produce a two-page CV for me? I need a total of 14 copies in A4 white quality paper.'

### Written enquiry 1
Will you provide prices (and total costs) for: 300 coloured compliment slips; 100 plain white business cards; and 600 A4 photocopies of an original (black and white). We are a registered charity, Homeless Action, 22 Hyde Park Road, London and our number is 071 223 1654. (The letter is signed by P. Boyd (Secretary).)

### Caller 1
'I need my dissertation of 86 pages word processed and two copies produced. How much is this going to cost me? I am a student at the university in the city.'

### Customer 2
'I am in a hurry to have an important piece of coloured design work photocopied. Could I have a price for 12 copies of high gloss film A3 size? How much more would it cost to have them linen textured?'

### Written enquiry 2
'I am a teacher at Main Road School - Mrs Jeffries (geography department). I need some urgent photocopying for exam purposes. Our school does not have a colour copier and I need colour copies of a map. The map is A4 size and I need 32 copies. How much will this cost?'

### Customer 3
A fax has to be sent quickly to Italy; it has a cover sheet and four pages. What will I be charged for this?'

### Caller 2
'The office computer has broken down and I need some letters sent out today. There is approximately three hours word processing involved. What is your hourly rate?'

### Caller 3
'I need 100 letterheads A4, 200 compliment slips and 100 plain white business cards produced quickly. 200 leaflets A5 coloured are also required for next Monday. The order is for the Boys Brigade. What is the total cost?'

### Caller 4
'I need a temporary secretary urgently. I think it will be for two weeks at least. Do you provide this service? How much will it cost me?'

**Task 3 ➤**    Use your initiative in this task. Consult the Services and Price Guide and write down the answers to these requests:

a) A new business has opened in the area. The owner wishes to order a small amount of stationery from you. He needs 40 plain business cards; 50 letterheads A4 size top quality paper with one-colour printing; and 40 leaflets A5 size. What would you charge for this?

b) A customer wants 10 photocopies of an A4 document enlarged to A3. She also needs a 20-page A4 manual photocopied, collated and stapled. What will this cost?

c) A businessman is attending a conference in town. He has run out of business cards but has one of his old ones left. He needs it reproduced exactly and needs 150 in colour.

d) A client is sending a mail shot to 500 prospective customers. Her costs have to be kept down and she needs to know if you will give a discount for volume? What would you do?

## Assessment activity 11.1

> **Remember! Keep your work from this activity for reference and assessment**

Carry out this activity as a role-play one. Take turns at playing the part of the employee working at the customer enquiry desk (who also answers the telephone). The other students should act as the telephone callers and visitors. Pause after every question you ask, wait for the reply, allow the employee to ask for details and then go on to the next question.

Students playing the part of telephone callers should also write down notes of answers they receive. At the end of the role-play get together and discuss how each of you handled the situations. Write down brief reports of action taken and produce summaries of complaints in an appropriate format.

### Telephone caller 1

'Hello, this is Margaret Williams. I have recently become self-employed and opened a florists in town. I need 1000 advertising leaflets printed on red paper. Could you tell me how much this will cost and how long it will take your company to provide them? Could you send me written details please? My address is 271 London Road.'

### Personal caller 1

'I had a CV and 10 copies produced yesterday. My friend picked them up for me last night. I was horrified to find that my educational details had been missed out. I am attending an interview this afternoon and urgently need this CV. What can you do about this error?'

### Telephone caller 2

'Hi, this is Joanne Mercer from Granny's Kitchen Tearoom. I hear you provide a book-keeping service for small businesses. Could you give me some details of the services you offer? My accounts are quite up-to-date at the moment but the person who normally looks after the books has recently moved to another area. What other services do you provide for small businesses which I may find useful? Do you have any brochures or catalogues which you could send me? My address is 161 High Street.'

### Telephone caller 3

'Good morning, Graeme Simons solicitor here. My secretary has co'
in sick and I urgently need some letters produced. The letters hav'

sent out by the last post today. There are 36 in all; 12 of these are three-page, eight are two-page and the remainder are single page. Can you do this for me in time? What will be the charge? I will send someone over with the drafts straight away. Could you give this person the account and I will send a cheque?'

### Personal caller 2
'I have a number of manuals to be produced for a first aid course you offer. These manuals are 20 pages, A4 size in total. They need to have a front and back cover (card) on them and the original needs to be photocopied and collated. What will I be charged and when they will be ready for collection?'

### Telephone caller 4
'Christine Collins here. I have just opened up a new catering service on the outskirts of town. When I am out delivering orders I am sure I am losing business as there is no one here to answer the telephone. I cannot afford to take on an employee to do so at this stage. My friend recommended I enquire about your communication service. Could you give me some details please?'

### Telephone caller 5
'My name is Richard Jackson of Jackson Brothers Building Contractors. I have just received delivery of the stationery order which I placed on Monday. I am unhappy with the quality of the letterheads which have been sent. They are definitely not up to the usual standard. The logo is smudged and the paper seems damp. I need this dealt with straight away as we only have a few of the old ones left.'

### Personal caller 3 (aggressive in manner)
(You throw some business cards on the counter. You are really angry.)
'I ordered 1000 business cards three weeks ago and was promised them the following day. Since then it has been one disaster after another. My first order was produced on the wrong material. I then received plain ones when I ordered laminated lightweight. Then the order was mixed up again and I was given middleweight. This is the last straw – the business card material is fine but they have my old address and telephone number on them. I have moved to another area and the whole purpose of having new cards printed was to alert people of my new details. I now have no new business cards and could be losing customers. I want something done IMMEDIATELY!'

### Telephone caller 6
'Good morning/afternoon this is Father McCluskey from St Theresa's Church. The Young Mother's Group is holding a Summer Fair next week and we need some urgent photocopying of posters. The original poster has been created by members of the Youth Club and is coloured, roughly A3 in size. Could you photocopy 20 of them for us within the next hour? How much will this cost? Do we qualify for our normal discount on photocopying services?'

**Telephone caller 7** (with a complaint)
'Good morning/afternoon, this is Nicola Pearson of Hunter Associates. We have received delivery of the advertising posters we ordered. However, the order is wrong. We ordered 1000 A4 size posters of two-colour printing and 500 A3 size in one-colour printing. We received 500 A4 posters in one-colour printing and 1000 A3 in two-colour printing. We are really surprised that this serious mistake has happened as we have never had any reason to complain about the service you provide. We can only assume that the person who took the order got a bit mixed up. What can you do?'

# Inform customers/clients about available products and services

The previous units have covered areas of customer relations and service provision. What happens when a customer asks you to provide goods or services which are unavailable? Your response will depend on whether the products required are:

- out-of-stock
- unavailable at the present time
- definitely not offered by your organisation.

## Out-of-stock goods

If a customer asks you to supply goods which are out of stock – **never** say 'We don't have any'. **Always** offer alternatives.

**Task 4 ➤**   A customer of the Business Centre asked to order lightweight, laminated, two-coloured business cards and you are completely out of lightweight material.
  Discuss with others in your group the alternatives you could offer in this situation and give your reasons for the choices.

> **Remember!**
> **Never try to**
> **pressurise**
> **customers**
> **into buying**
> **something –**
> **let the final**
> **decision be**
> **theirs.**

Any alternatives offered must be an **ASSET**:

| | |
|---|---|
| A | **available** immediately |
| S | **similar** to what the customer requires |
| S | **same** quality |
| E | **equal** (or close to) in price |
| T | **totally** acceptable to the customer. |

Suppose you chose middleweight cards for Task 4. **What about price?** There is a difference of £3.00 between the lightweight and the middleweight; the latter being more expensive. Depending upon individual organisation policy, you could offer the middleweight at the lightweight price – this would enhance customer relations. However, never take such decisions yourself – discuss the situation with your supervisor (especially if the final price difference is a large amount).

**Task 5 ➤**

1 Which alternatives would you offer customers if the following goods were temporarily unavailable from the Business Centre stock? Give reasons for your choices and say what you would do if there was a price difference.

a) 300 letterheads on standard paper

b) 100 A4 leaflets

c) 12 sheets of A3 colour photocopying

d) 500 white business cards

e) 20 A4 photocopies with satin laminated finish

f) 500 coloured compliment slips.

2 Are there any of the above for which no alternatives could be offered immediately? If any, which ones are these and why?

3 What would you do about a price difference in each case?

4 Could you assure the customer of the same quality in any alternative you offered?

## Unavailable goods

There will be times when alternatives are not acceptable to customers. Some customers are very wary of trying anything which is **new** to them. They may like to continue using tried and tested goods and have no wish to change. In this case you can only give assurances that you will let them know as soon as the item they require becomes available. If orders have already been placed for out-of-stock items you can probably access your computer to find out the expected delivery date.

## Goods or services not offered by your organisation

In reality you cannot provide every item to satisfy all the needs of every customer. You may be asked for a certain service or to provide a particular item which may never again be requested. It would be unwise for organisations to overstock on goods which tie up their capital unnecessarily. If you are **sure** that your company does not provide a certain item or service you can:

- suggest the customer tries another organisation you **know** will supply the goods or services;

- look up your list of companies similar to your own in the area who may offer the goods – if you have time telephone one on behalf of the customer as this enhances customer relations;

- bring the request to the attention of your boss at your next departmental meeting if you have frequently been asked for the particular item or service.

## Computer databases

Employees dealing with customer enquiries have the advantage nowadays of accessing computer databases. You can call up any item of stock to find:

- how many you have in stock;

- if the correct size, colour, type is available;

- current prices and discounts available;

- dates of deliveries of replacement stock.

Students who have worked through Book 1 will be familiar with using databases. If you have no experience of data input and output then either refer to Book 1 or ask your tutor for notes to use with the database package in use at your school/college.

**Task 6 ➤**

This task involves the creation of a database which you will name **MPSTOCK**. The database will have 20 **records** of 8 **fields**. The fields are:

| STNO | – 8 characters | MIN | – 3 numeric |
| ITEM | – 30 characters | REORD | – 3 numeric |
| PRIE | – 4 numeric | SOLD | – 3 numeric |
| MAX | – 3 numeric | BAL | – 3 numeric |

When creating the database form give instructions that the sold figure (SOLD) has to be deducted from the balance (BAL). You also must indicate that when the balance reaches on or below the reorder level (REORD) an order for new stock must be placed.

Save the master form and then enter the following details (your opening balance will be the maximum held):

| STNO | ITEM | PRICE | MAX | MIN | REORD |
|------|------|-------|-----|-----|-------|
| 1DDC2576 | Collins Desk Diary | 9.27 | 20 | 05 | 10 |
| 1FLP5518 | Nobo A1 Flipchart Pad | 7.75 | 30 | 10 | 15 |
| 1SVY0349 | Simplex D Account Book | 4.91 | 20 | 05 | 10 |
| 1SVY0360 | Simplex D VAT Book | 7.30 | 20 | 05 | 10 |
| 1PWP3110 | Bank Paper A4 Ream | 8.69 | 50 | 10 | 20 |
| 1PWP0413 | Bond Paper A4 White Ream | 10.61 | 80 | 20 | 50 |
| 1PWP0423 | Bond Paper A4 Blue Ream | 10.85 | 20 | 05 | 10 |
| 1PWP0433 | Bond Paper A4 Pink Ream | 10.85 | 10 | 02 | 05 |
| 1PWP0443 | Bond Paper A4 Green Ream | 10.85 | 10 | 02 | 05 |
| 3PILSPOT | Pilot Spotlighter Blue | 0.65 | 50 | 10 | 20 |
| 3PENF50F | Pentel F50 Felt Marker | 0.95 | 50 | 10 | 20 |
| 3PENN50G | Pentel Giant Marker N50 | 0.87 | 50 | 10 | 20 |
| 3PENN60G | Pentel Giant Marker N60 | 0.87 | 50 | 10 | 20 |
| 6WEBE500 | Ring Reinforcements (500) | 0.66 | 50 | 10 | 20 |
| 6WEBE999 | Ring Reinforcements (1000) | 1.15 | 12 | 03 | 6 |
| 6EASA4RB | Eastlight A4 Ringbinder | 1.43 | 10 | 02 | 5 |
| 6EASA4AB | Eastlight Ebony A4 Ringbinder | 2.11 | 20 | 05 | 10 |
| 6NRX8031 | Box Nyrex Wallets Clear | 15.60 | 10 | 02 | 5 |
| 6NRX8032 | Box Nyrex Wallets Coloured | 15.60 | 5 | 01 | 2 |
| 6MFM2851 | Roll Store Mailing Tube | 0.81 | 30 | 10 | 20 |

Save and print out the completed list for your folder.

## Information on goods and services

Customers often ask for your advice on items and services. You may be asked any, or all, of these questions about specific products your organisation supplies:

- What outstanding features does this product have?
- What benefits will I find from buying this item rather than another one?
- Does it suit the purpose for which I need it?
- Will it actually do everything you say it can?
- What other purpose will it serve?
- Are there any cheaper alternatives which will fit my requirements just as well?

This list could be endless. However, you must be aware of the **practise** you need to build up experience that will make you proficient at assessing clients' needs. Every client has specific preferences so treat her/his needs individually.

Remember!
If you provide a helpful, efficient service a client will come back and buy from you again. But do not frighten customers off by being too pushy.

**Task 7** ➤ Below are some examples of clients' requests for information about the services you can provide. Consult the Business Centre Services and Price Guide then list points you would bring to the attention of these clients. (Not all clients' requests can be met – pick out those that cannot and say why you think a reputable organisation would decline any such requests.)

### Client 1

'I have recently started up in business. It is only a small concern – car servicing and repairs. I am the only mechanic, but my teenage son helps out after school and at weekends. The problem is that I am often called out to car breakdowns. While I am out of the garage I believe I am losing custom. I am also a bit mixed up about the book-work and at present I'm not in the position to employ anyone full-time in the office. Which services could your organisation provide which will be efficient but not costly?'

### Client 2

'I have an important prospective customer arriving from France tomorrow. My problem is that I cannot speak the language – I need an interpreter who can also act as my Personal Assistant for a few days (it helps the image you know). I would prefer a tall, slim, intelligent blonde (a Marilyn Monroe look-alike would be nice) between the ages of 21 and 25 – one who is fun to be with. She will need to be at my apartment in town by 8 a.m. at the latest and I will pay for her services and hotel bill for two nights.'

### Client 3

'I am the Politics Departmental Secretary at the local university. For some years now I have been helping out honours students by typing dissertations for them. Word has got around and I have been inundated with requests from over 40 students this year. I do not have the same amount of spare time as before to help out as much. However, I feel really bad – as if I am letting the students down – if I say I cannot manage to help. Most businesses which provide this sort of service to students charge very high rates which are well out of the reach of these young people. Could your company offer affordable rates to these students if I can guarantee a minimum volume of work?'

### Client 4

'Help! I am a self-employed financial consultant working from home. My wife has left me and she used to look after all my accounts and secretarial needs. I am in a real mess and cannot begin to attempt to sort things out. What can you do for me – it is urgent!'

### Client 5

'My office cleaner has not turned up the last few days and the place is a right mess. I heard from a friend that your company provides office services to small businesses. Can you assist me with my problem? How much will it cost?'

### Client 6

'Now and again I have to send and receive faxes to and from Europe. I may have 10 or more transmissions and receipts one month and then nothing for another three months. I really cannot afford to invest in a fax machine at the moment. Can you help me and what will it cost?'

## Assessment activity 11.2

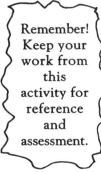

Remember! Keep your work from this activity for reference and assessment.

Carry out this activity as a role-play exercise. Use your database **MPSTOCK** and the Services and Price Guide to provide the information requested. Any complaints will have to be noted and reported to your supervisor in an appropriate format. Some customer enquiries will have to be answered by letter. At the end of the activity enter all details of stock which has been used onto the database.

### Telephone caller 1

'I am Rebecca Marsh, financial consultant. I work from home and am often called away to meetings in other parts of the country. When I am away I am losing clients because letters are not being answered, my telephone is not manned and faxes cannot be replied to. Does your company provide a service which may solve my problems? I would be grateful if you could either make me an appointment for a meeting with an advisor or write to me with details. My address is 166 Bromley Road West. Many thanks for your help.'

### Personal caller 1

'Do you stock the Pentel F60 Felt Marker Pens? (If the salesperson says 'No, but we do stock the F50 which is similar', ask for the price.) I am a student at the local college but I have forgotten my student card, will I still get a discount? If so, I will take 20 pens.'

### Personal caller 2

'I am Ron Gauld from the *Advertiser* newspaper. Look at this box of 20 Roll Store Mailing tubes which your driver delivered yesterday! I went to use them this morning to send out this year's calendars to customers. The tops are stuck fast and they cannot be used. They must have been stored in a warm place and the glue has melted. I need another 20 urgently as these calendars **must** be sent out today. Make sure the ones you give me this time are okay. I really should speak to Mr Brown about this. Surely, goods are checked before being sent out to customers?'

### Telephone caller 2

'Do you have any Collins Desk Diaries in stock? I thought I had placed an order with you for them last month. However, when I looked up the order I noticed I had forgotten to request the diaries. I need 30 for the office as soon as possible. (The employee will let you know that there are only 20 in stock.) I will take the 20 now and could you have the other 10 delivered with our next order? Thank you very much.'

**Personal caller 3** (Schoolboy)
'I would like to buy five A4 ringbinders please. How much change will I get from £10.'

**Telephone caller 3**
'Good morning/afternoon – this is Shareen Nardini. I am the Secretary of the local boys' club football team. I am organising a summer fete to raise funds for new football strips. Would your organisation be interested in either sponsoring, donating raffle prizes or giving cash donations to the cause?'

**Telephone caller 4**
'Naomi Matthews here from A1 Business Services. I have urgent typing to be processed and one of my staff has called in sick at the last moment. I am really understaffed at present so I wonder if it would be possible to hire one of your word processor operators for the afternoon? The operator will need to come to our premises in the High Street as the work is quite involved.

**Personal caller 4**
'Could I have 20 A4 copies of this sheet please? It is double-sided, black and white photocopying.'

**Personal caller 5**
'Do you stock Roll Store Mailing tubes – I need five?'

**Personal caller 6 (slightly deaf)**
(Act out this part accordingly – as if you do not pick up certain points the employee makes.)
'Good afternoon. Could you help me with a problem I am having? I purchased this calculator (use a solar calculator) from your shop as a birthday present for my nephew. I have been looking for the place to insert the batteries but I cannot find any openings for this. I know calculators **need** batteries to work them.

# Storing and supplying information

## Maintain an established filing system

Unit 1 of Book 1 dealt with filing in some depth. It covered the basic filing principles and classification methods. (Those students who have not already done so, will find it necessary to read up on this.) The emphasis in this unit will be placed on the importance of **maintaining** an efficient filing system.

### What is the purpose of filing?

Is it:

a)  to tidy up your desk?

b)  to look busy when you have nothing else to do?

c)  to be able to find information (paper based or electronic) easily and quickly at a later date?

d)  to do **something** with loose papers which are lying around because you do not know whether to throw out material which has been dealt with or keep it just in case?

e)  to make your office system **look** efficient?

**Remember! We file to FIND!**

Although c) is the only correct statement some people file for one or all of the other reasons. This, in turn, leads to inefficiency as there is no **logic** to systems resulting from the other reasons.

### How well organised are you at work?

Do you think filing is just another boring aspect of your job or do you appreciate its importance?

A large part of the efficiency of an office depends, not only on the existence of a reliable filing system, but also on the skill of staff in the art of methodical filing. All office workers needs to understand the methods of filing used within their organisations. Filing systems are designed in a way which will ensure your organisation can operate efficiently.

No two organisations' filing systems will be alike. Filing systems must be tailored to suit the needs of each business. However, the basic methods and principles of filing, illustrated in Book 1, can nearly all be written into the **office bible.**

**Task 1 ➤** Picture this scenario:

> I FILED THE LETTER THE BOSS IS ASKING FOR ONLY LAST WEEK - BUT WHERE ON EARTH DID I FILE IT?

Has this ever happened to you? How can you avoid this situation?

Write down the essential steps to take when filing documents which will ensure **easy retrieval** when necessary. Take into account classification methods and filing systems.

Remember!
Place documents in files where they can be found easily and quickly in future.

## Designing and modifying filing systems

When designing a new filing system or changing an existing one try to make the system as simple as possible. You must make sure that the filing methods and principles will be understood by all employees who need to access it.

Check that the system will be:

● quick and simple to use;

● easily accessible and space saving;

● flexible enough to add other records to or change if required;

● suitable for the type of material dealt with;

● secure and safe.

Check that documents and papers can be:

- retrieved easily and quickly once filed;
- maintained in a system which will allow you to know the location of a particular file or document at any specific time;
- secure from personnel who do not have authorised access;
- thinned out when necessary;
- kept safe from dust, damp, fire and theft.

When the system is set up and running properly keep it that way. Consultation between users of the system must be carried out prior to changes being made. All users must be kept up to date about **what goes where** and borrowing procedures.

> **Remember!**
> **A good filing system can be maintained only if it is used correctly by all who have access to it.**

For a filing system to work efficiently it needs to meet **all the requirements** of information storage and retrieval in an individual department or centralised unit. Each member of staff who uses the system, needs to know:

- what documents need to be filed;
- where they should be stored;
- how long papers or computer files need to be kept.

### What kind of information must be stored for future reference?

In offices throughout the world there are storage systems which are packed with pieces of paper which do not need to be retained. Advertising literature, for example, received by your organisation which is of no interest to any employee can be thrown out immediately. Other items which are often filed unnecessarily are:

- papers confirming appointments – these can be discarded after the date of the appointment;
- copies of internal memos – these can be discarded after the information has been noted;
- acknowledgments of correspondence received – a copy of the original letter or document will be held so the acknowledgement can be discarded;
- remittance advice notes – payments to account are recorded elsewhere.

Many people are afraid to discard any pieces of paper containing information. Systems then become clogged and it is more difficult to find **essential** information which may be needed quickly.

# Classification methods

Classification methods were dealt with in detail in Book 1. The following table lists the advantages and disadvantages of the main ones.

| Classification | Advantages | Disadvantages |
|---|---|---|
| ALPHABETICAL | • simple to understand and operate<br>• index is not required<br>• easy to group together related documents<br>• can be used for most filing requirements | • documents may need to be filed under more than one heading and will need to be **cross-referenced**<br>• common names can cause confusion<br>• files may become rather bulky and have to be split<br>• easy to access confidential information |
| NUMERICAL | • each document can be allocated a unique number<br>• easy to expand<br>• files number may be used as reference, e.g. customer account numbers<br>• confidential files harder to access | • necessary to maintain indexes<br>• operation is more difficult<br>• figures are easily transposed, resulting in mislaid documents |
| GEOGRAPHICAL | • useful where regional information is required, e.g. sales agents' customers<br>• keeps files relating to certain districts in same location<br>• useful where area information needs to be kept in individual files, e.g. for estate agents | • users of the system need to have a good knowledge of geography, district and regional boundaries<br>• boundaries can be altered periodically<br>• an index may also be necessary<br>• files can be mixed up and documents mislaid, e.g. when customers have same name but different location |
| CHRONO-LOGICAL | • useful for financial documents<br>• useful for minutes of<br>• meetings | • an index is essential<br>• can be meaningless if used for general correspondence |
| SUBJECT | • easy to understand<br>• no index necessary<br>• easy expansion of system<br>• beneficial for grouping related material | • files may be doubled up under different subject headings<br>• system can become over-loaded with too many files for related subjects |

# Filing point

Before you can decide where a letter or document is to be held you have to decide **what** the contents of the document refer to. For example, you could receive a letter from a customer asking for a credit limit increase. Would you file this letter in the accounts files by account number or in the customer file by name?

Realistically, this may not be left to the filing clerk or office junior to decide (except with obvious documents such as invoices, etc.). The recipient of the document or letter is responsible for indicating the **filing point** on a document. The filing point will refer to the classification and relate to one of these:

● surname or organisation name

● account number or reference number

● dates of personal correspondence

● invoice number

● subject of the document

● employee reference number.

The **filing point** may be indicated by being underlined, highlighted with a felt pen or circled, as below:

---

### MEMORANDUM

TO:      Salaries                    REF: New employee
FROM: Personnel                  DATE: 2 April 199-

---

Karine Newall has accepted the position of Computing Consultant with the Business Centre. She will commence her employment on the first Monday of next month. I have allocated an employee number to her which is (BC 333)
   Please enter the enclosed personal details on record and allocate a paper file in the personnel section.

Enc.

---

On a computerised filing system you will quickly locate Karine's record by searching on employee number. How would you retrieve it from a paper-based system if you did not know this number – only her name?

# Indexing

Alphabetical and subject classifications are the only methods which enable you to locate a particular file by searching through the records. If files are classified according to account number, geographical location, stock numbers, etc. would you have to look through every individual file until you came to the correct one? This would be time-consuming and very boring. So how can you avoid this?

### Referencing

Referencing files through strip, visible card or rotary indexes provides a simple method of locating records from a minimum of information supplied. The illustration below gives an example:

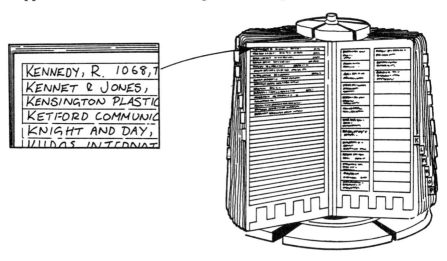

KENNEDY, R.  1068, T
KENNET & JONES,
KENSINGTON PLASTIC
KETFORD COMMUNIC
KNIGHT AND DAY,
KUDOS INTERNAT

Strip index

Personnel records may be classified according to employee number and filed logically using this method. A visible card index could be used to contain additional information. It may be arranged alphabetically, by surname. In this case, if you were asked for the personnel file on Robert Kennedy who works in the mail room, his employee number could be found easily and quickly from the card index.

### Indicators

Index systems can hold thousands of cards and paper-based filing drawers are home to hundreds of folders. It is often necessary to use **signalling devices** to indicate special points within the system. For instance, in the geographical system used in Microplus coloured tabs are used to indicate the area dealing with specific customers.

Colour can play an important part in office systems as it simplifies many filing tasks. Many organisations now use four-page documents for accounting purposes, for example:

● the advice note – green

● the delivery note – pink

● the invoice – blue, and

● the statement white.

## Filing systems

Filing can be carried out on any information storage system. The three that are commonly used are:

● **Paper-based** storage systems where documents are filed in horizontal, vertical and lateral systems.

● **Microfilm-based** storage systems where documents are microphotocopied and stored on rolls of film or as transparencies.

- **Electronic-based** systems where records are stored in computer memory on hard disk and backed up onto floppy disks.

### Filing routines

Remember the basic steps to be followed in preparing documents for filing. File regularly and do not let filing pile up.

| | |
|---|---|
| Step 1 | Gather papers and documents for filing and place them in a suitable filing tray or a pre-sorter. |
| Step 2 | Check all items for a **release** mark. |
| Step 3 | If the filing point is not indicated read through the document. Decide on the classification and mark the filing point. |
| Step 4 | Cross-reference papers which apply to more than one file. |
| Step 5 | Pre-sort to arrange documents in the order in which you will be filing them. |
| Step 6 | Enter details of new files into the relevant index. |
| Step 7 | Finally, insert documents in the correct files. |

**Task 2 ➤**

Form a group and discuss the following situations. Give some tips on how to avoid the same problems happening again.

a) You have spent the last two hours searching for a letter from a customer which should have been filed in customer records. Another filing clerk directs you to the accounts records. You find what you are looking for there and note that the filing point has been marked as account number when it should have been customer name.

b) Your boss asks you to locate the latest VAT return copy. You were using the document for information to record yesterday. You know it is **somewhere** on your desk.

c) The Business Centre Manager asked you to send a contract to a new customer last week. He arrives in your office and is visibly annoyed. The customer has telephoned to cancel the contract as the paperwork never arrived. You are sure you posted it immediately. You call up the word-processor file and search for the contract. However, an hour later you are still unable to locate it. You know you filed the contract logically but the search is not successful. Someone must have wiped it from the harddisk.

d) You are looking for the last invoice from a supplier. You find the supplier's file but the document is missing. You search through other suppliers' records to try to locate it. Helen Black is filing papers at another cabinet. She hands you the missing invoice and asks you to file it for her. Her boss was using the document to find the cost price of an item.

e) While filing some paperwork you notice that some documents have been torn. Obviously they have been caught in the rack. This has happened when the filing cabinet has jammed – no wonder as the files are too bulky.

## Removal and return of files

A few of the above situations could have been avoided if proper practices had been adopted in controlling the system. When working in an office which has departmental filing systems try to follow these **golden rules:**

● Individual papers or documents should not be removed from a file.

● Take out a complete file from the system when you wish to look at a particular document.

● Always insert a completed **out-card** when removing a file from the system. Insert the out-card in the relevant space.

● If a document needs to be retained for a long period make a photocopy and then replace the complete file immediately.

● As soon as you have finished with a particular file return it to its proper place.

● Check all filing cabinets/drawers periodically to ensure files are being returned to the system on time.

● Check the same to ensure that redundant material is not being retained.

● Chase up files from staff members who have failed to return them by the date shown on the out-card.

## Centralised filing systems

The greatest advantage of a centralised filing system is that it is easy to maintain. In a centralised system only authorised filing clerks have direct access to the files. Removal and return of files are strictly controlled.

These **golden rules** should be adhered to:

● Employees requiring access to a file must apply to an authorised filing room clerk.

● An out-card should be completed and inserted by a filing room clerk.

● The employee will be asked to return the file by a certain time or date.

● When the employee returns the file, the out-card will be removed and the file replaced in its original position.

● Filing registers are completed to record files which are out on loan. The employee may be asked to sign this register.

● Filing clerks check the register every morning to ensure files are returned. If an employee has an overdue file, a request will be made for its return or a reminder will be sent.

- All returns – with dates – are recorded in the register. This makes life easier for the filing clerks as they can see at a glance which files are missing from the system.

- In organisations where there is no filing register, filing clerks need to check physically for out-cards each morning.

# Document retention and disposal

### Thinning

To avoid filing systems becoming overloaded the oldest papers are usually removed periodically from the back of the files. Files are thinned by looking through papers and removing those unlikely to be referred to again.

Thinning normally takes place annually. You could look on thinning as a form of weeding. Gardens need periodical weeding or they become unruly and difficult to manage. The same applies to filing systems.

Thinning maintains an **orderly system**. The advantages are:

- Bulky files can be **reduced** when it is convenient to the supervisor. An ideal time would be when the office is quiet and work is slack.

- There is no need to **divide** bulky files into two as files are kept within a reasonable and manageable size.

- Out-of-date documents (over a year old) can be transferred to archival storage.

- Files are easier to handle.

- Less time is spent locating individual papers than would be taken up in searching through an overloaded system

- It is **safe** and practical. Each paper is scanned thoroughly before any decision to discard it is made.

Many companies find it useful to operate a retention policy which determines:

- how long documents are kept in the current files;
- when documents can be transferred onto computer or microfiche;
- after what length of time documents should be transferred to **dead file** storage. (Dead file storage means that older documents are normally boxed and taken to a store room for a certain period of time before being destroyed.);
- the legal requirements for retention;
- when documents can be destroyed.

Companies will usually discard day-to-day correspondence after a year or two. However, by law, they are required to keep financial accounts, VAT and legal documents for a minimum of six years.

### Disposal

A organisation's retention policy will also contain rules governing how documents should be destroyed. The options are to:

- put them in the waste-bin
- burn them, or
- shred them.

### Operation of a shredder

1    Ensure all paper clips and staples have been removed.

2    Be extra careful not to shred documents which may be required at a later date.

3    Empty the shredder regulary to ensure the machine does not become clogged.

4    Clean the machine regularly – at least once a week.

Using a shredder

**Task 3 ➤**    In recent years newspapers have reported the finding of confidential material in public places. Can you think back to events which have made news headlines? Form a group and discuss:

a)    Events surrounding personal papers which have been found on wasteland or rubbish tips. How could this have happened? **Think about** the implications for medical records, banking details, government papers, etc.

b)    What possible consequences could result if confidential information finds its way into the wrong hands.

c)    What steps you would take to avoid this happening to documents to be discarded from **dead file** storage.

## Security

Security is a major problem in any system of information storage. Records in any form need to be safeguarded against damage, eradication, unauthorised access and theft. There is no foolproof system available and employees need to be fully aware of the capabilities of each storage method.

A routine must be adopted to ensure security procedures are adhered to. In some offices rules are imposed which insist on locking all filing cabinets after use. However, it is no use locking the filing cabinet and leaving the key in the lock. The same applies to storing the keys at night after you lock up. How many people lock a filing cabinet, place the key in the top drawer of the desk and then do not lock the desk?

When designing or considering amending a filing system think about the advantages and disadvantages of the available options regarding security and storage:

| Method | Advantages | Disadvantages |
| --- | --- | --- |
| Horizontal filing cabinet | • Can hold large documents flat. | • Corners of documents become dog-eared and torn.<br>• Unauthorised access is a problem |
| Vertical filing cabinet | • Documents are protected from damp, dust and fire.<br>• Cabinets can be locked. | • Documents can be damaged when files become to bulky.<br>• Print on documents may become faded.<br>• Access to files is easy. |
| Lateral filing cabinet | • Space saving. | • Files are not offered the same protection against dust, fire and wear and tear. |
| Electronic storage | • Use of passwords means limited risk of unauthorised access.<br>• Files can be accessed quickly. | • Files need to be backed-up and floppy disks stored in fire-proof, lockable fire-proof, lockable disk boxes.<br>• Information may be copied or changed easily by unauthorised personnel. |
| Microfilm storage | • Safety and security is at a maximum. | • Individual document location is time-consuming.<br>• Can be damaged by heat. Microfilm can be torn. |

# Maintaining an established electronic filing system

How do you know what information is contained in your database filing system? You need to adopt **good housekeeping** practices when dealing with electronic files. Follow these guidelines:

- file names must always be kept **short** (no more than eight characters may be used) – try to aim for four or five;

- file names are used as a **pointer** to the contents of the file so when naming new files apply a word which will make the connection easy, for example, a database of customer addresses might be named CUSTADD;

- the computer will automatically allocate an extension to any file you create according to the application package you are using. Use the same extensions when recording an index of files, for example:
  - **word processed** documents have the file extension **.doc**
  - **database** files have the extension **.dbf**
  - **back-up** files have the extension **.bak**
  - **spreadsheet** files have the extension **.wks.**

### Indexing electronic files

When using manual filing systems, indexes are used to locate files we need to use. Similarly, when using electronic files it is a good idea to use indexes. Not only can they indicate the correct file to recall they can be useful sources to refer to when **tidying up** or **thinning** out-of-date files.

You can make up your own index systems for recording electronic files or use one similar to this:

| CODE | FILENAME | PROGRAM USED | CONTENTS | DATE |
|------|----------|--------------|----------|------|
|      |          |              |          |      |
|      |          |              |          |      |
|      |          |              |          |      |
|      |          |              |          |      |

Index of computer files

Photocopy the blank index of computer files form on page 267 and fill in the details **every** time you create a new file on disk.

Good housekeeping also means you have to delete out-of-date files from your hard and floppy disks regularly. Those files which must not be deleted can be **protected** or copied to a floppy disk and put away in archival storage.

## Assessment activity 12.1

Remember! Keep your work from this activity for reference and assessment.

You are asked to design a filing system suitable for holding the information on the training and development courses which are offered by the Business Centre.

The system needs to be easily accessed and details of courses located quickly when telephone queries and personal enquiries arise.

The individual files for **each** course will store these details:

Type of course
Suitable entrants
Entry requirements
Fees
Lecturer
Room number
List of days with dates for next two months
Applications for entry to course.

**Note:** Keep the computer file log (**index of computer files**) in a safe place and use it when you need to recall files you have created.

# Supply information for a specific purpose

## Processing information

In your work you may be called upon to provide information regularly. This information may sometimes be routine but at other times you may find details difficult to find.

**Task 4 ➤**

1 How many sources of information within the office could you write down in ten minutes? Try to think of at least ten and then discuss your answers with another member of your group.

2 Here is a table of common sources of information and others which could be harder to locate. How many of these have you used before?

| Common sources | Harder to locate sources |
|---|---|
| Your own memory | ABC Rail Guide |
| Internal telephone directory | ABC Airline Guide |
| Local telephone directories | Whitaker's Almanac |
| Yellow Pages | Civil Service Yearbook |
| Thomson's Directories | Employment Gazette |
| Supplier's catalogues | House of Commons papers |
| National daily newspapers | Hansard |
| Local newspapers | Europages |

| Common sources | Harder to locate sources |
|---|---|
| Post Office leaflets | Conference Blue Book |
| Royal Mail Mailguide | International Association of Conference Interpreters |
| Dictionary | British Tourist Authority guides |
| Rail and coach timetables | Travel Trade Directory |
| Airline timetables | Michelin Guides |
| Librairies | Annual Abstract of Statistics |
| AA and RAC handbooks | BLAISE |
| Roget's Thesaurus | Prestel |
| Information from colleagues | Government departments |
| Office files | Professional and trade associations |
| Databases | |
| Ceefax and Oracle | |

**3** Using the **harder to locate** list find out what information is provided by these publications.

**4** List some ways in which you would find them useful if you were employed as a Personal Assistant within a large organisation.

## Reference books

In your work you may have to supply other members of staff with information. Most information can be obtained from reference books in the office or internal office information retrieval systems.

You may be asked for many kinds of information. For example, a quiet four-star hotel in a foreign country, times of flights to and from other countries or a local reputable car hire organisation. It is highly unlikely that you would be able to give out these details from memory. Try to use your initiative and look up the appropriate reference material. If you get into the habit of doing so you will soon get to know which source of information has the material you require.

Unit 2 of Book 1 has a useful list of common reference sources and types of information provided.

## Methods of presenting information

Information can be provided:

● orally (spoken)

● in writing

● by tables, graphs, charts or diagrams.

When a member of staff asks you to find information she/he may also indicate how this information should be relayed. Alternatively, you may have to use your own initiative in deciding the best possible way of presenting the data.

Decide on the most suitable methods by considering the advantages and disadvantages of each one:

| Advantages | Disadvantages |
|---|---|
| **Oral**<br>There is no time wasted in providing the details required.<br>If the recipient is not clear about a certain point it can be clarified immediately.<br>The information can be discussed between the provider and recipient.<br>If other information is required the recipient can ask for this immediately. | The recipient may fail to pick up an essential detail.<br>Information could confuse the recipient if not presented clearly.<br>The recipient may not be available when the information comes to hand – it may then be forgotten or essential data omitted. |
| **Written**<br>Easier to pass on intricate details correctly.<br>Identical information may be supplied to more than one recipient.<br>Information supplied can again be referred to at a later date. | It takes more time to present the data.<br>It may be harder for the recipient to understand<br>There is no one-to-one communication so information cannot be expanded upon. |
| **Graphs, charts, diagrams**<br>Statistical information is presented in a form which will be easily understood.<br>Figures are produced in reports in a way which the recipient can interpret easily.<br>Can be used to show changes over a period of time. | Usually needs to be presented along with other written or spoken communication. |

## Relaying information orally

Only use this form of presentation when the data required is:

- urgent
- brief
- distinct.

Try to avoid relaying information verbally that contains figures or statistics. **Think** about:

- the purpose of the information
- the needs of the recipient
- the need to omit any surplus details.

### Presenting written information

Ask yourself:

- Is the information better presented in writing or in a pictorial form (diagram, sign, graph, chart, etc.)?

- Will it assist the recipient's understanding if the information is displayed using a combination of text and pictorial forms?

- Is a short note sufficient?

- Is a memo required?

- Is an official letter required?

Whatever form you decide upon try to remember to pass on information in a way which will be easily understood.

**TIPS ➤ ➤**

**Written communication**

- Use simple words and phrases.

- Use short sentences.

- Be clear in your meaning.

- Be direct.

- Only use words which will be understood by the recipient.

- Proof-read all written documentation, checking spelling, grammar and punctuation.

**Task 5 ➤**

Rewrite this passage correctly using an appropriate format. Punctuate and check spelling and grammar.

computer sales amounted to £276098 for the quarter july to september and rose to £352711 by the end of the december quater there was an increese recorded in each month from july to october but sales reduced in novemeber sales in december then increased dramaticaly the busness centre reported a growth in sales for each month of the second half of the year with the exception of november when result were stattic from july to september sales amounted to £109245 and october to december figures are £113220.

**Task 6 ➤**

Find the information asked for in the memos overleaf and present the data in an appropriate format.

1

---

# MEMORANDUM

TO:      General office
FROM:    Jim Dunlop        DATE:   Today's date

---

I am presenting the **Time Management** course to members of
staff of the local council next week. I have been asked
to attend the council offices to deliver the course as
some participants need to be on hand in the building.

Would you please send confirmation of the course
delivery on the first week of next month to Mr Raj
Singh, The Director of Personnel. Also inform Mr Singh
that the maximum number of employees who can be
accommodated at any one time is 15. He has requested
details of the costs involved and I have agreed our
normal price less 25% discount. Please confirm this in
the letter.

---

2

---

# MEMORANDUM

TO:      General office        DATE:   Today's date
FROM:    Theresa McPherson

---

I attended a seminar in Germany last week and stayed at
the Hilton International Hotel in Munchen. I left some
important papers in my room (No 369) which I need
returned quickly. I have a report to compile for the
managerial meeting on Wednesday and need these papers
before then.
    Could you please attend to this for me?

---

## Visual information

Visual information can have an immediate impact on the viewer as it
relays details quickly and is easily understood.

What kind of visual information are you familiar with? How do you
know for instance when you enter a no-smoking area or can cross the
road at a set of lights. Pictures, graphs and charts can provide information
at a glance – there is no need to pour over pages and pages of data.

**Task 7 ➤**

1 Form a group and discuss other signs or symbols you may come
across every day. For example, the symbols which show up on the
control pad of the photocopier.

2 Design a symbol of your own which could be used in the office to
indicate an important rule which needs to be displayed, for example
'No standing on chairs'.

### Displaying statistical information
In business, staff often have to deal with statistics. You need to have an understanding of the types of charts and graphs which are used – both manually drawn and computer generated.

### Flow charts
A flow chart shows the steps to follow in order to achieve a final outcome. It illustrates the **flow** of the procedure and allows for alternative paths to be taken. Symbols or pictures are used as a guide to the process.

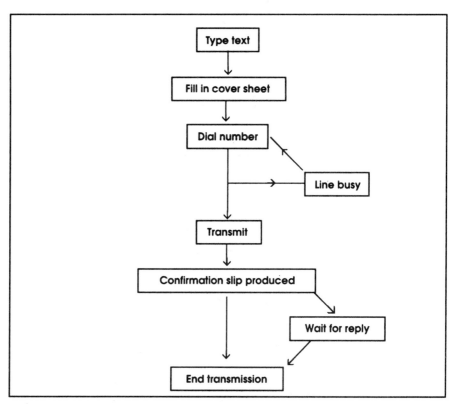

Flow chart to show how to transmit a fax

Flow charts are very useful as instructional aids. In the office environment new members of staff can find them a great help in working unfamiliar machinery or carrying out organisation procedures such as mail handling or processing payments.

**Task 8 ➤**    Make up a flow chart which will guide a trainee in your office in producing text to mailable copy.

### Line graphs
Line graphs are used to show comparisons or trends over time. Take **unemployment** levels, for example. Yearly increases and decreases can be used to show the levels and changes in sucessive years, and comparisons can be drawn. The **horizontal axis** (x axis) may show the years and the **vertical axis** (y axis) the numbers unemployed. Line graphs can be used to show most kinds of statistical information.

**Creating a line graph:**

1    Work out the spacing according to the information you have to provide. For example, if you have to record statistics covering each month of the year then plot 12 even spaces along the horizontal (x) axis.

2    Decide on the spacing required for the vertical axis – work in units which correspond with the squares on the graph paper. Depending upon the information to be recorded use appropriate units, for example, 10, 20, 30, or 10,000, 20,000, 30,000, etc.

3    Include easy to follow labels, for example, 1992, 1993, 1994 or Jan, Feb, March, etc.

4    Use a pencil to mark a dot at each point and then join up the dots using a ruler.

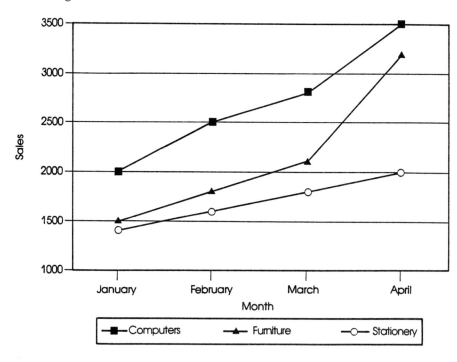

Line graph to show monthly sales by product

**Task 9 ➤**    Produce a simple line graph (using graph paper) from this information. Then produce the same graph by computer.

**Sales figures:**

| 1987 | 1988 | 1989 | 1990 | 1991 | 1992 |
|------|------|------|------|------|------|
| 27,000 | 31,000 | 29,500 | 32,000 | 28,500 | 26,000 |

**Bar charts**

Bar charts are a popular method of producing information which can be interpreted easily. A bar chart can be drawn horizontally across the page or vertically upwards. A simple bar chart uses a single bar for each item. This type of chart is useful when comparing sales of certain goods as increases and decreases in sales are clearly shown. Each item can be presented by a bar (block) labelled along the x axis. The height of the blocks correspond to the figures along the y axis.

A multiple bar chart can be used to compare a number of items over a period of time. Shading or different colours are normally used in multiple bar charts and keys are included to describe what the shading or colour means.

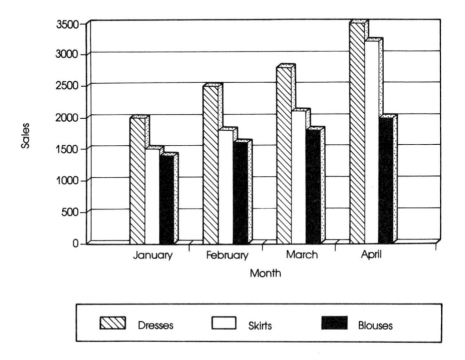

Bar chart to show monthly sales by product

**Task 10 ➤**

1  Draw a bar chart which shows the monthly sales of computers, dot-matrix printers, laser printers and typewriters over a six-month period. Remember to use a key.

|  | Computers | DM printers | Lasers | Typewriters |
|---|---|---|---|---|
| **January** | 14,500 | 7900 | 13,000 | 2500 |
| **February** | 13,000 | 6500 | 11,500 | 1900 |
| **March** | 15,000 | 4750 | 12,750 | 1500 |
| **April** | 14,000 | 4250 | 11,750 | 1500 |
| **May** | 15,000 | 4000 | 13,500 | 1000 |
| **June** | 15,500 | 3500 | 14,000 | 1250 |

2  Suggest to the Sales Manager which item requires an advertising campaign to increase sales and how you might tackle the campaign.

### Pie charts

Pie charts are used to show proportions or percentages of a whole. A circle is drawn and divided into slices called **sectors**. Each slice represents a portion or percentage of the whole pie. A pie chart could be useful to management to show the proportion of staff in certain departments or nature of employment. Here is an example of a pie chart showing company expenditure over a six-month period.

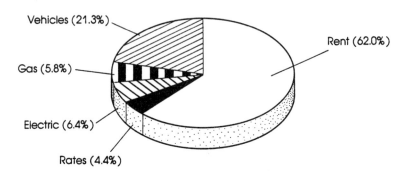

Pie chart to show typical expenditure over a six month period

**TIPS ➤ ➤**

**Creating a pie chart**

- Total the values of all the elements to be represented. This figure will be equivalent to 360°, ie the whole circle or pie.

- Take the value of the first element, divide it by the total value of all the elements, and multiply it by 360°. This gives the size of the segment or slice of the pie that represents this element.

- Do the same for all the elements until you have a set of values which should add to 360°.

- Use a protractor to divide the circle into these values and label each segment appropriately.

**Task 11 ➤**    Produce a simple pie chart which shows the percentage of consumer expenditure from this information:

| | |
|---|---|
| Housing | 20% |
| Cars and travel | 15% |
| Food, drink, tobacco | 14% |
| Leisure | 10% |
| Clothing | 12% |
| Other | 29% |

**Diagrams and maps**

If you are asked to attend an interview in a strange location a map with directions is often provided. A diagram may also be given showing the floor plan and layout of the building. Maps and plans are used for various purposes and can range from being very simple to very complex.

**Task 12 ➤**    Draw a simple map which indicates the route you take from home to your college or place of work. Draw a diagram which shows the location of departments within the college or office.

# Itineraries

An itinerary outlines a plan for a business trip or visit and provides information on a list of events in date and time order. It highlights:

- departure and arrival times
- length of stay
- method of travel
- appointments
- locations
- individuals to be met
- hotel reservations.

Itineraries are helpful reference sources for business people who engage in any travel. An itinerary lets people check details while travelling. If it is a short visit it is best to produce the itinerary on a card which can be placed in a handbag or pocket for quick reference. When the trip is a lengthy one involving various meetings you can produce a card for each day's events. Look at this example:

```
Mr A Brown - visit to Turnberry (week-end)


Friday 29 January

1630 hrs  Taxi from home to Heathrow Airport
          (Executive Travel - 081 544 6480)
1715 hrs  Check in at London Heathrow
1745 hrs  Depart London Heathrow - Flight BA4663
1830 hrs  Arrive Glasgow Airport
1845 hrs  Taxi from Glasgow Airport to Turnberry
          Hotel, Girvan
          (Central Taxis - 0292 267655)
2015 hrs  Check-in Turnberry Hotel
          (Single suite reserved. Confirmation
          attached.)


Mr A Brown - visit to New York


Monday 1 February

0615 hours    Taxi from Turnberry Hotel to Glasgow
              Airport
              (Central Taxis - 0292 267655)
0745 hours    Check in Glasgow Airport
0815 hours    Depart Glasgow - Flight BA4863
0930 hours    Arrive London Heathrow
1100 hours    Depart London Heathrow - Flight BA175
```

```
1350 hours      Arrive New York - J F Kennedy Airport
1400 hours      Check in at Excelsior Hotel
                (Single room with bath reserved.
                Confirmation attached.)
```

**Task 13 ➤**   Complete Mr Brown's itinerary for the return journey. He leaves New York the following Friday on flight BA176 departing at 9 p.m. and arrives in London at 8.45 a.m. the following morning. The minimum check-in time for flights is 30 minutes. Decide which flight will take Mr Brown from London to the airport nearest to your town and the time of arrival. Mr Brown will be met at the local airport by an organisation car.

## Assessment activity 12.2

**Remember! Keep your work from this activity for reference and assessment.**

This activity needs to be carried out as a mixed assessment. Some role-play situations are combined with practical exercises. Where you are asked to present information orally you need to work with another student.

1   Produce the information asked for in this memo:

---

### MEMORANDUM

TO:     General office
FROM:   John Allen            DATE:  Today's date

---

Can you produce these figures in bar chart form on graph paper for me. Label axes clearly and give the chart a suitable title. Use an appropriate scale and key. I need this done quickly for a report on marketing to be presented to the management meeting on Thursday.

| Service | Jan | Feb | Mar | Apr | May | June |
|---|---|---|---|---|---|---|
| Word processing | 9000 | 8750 | 8250 | 9500 | 7500 | 10000 |
| Computing | 4300 | 6000 | 5500 | 7500 | 5000 | 8500 |
| Training courses | 11000 | 10000 | 9900 | 9000 | 9500 | 13000 |
| Business advice | 4000 | 4900 | 6500 | 7000 | 8500 | 9600 |

---

2   Margaret Murphy has contacted you via the internal telephone system. She has asked you to find the telephone number of Media Europe Italian at 60 c M D'Azeglio, 10126 Torino.

3   Mr Brown is making a business trip to Canada tomorrow. He wants to know the current exchange rate and how many dollars he will get for £540. (Remember to allow for the bank or travel agent's commission.) Telephone him at his extension with the information as soon as you have it.

4   Find out today's share prices for these organisations:
    Abbey National      National Power    British Airports

| | | |
|---|---|---|
| TSB Group | Power Gen | British Steel |
| Ferranti | Trafalgar House | Rank Organisation |
| Marks & Spencer | Midland Bank | Kwik Fit |
| British Aerospace | Eleco Holdings | Grampian TV |
| Lonrho | RMC Xerox | Weir Group |
| Pilkington | Macallen-Glenlivet. | |

5 Produce a flow-chart to guide the new trainee on the mail in and out procedures.

6 George Hendry telephones from a customer's premises to ask you when the next training course on **Extending WordPerfect** begins and what the cost is.

7 Michelle Thomas is considering purchasing some new workstations for the general office to accommodate the new computer systems. You are required to select five different workstations from office suppliers' catalogues; these can either be static or mobile and must be between £200 and £300.

   When you have selected the most suitable quality workstations, type out a list detailing the reference number, supplier, make and price. Also give a brief description of each one and list special features.

   This information is needed by 10 a.m. tomorrow. If you are unable to meet the specifications please suggest alternatives which could be above or below the price range.

8 The Business Centre Manager has asked that you produce a graph which shows the comparisons between profits over four years.

| | 1989 | 1990 | 1991 | 1992 |
|---|---|---|---|---|
| | | | (£000) | |
| January | 88 | 93 | 86 | 84 |
| February | 76 | 72 | 68 | 70 |
| March | 78 | 80 | 76 | 75 |
| April | 80 | 84 | 82 | 78 |
| May | 92 | 96 | 86 | 84 |
| June | 90 | 90 | 84 | 82 |
| July | 88 | 90 | 86 | 80 |
| August | 84 | 86 | 82 | 78 |
| September | 86 | 78 | 84 | 82 |
| October | 88 | 88 | 86 | 84 |
| November | 86 | 88 | 84 | 80 |
| December | 85 | 87 | 83 | 81 |

a) Produce the graph in an appropriate format.

b) Draft and attach an initial report commenting on the position revealed by the graph.

# UNIT 13 | Information processing

## Process records in a database

### What is a database?

A database is an electronic filing system which stores information in an organised way. A computer database is an electronic equivalent of the paper-based filing methods which are used in office systems.

A **database** is composed of a collection of records all containing the same sort of information.

Office filing cabinets are used to store information such as personnel records and correspondence. Similarly, card indexes may contain names, addresses and telephone numbers, and you can write down a list of stock held by your organisation. These are all examples of databases. However, a filing cabinet does not constitute a database – it is the way information is organised in the cabinet which makes it a database.

#### Advantages of electronic databases

Manual filing systems and electronic databases are an aid to storage and retrieval of information. Electronic databases have the advantages of being:

- space saving – there is no need to keep vast amounts of paper in files;

- very fast – information is retrieved in an organised manner quickly;

- up-to-date – information held on a database can be easily altered and kept up to date;

- efficient – there is no need to search through large amounts of paper to find information. File management is simple and mistakes can be rectified quickly.

**Task 1 ➤**    1  Form a group and discuss how you would find or change this information which is stored in manual filing systems:

a)  Customer records in the filing cabinet are classified alphabetically. You have been asked to provide the Sales Manager with two lists – one of customers who are based in Birmingham and another of those based in Manchester.

b)  The telephone number of a cash-and-carry warehouse which is located on the outskirts of town. Your boss cannot remember the name but has the address. Would it be possible to find the telephone number? If not, why not?

c)  The visible card index has been written up alphabetically listing names and telephone numbers. Will you manage to fit in another five records which have different letters as surnames? What would you have to do to update the listing?

d)  British Telecom have sent you correspondence informing you of a change to some area codes within London. It is necessary to update this information on all records of customers, suppliers and contacts in this area. How would you start? Will this be an easy task?

e)  The departments within the office have been re-organised – some have been merged and others split. The personnel records have to be altered to show new employee numbers, departments and locations. Will you need to make out new records for all employees who are involved in the re-organisation? If so, why?

2  In all of the above situations do you think the final outcomes would be accurate? If not, why not?

3  How long do you think it will take you to produce the information in the required format in each case?

## Benefits of electronic filing

When you use a computer database as a filing system, problems such as those encountered in the task above will be eliminated. The major benefit of electronic filing is the **speed and accuracy** with which information is provided in an organised format. For example, finding a customer's details from thousands of records takes less than two seconds. Likewise, sorting a database file into alphabetical order only takes a few minutes.

A computerised database also has the ability to examine information from a number of angles. For example, you could search for a customer account number by name or reference.

A computerised database that can do all these functions is known as a **database management system**.

## Designing a database

Before you begin to create a database you have to think about:

• what information it needs to hold

- who will be using the database
- what purposes it will be used for
- whether the database format meets the objectives.

For example, you may wish to design a database which holds supplier information. The obvious **fields** (information areas) to create would be:

- supplier name
- address and telephone number.

However, other members of staff might need other details to be recorded such as:

- contact name
- date of last order placed
- items normally purchased
- balance of account
- credit limit, and so on.

> **Remember!**
> **Before**
> **creating a**
> **structure**
> **think about**
> **the**
> **foundations!**

**TIPS ➤ ➤**

**Database design**

- Write down everything you can think of that **could** go into a database file.
- Consult other users of the proposed system about their needs.
- Take time to consider the order in which information should appear.
- Think about field names, descriptions, types of data, sizes of fields, calculations, indexes, etc.
- Allocate field names which refer to the data stored in those fields.
- Eliminate fields which are not necessary for your organisation's purposes.

## Creating a database file

### Loading the database
When you switch on the computer, a menu of program names might appear similar to this one:

```
1.   Word processing
2.   Spreadsheet
3.   Database
4.   Accounting
5.   Computer-aided design
6.   Desk top publishing
0.   Utilities
```

Select the number on your menu which corresponds with the software you will be using to access the program. This activates the application package and loads the database program. Displayed on screen will now be a menu similar to this one:

| **Catalog** | **Tools** | | **Exit** | | | **Time** |
|---|---|---|---|---|---|---|
| | | | CATALOG: C\DBASE\ | | | |
| Data | Queries | Forms | Reports | Labels | Applications | |
| (create) | (create) | (create) | (create) | (create) | (create) | |

File:
Description:

Once you start to use a database you will find that the names of the **files** will be displayed somewhere near the status line on the screen.

### Structure and data

> **Remember!**
> **Change the active drive to A to save material onto your own disk.**

The file contains the **structure** and the **data**. These terms can best be explained by looking at an example record:

| Structure | Data |
|---|---|
| Surname | Jones |
| Forename | Anne |
| Date of birth | 31.12.76 |

The structure remains the same for each record while the data changes.

### Character

A character is a letter of the alphabet, a number, a symbol (for example, a full stop or £ sign) or a space.

### Field

> **Remember!**
> **Never include blank spaces.**

Each piece of information is called a **field**. In the above example, Jones is a field. Surname is the **field label** or **field title** which identifies the field. Always choose a name which relates to the data which will be stored in a field.

Names can be from one to ten characters long and contain letters, numbers, symbols and the underscore character. The first character must be a letter. For example, if you have a field which is to hold the account numbers of customers you could name this field either ACCNUM or ACC_NUM.

### Record

All the fields relating to a particular item or person are known as a **record**.

### File

Each set of related records is called a **file**. For example, a company may hold a database file of stock records, personnel records or customer records.

### Form

The first step is to create a blank master form onto which various items of information can be recorded. This is the screen display showing the fields into which the data is inserted.

### Creating a database file (worked example)

Although it would be impossible to give complete instructions for every database package this worked example will provide you with a guide. We have used basic database terms to help you with selecting functions.

> Remember!
>
> A database file has two distinct parts:
>
> - the structure (a form like a record card)
>
> - the data (the information you key in via the keyboard).

USE THE CURSOR KEYS TO MOVE AROUND THE SCREEN

### Creating the structure

Check that the flashing cursor is sitting on the word **Create** in the data panel and press the **Enter** key to select this option. A **form** like the one below will be displayed for you to create the **structure**:

| NUM | FIELD NAME | FIELD TYPE | WIDTH | DEC | INDEX |
|-----|-----------|-----------|-------|-----|-------|
| 1 | – – – – | – – – – | – – – | | |
| 2 | – – – – | – – – – | – – – | | |
| 3 | – – – – | – – – – | – – – | | |

You will then be asked to define the **structure** or create the **form**. Then you will be prompted to enter each **field** name followed by the field type. This allocates a data classification to each field. You can normally select one of five data types:

$$
\begin{aligned}
C &= \text{character} \\
D &= \text{date} \\
N &= \text{numeric} \\
L &= \text{logical} \\
M &= \text{memo.}
\end{aligned}
$$

**Numeric-type** data is for all numbers which have to be used for calculation purposes. For numerical data such as telephone numbers and stock code numbers which are not used in calculations always use **character-type** data.

**Logical-type** data is used for fields which contain a value representing true or false. You can type the value as upper or lower case T (True), F (False), Y (Yes) or N (No), as appropriate.

**Memo** is used to attach reports about the current record when you do not want a limit to the amount of data in the field.

### Specifying the field width

Use the field **width** specification to indicate the maximum number of characters or digits a field can hold. You must specify widths for character and numeric fields. The widths for date, logical and memo are automatically inserted.

### Specifying decimal places in the field width

You must indicate the number of decimal places (Dec) for a numeric field.

Enter this structure:

| Field name | Type | Width | Dec |
|---|---|---|---|
| SNAME | C | 12 | |
| FNAME | C | 10 | |
| DOB | D | | |
| POS | C | 20 | |
| SALARY | N | 07 | 02 |

### To finish creating the structure

After entering field 5 the cursor will be sitting on empty field 6; press the **Enter** key at this point. Save this structure and select the option which allows you to continue the operation. You will then be asked for a filename; type PAYROLL.

### Inputting records

The screen prompt will then prompt to ask if you wish to **Input data records now**; press **Y** for yes.

Enter the ten records below in the **exact** order as shown. **All** data entered on records must be in the same format, for example:

BLOCKED CAPS, or
Initial Caps.

It may be sensible to put on the CAPS LOCK facility.

**Hint**
Make sure the **flashing cursor** is sitting on the SNAME field of the first record before entering your data.

| Name | DOB | Position | Salary |
|------|-----|----------|--------|
| Pearson Lorraine | 02/04/54 | Computer Operator | 15795 |
| Wells James | 02/01/65 | Supervisor Mailroom | 12955 |
| Kenny Michael | 23/06/67 | Clerk Sales | 11069 |
| Karsan Sean | 08/09/71 | Clerk Purchasing | 11069 |
| Santos Linda | 12/12/68 | Personal Assistant | 13992 |
| McPherson Theresa | 01/09/63 | Manager Training | 17432 |
| Black David | 09/04/70 | Clerk Accounts | 11069 |
| Freeman Angela | 10/08/67 | Personal Assistant | 13992 |
| Gilmour Tracy | 13/10/63 | Manager Print Room | 17432 |
| Keenan Carly | 02/04/66 | Computer Programmer | 16666 |

Each row of the above database contains an employee name, date of birth, position and salary and is related to the other rows because they all contain the same **types** of information:

- The **rows** are individual **records** as the information contained in each row relates to the same person.
- The **columns** are **fields** because they hold the same type of information on each record.

### Saving the records

When you have finished entering the ten records the cursor will be sitting on an empty record form. Press the **Enter** key on the empty record to finish and save the records you have just completed.

### Proof-reading your records

As with any other text produced it is essential to proof-read the contents of your file to ensure details have been entered correctly.

Remember!
Check:

- **text for spelling mistakes;**

- **numerical data to ensure figures have not been transposed;**

- **each record to make sure you have not mixed details from other records.**

Make sure all records are correct **before printing**.

### Printing the contents

Each package has different commands for printing. Consult your manual or ask your tutor for guidance. Print out the contents of the PAYROLL file.

### Making changes to an original database file

Information held on file needs to be up-to-date and accurate. You have entered ten employee records into a database file, PAYROLL, which is accurate at the time of entry. But what happens if one of the employees moves to another department, is promoted or has a salary increase? You will need to change this information on your records.

This is where an electronic filing system has the advantage over a paper-based one. You can recall the original file to the screen and choose to Browse or Edit. In a matter of seconds the information will be updated and you will have an up-to-date record.

We are now going to make changes to the original PAYROLL file. Select the option to use **PAYROLL**.

Choose to **browse** the file. This will take you into what is known as the **browse screen**. You can use the cursor keys to browse up and down or from side to side in this mode. Browse allows you to check details or find records which need to be edited.

Change these records:

a)     David Black's date of birth is 09/04/71.

b)     Lorraine Pearson's salary is £14598.

c)     Carly Keenan's date of birth is 13/05/66.

### Adding new records to an existing file

When you expand a paper-based filing system space is at a premium. Depending upon the classification method used it may take a great deal of time to reorganise the system in order to enter new records. With an electronic system adding records is quick and simple. Choose the option to **Append** or **Add** which allows you to insert further records to the file.

Enter these new records:

| Name | DOB | Position | Salary |
|------|-----|----------|--------|
| McMillan Jane | 16/03/59 | Manager Accounts | 17432 |
| Murphy Margaret | 09/02/68 | Personal Assistant | 13992 |
| Allen John | 30/03/61 | Manager Marketing | 17432 |

Print the updated file.

### Deleting records

As with adding, deleting records is quick and easy. Records which are no longer active need not be kept on file until a disposal date. These can be marked for deletion and hidden away from the active database. If records need to be recalled to use they can be unmarked and brought back into the system. Alternatively, you may wish to copy the records to a separate inactive database which allows you to remove them from the current records.

Two employees' records have to be transferred to another file. The records will have to be erased from this file. Mark for deletion or delete the records of Sean Karsan and James Wells.

Print out the new contents of the file.

# Maintaining a database

From the previous text you will understand that for accurate details to be kept on a database new records have to be added, changes have to be made to existing records and old records should be deleted from the current database.

### Organising the file

With paper-based filing systems documents are sorted and stored according to a classification, for example, numerical. Indexes have to be used to direct you to material which has been filed in various systems. It takes up a lot of time searching through indexes and files looking for the correct item.

Electronic records can be rearranged quickly to find a record by any given **field**, for example, area, post code, account number or surname. You can **sort** a database on any field or combination of fields.

### Sorting the database file

You have managed to enter, edit, and add records to the PAYROLL file. However, the file is not in a **logical** order. It can be arranged into alphabetical order, or by age, salary or position.

By **sorting** the file into a logical order you create a new file (in the order you require) from the master one. Therefore, a new table will be created with the records in a specific order.

To classify the file and arrange it in alphabetical order.

- Choose the option to **use** the PAYROLL file.

- Choose to **sort**.

- Sort the file on **surname**.

- Name the sorted file **PAY2**.

Print out the sorted database file PAY2.

# Searching the database to locate particular records

When you use a paper-based manual filing system, finding particular letters or documents can be like looking for a needle in a haystack. Suppose you are working in a college in East Sussex and your boss asks you to give her/him a list of all students who live in Eastbourne. The student records are filed according to student number. It would take you days or weeks to physically check every record. Using an electronic filing system this list can be produced in minutes.

Using the **search** command the PAYROLL file could provide details of all managers' records. Ask your course tutor to provide you with guidelines on your particular database package for this function and then print out the following listings:

- all employees earning over £15,000 per annum;

- all employees aged 30 years and above;

• all Personal Assistants.

It is also possible to search the file to provide a listing which meets more than one criteria, for example, all employees over the age of 30 who earn less than £15,000 per annum.

Search and then print out the following listings:

• all clerks under the age of 30;

• all employees under the age of 25 who work as Personal Assistants.

Save and print the file.

**Remember! Back up the file.**

## Function keys

Function keys appear on all keyboards. You may have a set of keys marked from F1 to F12. Pressing function keys provides a quick entry to various operations. For example:

HELP – Displays on-screen help messages and instructions.

Find out which function key accesses the help screen and use it when necessary.

Help is normally **context responsive**, which means that Help messages and screens refer to the task or command you are performing when you request Help.

## Data security

Unit 3 of Book 1 covers data security in detail.

**Task 2  ➤**  Explain the features of a database in your own words by answering these questions with a brief summary.

1  June Oliver has asked you to create a simple database to hold information on accounts received by suppliers. The data is to be kept in a file called SUPP. It will contain the following information from each supplier:

| | |
|---|---|
| OUR ACCOUNT NUMBER | SUPPLIER'S NAME |
| STREET ADDRESS | STREET ADDRESS 2 |
| TOWN | COUNTRY |
| SUPPLIER CONTACT NAME | TELEPHONE NUMBER |
| BALANCE WE OWE SUPPLIER | |

Explain how you would set this file up – what would the field names be, the sizes, types, etc.?

2  How do you look through records on a database?

3  How do you search for particular records?

4   What does **append** mean?

5   What will you do to provide a listing of information from all the records on your file, for example, name and telephone number?

6   What is the best method to use to alter data in a large file?

7   How would you go about increasing the length of a **field**?

8   Design a structure for a database of your choice.

You can now proceed to create some small database files. Always back up the original file on floppy disk.

**Task 3 ➤**

Here is a listing of the top 20 records at the beginning of February 1993. Plan and create a database to hold the information from this list:

| Title | Chart position | Recorded by | Previous position |
|---|---|---|---|
| I Will Always Love You | 02 | Whitney Houston | 01 |
| Little Bird | 03 | Annie Lennox | New Entry |
| I Lift My Cup | 20 | Glow Worm | New Entry |
| I'm Easy | 19 | Faith No More | 12 |
| We Are Family | 15 | Sister Sledge | 10 |
| How Can I Love You More | 08 | M People | 09 |
| No Limit | 01 | 2 Unlimited | 02 |
| All You Need Is Love | 20 | Tom Jones | 19 |
| Ordinary World | 06 | Duran Duran | 06 |
| The Love I Lost | 04 | West End | 03 |
| Exterminate | 07 | Snap | 04 |
| Independence | 14 | Lulu | 11 |
| Tragic Comic | 16 | Extreme | 15 |
| Sweet Harmony | 10 | Beloved | 08 |
| Deep | 05 | East 17 | 05 |
| Open Your Mind | 11 | Asura | 07 |
| Stairway to Heaven | 09 | Rolf Harris | New Entry |
| You're In a Bad Way | 12 | St Etienne | New Entry |
| Vienna | 13 | Ultravox | New Entry |
| If I Ever Lose My Faith | 17 | Sting | New Entry |

1   Print out a listing which shows the top 20 records in this order:

   a)   Place in charts this week.

   b)   Song title.

   c)   Recorded by.

   d)   Last week's placings.

2   List all the details of new entries and print out this information.

3   Reconstruct last week's top 20 list and show the new entries at the bottom of the list.

**Task 4 ➤**     A self-employed travel consultant has asked the Business Centre to prepare a database which will show peak season average monthly temperatures at various holiday resorts.
Plan and create the database from this information:

| Resort | Apr | May | June | July | Aug | Sept | Oct |
|---|---|---|---|---|---|---|---|
| Florida | 81 | 85 | 88 | 90 | 90 | 88 | 84 |
| Malta | 64 | 72 | 79 | 84 | 84 | 81 | 75 |
| Turkey | 68 | 77 | 82 | 91 | 91 | 81 | 73 |
| Crete | 68 | 73 | 81 | 84 | 84 | 81 | 75 |
| Zante | 66 | 73 | 82 | 88 | 88 | 82 | 73 |
| Corfu | 66 | 73 | 82 | 88 | 88 | 82 | 73 |
| Cyprus | 75 | 84 | 93 | 99 | 99 | 91 | 82 |
| Ibiza | 66 | 72 | 79 | 84 | 84 | 81 | 73 |
| Majorca | 66 | 72 | 79 | 84 | 84 | 81 | 73 |
| Minorca | 66 | 72 | 79 | 84 | 84 | 81 | 73 |
| Costa Del Sol | 70 | 73 | 81 | 84 | 86 | 81 | 73 |
| Costa Blanca | 70 | 75 | 82 | 88 | 88 | 84 | 77 |
| Gran Canaria | 73 | 75 | 79 | 84 | 84 | 82 | 79 |
| Tenerife | 73 | 75 | 79 | 84 | 84 | 82 | 79 |
| Lanzarote | 73 | 75 | 79 | 84 | 84 | 82 | 79 |
| Algarve | 68 | 72 | 77 | 82 | 82 | 79 | 72 |

1   Which is the warmest country in July?

2   Which is the coolest in June?

3   Sort the data alphabetically to a new file.

4   Print out a listing showing the warmest country in August down to the coolest.

5   Print a report listing resorts in order of temperature for June, July and August.

**Task 5 ➤**     Microplus needs to have a database of monetary exchange rates which can be updated daily. The database is a simple one and will provide details of:

**COUNTRY     CURRENCY     £EXRATE**

1   Create the database and decide the length of each **field**.

2   Save the form and enter the data on the following page.

| Country | Currency | Exchange rate |
|---|---|---|
| Denmark | Krone | |
| Germany | D Mark | |
| Austria | Schilling | |
| Hong Kong | Dollar | |
| Finland | Markka | |
| Belgium | Franc | |
| Luxembourg | Franc | |
| Norway | Krone | |
| Netherlands | Guilder | |
| France | Franc | |
| Iceland | Krona | |
| Cyprus | Pound | |
| Italy | Lira | |
| Portugal | Escudo | |
| Yugoslavia | Dinar | |
| Turkey | Lira | |
| USA | Dollar | |
| Canada | Dollar | |
| Switzerland | Franc | |
| Sweden | Krona | |
| Spain | Peseta | |
| USSR | Rouble | |
| New Zealand | Dollar | |
| Australia | Dollar | |
| Greece | Drachma | |
| Israel | Pound | |
| Pakistan | Rupee | |
| Egypt | Pound | |
| China | Yuan | |
| United Arab Emirates | Dirham | |

3   Find the current exchange rate from a reference source and enter the details.

4   Print out a separate listing of all countries whose currencies are:

   a)   pounds

   b)   dollars

   c)   francs.

5   Find the country with krone for currency and print out the exchange rate.

6   State from which source you found the exchange rate.

7   Print out a report listing the countries in alphabetical order and showing currency and exchange rate.

8   Save and keep this file and update it regularly.

**Note:** You will have to use this information for tasks in Unit 19.

## Assessment activity 13.1

*Remember! Keep your work from this activity for reference and assessment.*

In this activity you have to set up a database of agents' customers in Britain. Name the file AGENTCUS and use these fields and formats:

| Fields | Type of field | Size of field |
|--------|---------------|---------------|
| Accno | Character | 6 |
| Area | Numeric | 2 |
| Company | Character | 30 |
| Credlim | Numeric | 6 + 2 DP |
| Agent | Character | 12 |

1  Enter these 30 records:

| Accno | Area | Company | Credlim | Agent |
|-------|------|---------|---------|-------|
| TO601 | 6 | Typewrite Ltd | 7456.00 | D Barclay |
| TO602 | 6 | Kenwell Electrics | 1000.00 | D Barclay |
| TO605 | 6 | Rowallen Tools | 987.00 | D Barclay |
| RO604 | 6 | R M Castings | 5766.50 | D Barclay |
| GO105 | 1 | GRC Ltd | 1200.00 | D Smart |
| WO104 | 1 | Walsh Travle | 3800.00 | D Smart |
| SO106 | 1 | Selex | 3000.00 | D Smart |
| DO902 | 9 | Dolphin Knitwear | 6745.00 | E Grant |
| CO903 | 9 | Cotswald Catering | 9576.58 | E Grant |
| PO901 | 9 | Pentwyn Design | 1000.00 | E Grant |
| AO303 | 3 | APS Coachworks | 5000.00 | G Renton |
| MO311 | 3 | Mowbray Fabrications | 4500.00 | G Renton |
| CO304 | 3 | Cumbria Classics | 2900.00 | G Renton |
| PO207 | 2 | Phoenix Motors | 9560.00 | H Boyd |
| AO201 | 2 | ABC Ltd | 4800.00 | H Boyd |
| CO204 | 2 | Copyclub | 1600.00 | H Boyd |
| BO208 | 2 | BND Electronics | 3645.00 | H Boyd |
| AO802 | 8 | Ace Management | 6450.00 | J Selby |
| EO806 | 8 | ECT Consultants | 9500.00 | J Selby |
| EO804 | 8 | Flotta Services | 9875.00 | J Selby |
| BO409 | 4 | Bradford Heating | 1500.00 | L Jones |
| WO408 | 4 | Wilmslow Communications | 9000.00 | L Jones |
| AO405 | 4 | Ashley Leisure | 1500.00 | L Jones |
| PO404 | 4 | Priestley & Sons | 2800.00 | L Jones |
| RO702 | 7 | Rigsby & Sons | 4500.00 | M Austin |
| KO703 | 7 | Kostain Engineers | 9876.00 | M Austin |
| TO705 | 7 | Tatler Publishing | 1750.00 | M Austin |
| DO501 | 5 | Domino Limited | 7800.00 | S Stavros |
| RO503 | 5 | AVX Ltd | 4550.00 | S Stavros |
| AO503 | 5 | Astor Company | 7896.00 | S Stavros |

2  Print out a list of the original data.

3  One of the records has the customer's name spelt wrongly – find and edit it.

**4**  Save the file and make a back-up copy.

**5**  Sort the records into area order onto a file named AREACUST.

**6**  Print out a list and save this file.

**7**  Sort the original file into alphabetical order on the basis of company names. Save this file as CUSTNAME and print out a listing of the contents.

**8**  Print out a list of G Renton's customers.

**9**  Print out a list of Area 7 customer names and credit limits.

**10**  Delete the record of Cumbria Classics.

**11**  Add these new records:

| Accno | Area | Company | Credlim | Agent |
|-------|------|---------|---------|-------|
| RO503 | 5 | Radbrook Systems | 9098.00 | S Stavros |
| PO701 | 7 | Pricewise Office Design | 8765.00 | M Austin |

**12**  Bradford Heating has been merged with Yorkshire Heating and is now know by the latter name – change this record.

**13**  Customers with a credit limit of £1000.00 have had this reviewed and the limit has been upped to £2000.00 – change these records.

**14**  Print out a listing from the new file.

# Process information in spreadsheets

## What is a spreadsheet?

A spreadsheet is a computer program which can be used for any sort of arithmetical, statistical or mathematical calculation. It is used to store and edit information in a framework which will produce data in numerical or graphical form. Within the framework numbers, text and formulae are used to carry out financial calculations quickly and efficiently.

Once a spreadsheet program has been created it can be used over and over again with different figures (data) inserted. This can be useful when you have the same reports to produce on a weekly, monthly, quarterly or yearly basis. The only information which may change on some reports is the financial data; the calculation formulae and text may remain the same. All you need do with a spreadsheet is insert new figures.

The **framework** of a spreadsheet is a series of boxes in a grid pattern which contain:

- columns identified by letters (or sometimes numbers)

- rows identified by numbers

- cells – the point at which rows and columns intersect.

Look at the example opposite:

| | A | B | C | D | E | F | G | Column letter |
|---|---|---|---|---|---|---|---|---|
| 1 | | | | | | | | |
| 2 | | | | | | | | |
| 3 | | | | | | | | |
| 4 | | | | | ← | | | Cell E4 |
| 5 | | | | | | | | |
| 6 | | | | | | | | |
| 7 | | | | | | | | |

**Row number**

Spreadsheets provide a means of displaying and calculating information. They allow the user to **PERFORM**:

- Present information

- Edit information

- Rearrange information

- Format information

- Organise information

- Re-use a master form to insert up-to-date information

- Make decisions based on the information provided.

## Types of spreadsheets and their uses

**Accounting** – to calculate profit and loss accounts, make cash projections, present cash balances, etc.
**Advanced statistics** – for data analysis.
**Analysing data** – for analysing results of surveys and polls.
**Analysing financial data** – to calculate interest, percentages, etc.
**Budgeting** – to keep up-to-date on company expenditure.
**Business estimates** – to calculate income tax, job costings, stock control, etc.
**Cash flow analysis** – forecasting probable income and expenditure which may identify possible cash flow problems.
**Conversions** – to work out exchange rates and other conversion tables.
**Mathematical functions** – for calculations and geometric operations.
**Presenting information** – to display numerical information in tabular form which is easy to understand.

There are numerous spreadsheet packages available. Whichever package you use the basic functions needed for the tasks which follow will be the same.

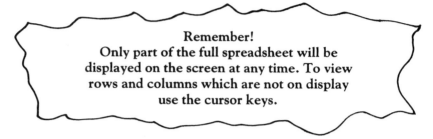

Remember!
Only part of the full spreadsheet will be displayed on the screen at any time. To view rows and columns which are not on display use the cursor keys.

## Constructing a spreadsheet

There are eight stages involved in the production of a spreadsheet. Of these the first – which does not involve the computer – is by far the most important. The stages must be completed in this sequence:

1.  **Plan** the layout:

    ● use a main heading

    ● insert column and row headings

    ● choose the correct placing for text

    ● decide whether figures have to be in £s, whole numbers or have decimal places included.

2.  Keep the **design** as simple as possible.

3.  Create the **structure**.

4.  Enter the **formulae**.

5.  Enter the **data**.

6.  **Test** the spreadsheet by having a 'trial run'.

7.  Name the spreadsheet according to your organisation's rules, giving it a sensible title and extension if necessary (see Unit 12).

8.  Produce the **output**.

Data is stored in each cell of a spreadsheet in one of four ways by:

● entering text

● entering numbers

● entering a formula

● leaving the cell blank.

Text is used for descriptive purposes such as column headings, row descriptions, report titles, etc.

## Preparing a 'skeleton' spreadsheet

What do you want the spreadsheet to produce? As in the example below you may want to create a spreadsheet which will provide details of total monthly expenditure, half-yearly totals or yearly figures.

To do this:

- set up the **column headings** first, for example, Jan through to Dec (remember to leave **cell A1 blank** as this will be used for descriptive purposes);
- use the **A column** to set up **row headings**, for example, Rent, Rates, etc;
- insert **formulae** for calculations to be carried out;
- **adapt** column widths to suit the descriptions and figures;
- **save** the skeleton.

|   | A | B | C | D | E | F | G |
|---|---|---|---|---|---|---|---|
| 1 | HALF-YEARLY EXPENDITURE | | | | | | |
| 2 | | | | | | | |
| 3 | | Jan | Feb | Mar | Apr | May | Jun |
| 4 | Rent | 1400 | | | | | |
| 5 | Rates | 300 | | | | | |
| 6 | Electric | 140 | | | | | |
| 7 | Gas | 125 | | | | | |
| 8 | Vehicles | 495 | | | | | |
| 9 | TOTAL | @SUM (B4..B8) | | | | | |

Set up the above spreadsheet on your computer – enter your own figures in columns C4 – G8.

### Entering numbers
In column B of the above spreadsheet, cells B4 – B8 have individual figures entered showing the monthly expenditure on each item. Figures will also be entered in the cells for other months.

### Entering formulae to calculate figures
Using a computer spreadsheet package means that you do not have to calculate manually and enter figures for additions, subtractions, multiplications, percentages, etc. This is where a spreadsheet will save you work – the calculations are done for you.

In order to let the computer carry out the calculations you need to enter a **formula** into a cell. For example:

cell B9 has the formula **@SUM(B4..B8)** entered. This tells the computer that the figure to be entered in this cell is the total of cells B4+B5+B6+B7+B8.

If after entering the figures you found that the amount for electric was £180 not £140 all you need do is change the figure in cell B6 and the total amount displayed in cell B9 will automatically alter to the correct amount. Try this and see.

The same **formula** can be copied from cell B9 to H9. Insert a total column on your spreadsheet.

|   | A | B | C | D | E | F | G | H |
|---|---|---|---|---|---|---|---|---|
| 1 | HALF-YEARLY EXPENDITURE | | | | | | | |
| 2 | | | | | | | | |
| 3 | | Jan | Feb | Mar | Apr | May | Jun | Total |
| 4 | Rent | 1400 | | | | | | |
| 5 | Rates | 300 | | | | | | |
| 6 | Electric | 140 | | | | | | |
| 7 | Gas | 125 | | | | | | |
| 8 | Vehicles | 495 | | | | | | |
| 9 | TOTAL | | | | | | | |

Cell H4 could have the formula **@SUM(B4..G4)** entered and copied down to cell H9 which would then provide the gross total of each individual item of expenditure plus the total of all expenses in cell H9.

### Other formulae

| | |
|---|---|
| E7/5 | This formula means that the value stored in cell E7 is divided by 5. |
| (E7/2) * 10 | This formula means that the value stored in cell E7 is divided by 2 and then multiplied by 10. |
| net * vat | This formula will be used when cells have been given names to multiply one by another to calculate a new value, in this case gross amount. |
| @AVG(....) | Finds the average of a range of numbers. |
| @MAX(....) | Finds the biggest number in a range. |
| @MIN(....) | Finds the smallest number in a range. |
| @COUNT(....) | Counts the number of items in a range. |

## Editing a spreadsheet

All you have to do to change the contents of any cell is use the cursor keys to take you to the cell you wish to edit, type in the new contents and **enter**. When calculations are involved in the spreadsheet new figures will automatically be inserted in the appropriate cells. To **delete** the contents of a cell – find the cell and simply use the **space bar** or **del** key to erase the contents and **enter**.

## Formatting the spreadsheet to produce reports

When you are producing reports it is best to have them clear and concise with information well displayed and meaningful. You need to be able to produce documents where information can be found easily. The spreadsheet must also be easy for others to understand.

**TIPS ➤ ➤**    **Formatting**

- **Text and data** can be right-aligned, left-aligned or centred.

- **Numbers** can be displayed in many ways – in £ and p format, as whole numbers or show decimal places.

- Most packages allow you to select some of the features of a word-processing system such as embolden, change fonts, enlarge or reduce – use these to improve your display.

As with every other office function to become adept at creating and using spreadsheets you must actually have 'hands-on experience'. Work through the tasks which follow. If you need assistance ask your tutor for help.

**Task 6 ➤**    1    Plan and create a spreadsheet to show this information:

| Clock Number | Name | Initial | Monthly Salary |
|---|---|---|---|
| 0001 | Thomas | M | £876.54 |
| 0002 | Cook | R | £1023.45 |
| 0003 | McPherson | T | £1400.00 |
| 0004 | Wagstaff | S | £777.54 |
| 0005 | McMillan | J | £843.21 |
| 0006 | Adams | J | £923.45 |
| 0007 | McClune | T | £1111.37 |
| 0008 | Kenny | M | £763.42 |

2    Then do the following:

| | | |
|---|---|---|
| a) | Total the monthly wage bill | @SUM(D4..D11) |
| b) | Total the yearly wage bill | @SUM(D4..D11)*12 |
| c) | Average the monthly salary | @AVG(D4..D11) |
| d) | Find the highest monthly salary | @MAX(D4..D11) |
| e) | Find the lowest monthly salary | @MIN(D4..D11) |
| f) | Find the number of employees | @COUNT(B4..B11) |

**Task 7 ➤**   You are asked to draw up a spreadsheet calculating the monthly sales of stationery from these three regions:

| ITEM | AREA1 | AREA2 | AREA 3 |
|---|---|---|---|
| Paper sales | 2648.95 | 1999.80 | 3076.65 |
| Computer software | 3492.44 | 2223.32 | 4061.15 |
| Writing equipment | 905.47 | 557.66 | 1037.43 |
| Typewriter aids | 1047.65 | 437.99 | 1798.02 |
| Books and pads | 536.33 | 330.09 | 808.06 |
| | | | |
| **Total sales** | | | |
| **Overheads** | 2254.46 | 1865.32 | 4059.45 |
| | | | |
| Profit | | | |

1  Insert a suitable title for the spreadsheet.

2  Insert the appropriate formulae and save the skeleton spreadsheet.

3  Format the data to appear as currency.

4  Save and print the completed spreadsheet.

## Absolute and relative values

When planning and constructing a spreadsheet you need to be aware of the difference between **absolute** and **relative** values. This is of particular importance when you are copying from one cell to another. On most spreadsheets the numerical values you insert will be **relative** values unless you specify otherwise.

> **Remember!**
> If a relative value is copied the references are changed to that of the new cell; for example, the formula in B4 is relative when it is copied to C4 and D4 so that when copying B2+B3 into column C it becomes C2+C3. If an absolute value is copied the references stay the same at the new cell.

Look at this spreadsheet:

| | A | B | C | D |
|---|---|---|---|---|
| 1 | | Leisure | Fares | Rent |
| 2 | January | £99.20 | £34.50 | £150.00 |
| 3 | February | £86.00 | £34.50 | £160.00 |
| 4 | TOTAL | @SUM(B2..B3) | @SUM(C2..C3) | @SUM(D2..D3) |

An **absolute** value is displayed as $B$2+$B$3. This reference means that if you were to copy it into another cell it would remain as $B$2+$B$3.

Copy this spreadsheet. Note how the cells referring to column D are **relative values** but cell B is **absolute**. Copy the formula from cell D4 to cells D5..D8 – **do not type them in**. Change the interest rate and the amount deposited a few times to see what happens.

|   | A | B | C | D |
|---|---|---|---|---|
| 1 | INTEREST ON SAVINGS | | | |
| 2 | | | | |
| 3 | Interest rate | Amount deposited | Year | Amount at year end |
| 4 | 12.5% | £2000 | 1 | +B4+B4*$A$4 |
| 5 | | | 2 | +D4+D4*$A$4 |
| 4 | | | 3 | +D5+D5*$A$4 |
| 6 | | | | |
| 7 | | | | |
| 8 | | | | |

**Task 8 ➤**

Overleaf is some information relating to the marks scored by staff members during a recent college course. Design a spreadsheet containing a title and headings which make it easy to understand. Enter suitable formulae for the calculations to be carried out.
    Then:

1   Find the highest mark scored in each unit.

2   Find the lowest mark scored in each unit.

3   Find the average mark over the three tests for each employee.

4   Find the group average mark for each unit.

Unit marks out of a possible 100

| Name | Communication | Text processing | Administration |
|---|---|---|---|
| Anderson R | 88 | 72 | 81 |
| Armour J | 76 | 84 | 68 |
| Barbour B | 79 | 69 | 84 |
| Bell P | 63 | 96 | 92 |
| Black H | 62 | 69 | 84 |
| Black D | 89 | 51 | 92 |
| Brown J | 77 | 92 | 79 |
| Cairns P | 98 | 65 | 80 |
| Cowlie G | 96 | 82 | 88 |
| Cummings C | 52 | 61 | 75 |
| Dempsey J | 67 | 65 | 64 |
| Fisher J | 86 | 84 | 85 |
| Kennedy R | 71 | 48 | 44 |
| McDonald J | 65 | 88 | 82 |
| Watson J | 90 | 89 | 83 |

**Task 9 ➤**

1   Prepare a spreadsheet to calculate the profit eachregional office has made in the past month on various products. Enter the headings and descriptions on a skeleton   spreadsheet and save the file.

| | Equipment | Stationery | Services | Repairs | Overheads |
|---|---|---|---|---|---|
| Midlands | 11003.53 | 912.59 | 1279.48 | 611.85 | 9075.35 |
| North East | 6977.44 | 736.20 | 922.52 | 306.38 | 4761.11 |
| Scottish | 9086.45 | 822.22 | 1008.90 | 555.55 | 5241.44 |
| Southern | 15504.81 | 1621.12 | 3969.10 | 243.06 | 9999.06 |
| West | 8866.43 | 1317.82 | 1446.75 | 204.40 | 6124.74 |
| Yorkshire | 5445.37 | 942.28 | 1390.04 | 366.33 | 3890.67 |

Remember!
Proof-read
all entries.

2  a)   Plan out your spreadsheet and give it a suitable name.

   b)   Insert the data and formulae to show:

   i)   the monthly sales of each item
   ii)   the monthly sales of each region
   iii)   the net profit (less overheads) for each region
   iv)   the total sales of all regions
   v)   the total profit of all regions.

3   Print out the final report.

## Assessment activity 13.2

> **Remember!** Keep your work from this activity for reference and assessment.

Plan and construct a spreadsheet which will give a breakdown of the company's overheads for the year ended 199-. Use this information:

a)     The period covered is January-December inclusive.

b)     The expenditure items are Telephone; Gas and electricity; Vehicles and haulage; Rent and rates; Insurance; Legal fees.

c)     The details of expenditure are:

### January-December:
### Rent at £1150 per calendar month.

**January expenditure**

| Electricity | £356.54 |
|---|---|
| Telephone | £583.63 |
| Haulage | £607.77 |
| Insurance | £124.95 |

**February expenditure**

| Gas | £298.65 |
|---|---|
| Vehicles | £409.22 |
| Insurance | £190.45 |

**March expenditure**

| Electricity | £321.12 |
|---|---|
| Rates | £756.00 |
| Insurance | £115.22 |

**April expenditure**

| Telephone | £478.60 |
|---|---|
| Haulage | £555.22 |
| Legal fees | £411.13 |

**May expenditure**

| Gas | £319.33 |
|---|---|
| Vehicles | £200.56 |
| Insurance | £102.77 |

**June expenditure**

| Electricity | £291.17 |
|---|---|
| Rates | £756.00 |
| Vehicles | £99.03 |

**July expenditure**

| Telephone | £612.31 |
|---|---|
| Haulage | £481.55 |

**August expenditure**

| Gas | £269.90 |
|---|---|
| Electricity | £277.57 |

**September expenditure**

| Legal fees | £158.90 |
|---|---|
| Insurance | £222.40 |

**October expenditure**

| Vehicles | £333.09 |
|---|---|
| Rates | £756.00 |

**November expenditure**

| Electricity | £359.20 |
|---|---|

**December expenditure**

| Gas | £411.10 |
|---|---|
| Telephone | £662.77 |
| Haulage | £566.44 |
| Vehicles | £406.03 |
| Rates | £756.00 |

1   Enter this information and print out one copy.

2   Enter the formulae to give these statistics:

    a)   Total gross expenditure on overheads for the year.

    b)   The highest area of expenditure.

    c)   The lowest area of expenditure.

    d)   Average monthly expenditure.

    e)   Total expenditure on each individual overhead for the year.

3   Format the spreadsheet for numbers to appear prefixed by the £ sign and fixed to two decimal places.

4   Format a blank disk and take a back-up copy of all the files you have created while working through the tasks.

5   You will be using this spreadsheet again for next year's expenditure. Copy the file renaming it for this purpose.

**6**  Collate the copies of the spreadsheets you have printed and present them to your tutor.

# Access and print hard copy reports, summaries and documents

## Hard copy

By now you will be familiar with producing hard copy printouts from computer applications programs. You most probably have used a daisy-wheel, dot-matrix, laser or ink-jet printer.

All printers are capable of producing letter-quality documents. Depending upon the type of document you wish to present there are advantages and disadvantages for each sort of printer:

| Printer | Advantages | Disadvantages |
|---|---|---|
| **Daisy-wheel** | Good quality printing<br>Can change wheel to produce different type styles | Very slow<br>Slightly expensive<br>Noisy |
| **Dot-matrix** | Fast<br>Can use colour | Noisy<br>Poor-quality printing |
| **Laser** | Very fast<br>Quiet<br>Uses colour<br>High-quality printing<br>Different print fonts available | Very expensive |
| **Ink-jet** | Fast<br>Quiet<br>Uses colour<br>High-quality printing | Jets clog<br>Special paper required<br>Expensive to buy printer and paper |

## Inserting paper

One of the basic problems students find when printing a document is that of loading the paper correctly. Most printers offer the facilities to use either **single sheet** paper or special **computer paper** (fanfold paper) which has holes along the sides and perforations between the sheets.

### Using single sheet paper

When using single sheets of paper to print adjust the paper guides to match the size of the paper you will be using.

> **Remember!**
> Printing will start some distance from the left-hand edge of the carriage.

### Using fanfold paper

Place a stack of paper behind the printer. Open the **sprocket** covers and mount the paper by aligning the holes with the pins on the sprockets.

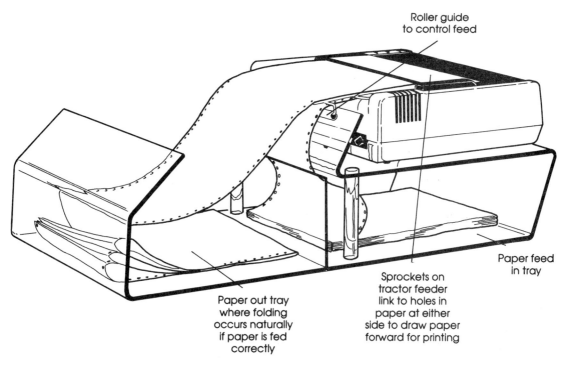

Roller guide
to control feed

Paper feed
in tray

Sprockets on
tractor feeder
link to holes in
paper at either
side to draw paper
forward for printing

Paper out tray
where folding
occurs naturally
if paper is fed
correctly

Using a tractor feeder with fanfold paper

Adjust the spacing of the sprockets by sliding them along the bar, using the clamp lever at the back of each sprocket to release, and lock them in position. Close the sprocket covers again making sure that the paper holes are aligned with the pins on the sprockets.

> **Warning!**
> **If sprockets are not aligned properly, you will have problems with paper feeding, possibly resulting in tearing or jamming of the paper.**

Feed the paper on until the print bar meets the perforation line between the first and second page.

### The on-line button

When a printer is **on-line** it can receive and print data from a computer. When it is **off-line** it stops printing and sends the computer a signal indicating that it cannot accept data. Always make sure that the printer is on-line before instructing the computer to print.

Use the off-line instruction when you wish to:

● **pause** during printing

- **pause** during printing

- **cut** fanfold paper at the end of printing.

### Paper feed

If you press the **paper-feed** button when the printer is off-line the paper will feed forward. If you hold the button down the printer will perform consecutive line feeds.

If you press the **on-line** button while you are line-feeding the paper will feed automatically to the top of the next page.

**TIPS ➤ ➤**    **Using a printer**

■ Make sure the printer is **switched on.**

■ Insert the paper in the printer, lining it up correctly (if using a daisy-wheel or dot-matrix printer).

■ Check there is sufficient paper in the holder when using a laser or ink-jet printer.

■ Make sure the **on-line light** is on.

■ Check **on-screen** instructions and proceed to print.

## Assessment activity 13.3

Remember! Keep your work from this activity for reference and assessment.

Choose any six reports you created for the database and spreadsheet tasks and print them out in a form which will be suitable for management to receive. **Proof-read** all hard copy before handing it in to your tutor.

# UNIT 14 | Telecommunications and data transmission

Brr. Brr. Brr.

## Process incoming and outgoing telephone calls using a multiline or switchboard system

Refer to Unit 2 of Book 1 for details of processing incoming and outgoing telephone calls, taking messages, telephone techniques and a summary of telephone equipment.

Are you afraid of answering the telephone? A surprising amount of people who use the telephone at home worry about doing the same thing at work. **Why?** It could be for any one or all of these reasons:

- they do not know how to operate the equipment;
- they do not know what to say when answering a call;
- they are afraid they will not be able to answer a caller's questions;
- they are afraid they will become flustered and make mistakes;
- they have little confidence in their own abilities.

**Task 1 ➤**   Form a group and discuss occasions when you have been wary about answering the telephone at work. Talk about the reasons for this, how you overcame your fears and the hints you would give to a new member of staff who was in the same position.

### Multiline switchboard systems

What type of telephone do you use at home? Most have a **memory** facility for storing frequently used numbers. Users can contact the last number dialled (without dialling the number again) at the touch of a button with the **last number redial** option. These facilities and many more are incorporated into modern multiline switchboard systems used in business.

**The call connect system** is the most popular system in use in the modern office. It is electronically operated to provide fast and efficient communication links both within an organisation and externally. It is quite easy to use and offers a wide range of facilities to help the switchboard operator become efficient at the job.

Some (or all) of these facilities may be provided:

**conferencing** – conversations can take place simultaneously among several extension users;

**diversion** – calls are automatically diverted to another extension when an extension is engaged or there is no reply;

**call holding** – calls are **held** to allow you to speak to another extension or transfer the call;

**interrupt** – designated terminals can interrupt calls to relay urgent messages

**loudspeaker** – a microphone and loudspeaker are built into the equipment which operates with or without the use of a handset, allowing other tasks to be performed while speaking;

**music on hold** – music is played on the line while callers are waiting to be transferred to the requested extension;

**mute** – using the mute facility allows you to speak to others in the room without being overheard by the caller;

**repeat dialling** – automatic dialling from a directory of frequently used numbers stored in **memory**;

**queuing** – incoming calls are placed in a **queue** to be answered in rotation.

**Task 2 ➤**

The switchboard your organisation uses at present is no longer sufficient for its requirements. Your boss has asked you to look through various leaflets provided by British Telecom and Mercury to find an alternative. She wants you to decide on two options which will provide these facilities:

a)   eight external lines

b)   60 extension lines

c)   call barring

d)   queuing

e)   conferencing

f)   diversion

g)   interrupt

h)   music on hold.

You have to list the specific points of interest provided by each chosen option and the costs, and report on the reasons why you have chosen these particular two systems from all those available. (You may have to telephone the companies to obtain literature.)

Although modern telephone systems make life easier for the switchboard operator you need to be very careful when using them and never lose the **personal touch**. You must always maintain good telephone techniques and keep the caller informed about what you are doing. Always remember to:

- keep checking with callers to find out if they still wish their calls to be held;

- make sure the **music** is played at the right volume and speed;

- let callers know when you are using **conferencing** facilities;

- be discreet when using the **mute** button – callers can usually detect this and may begin to wonder what is going on;

- tell callers if you need to switch to **loudspeaker** – especially when others will be listening to the conversation;

- if callers are kept waiting too long for extensions to become free, ask if you can have their calls returned.

Try to become familiar with the use of modern facilities by practising on the system used in college or at work. If you do not have access to a suitable modern system call in at your local British Telecom shop and ask for some brochures to read.

# Telephone communications

Everyone employed in an office needs to be able to process incoming and outgoing telephone calls. In business, good communication skills are very important. We communicate to pass on information so that it is understood.

TIPS ➤ ➤

### Communication skills

- **Think** before you say anything.

- Speak slowly and **clearly.**

- Use **words and language** which will be **understood** by the person to whom you are speaking.

- Try not to waffle – keep information **short** and **make your point(s) concisely.**

- **Tone** your voice to suit the occasion.

# Developing telephone skills

When you answer a telephone call at work try to create a favourable impression. Telephone calls play a major role in creating the image of the organisation you work for so it is important for all employees to develop skilful telephone techniques. If you listen to some telephone conversations you will find that there are many common errors caused by a failure to consider the person at the other end of the line.

TIPS ➤ ➤

### Answering and dealing with incoming calls

- Have to hand a note pad, message pad, pen, internal telephone directory and company organisation chart.

- Answer incoming calls quickly (before the fifth ring if possible).

- Identify the organisation clearly.

- Ask for the name of the caller and the company she/he is calling from and address the caller by name.

- **Listen** to the caller's requests and be responsive.

- Ensure that the person the call is for wishes to receive it before routing it.

- Route the call quickly, telling the caller exactly who you are transferring the call to.

- Keep the caller informed if there is a delay. If an extension is engaged or not being answered ask the caller if anyone else could help or if a message can be passed on.

- Aways remember that the caller is relying on **you** for information.

- Be positive and always close the call politely.

## Logging incoming calls

Some organisations like to keep a record of all incoming calls received. These records may be in the form of a book or loose-leaf sheets which register the time of incoming calls, the name and organisation of the person calling and **action taken**. Why do you think this is necessary? Discuss this with others in your group.

Here is an example of a log of incoming calls.

| LOG OF INCOMING TELEPHONE CALLS | | | | | |
|---|---|---|---|---|---|
| Date | Time | Caller | Firm | Contact | Action taken |
| 10/8/93 | 09.16 | Mr. Menzies | Jacob's | Jim Dunlop | Call routed |
| | | | | | |
| | | | | | |

## Dealing with difficult callers

At times you may be expected to deal with delicate situations, for example, customers calling to complain about the service they have received or a product they have bought.

Deal with these telephone calls by:

- Being understanding – try not to interrupt the caller when she/he is trying to explain the reason for the call.

- Taking notes of details and reading them back to the caller.

- Letting the caller know that you will take any necessary action but do not make promises that are unrealistic.

- Promising to have the matter looked into immediately and have someone call back at a suitable time.

## Wrong numbers

While working at the switchboard you will often answer calls which are not for your organisation. People may have dialled the wrong number or wrong area code. Always remember that callers do not dial wrong numbers intentionally – be polite and repeat your organisation's number to let callers know where they went wrong.

If you answer an extension telephone and a caller has been put through to the wrong department apologise and redirect the call – again it is unlikely that the call was intentionally wrongly routed.

### Callers with strong accents

In business, you will receive calls from many different people. Although most Europeans have a good grasp of the English language telephone communications can be difficult. It is much easier to understand someone who is talking to you face to face, when expressions and body signals can help. Picture this scenario:

**TIPS ➤ ➤**    **Conversing with people who have different dialects/accents**

- Listen carefully and speak slowly.

- Do not raise your voice unnecessarily.

- Use short simple sentences.

- If the caller is speaking quickly ask, politely, if she/he could speak slowly.

- Repeat essential details back to the caller and spell out words you are unsure of.

- If you have great difficulty in understanding the caller ask a colleague or senior member of staff to help out or take over the call.

## Nuisance calls

Nuisance (or annoyance) calls can upset the recipient as they often have sexual overtones or suggestions. However, if you receive a call which is meant to annoy or frighten you follow these procedures:

- Keep calm and do not engage the caller in conversation.

- If the caller goes on and on simply replace the receiver gently – do not bang it down or the purpose of the call will seem successful and appear to have unnerved you.

- Report the call to security and your boss.

- If the calls become regular report the situation to the police and your telephone company.

### Hoax calls

You may sometime be the recipient of a hoax call, for example, a caller saying there is a fire in the building or that a bomb is due to go off. **Do not panic or ring off – try to keep the caller talking.** Attract the attention of another member of staff to inform security to listen in to the call.

### Threatening calls

Bomb threats can never be taken lightly. With the rise in terrorist activities in mainland Britain every call should be taken **seriously**. As with hoax calls you must alert someone else while the caller is still on the line and **never ring off.**

**TIPS ➤ ➤**

**Dealing with threatening calls**

- Listen for subtle hints of identity by trying to place the accent of the caller or any familiar background noises.

- **Write down as many notes as possible of details of the conversation.**

- **Never** unnerve the caller by asking her/him to hold on – keep talking.

- Ask for as many details as possible:
  - a)  where the bomb is hidden
  - b)  what time it is due to go off
  - c)  what the bomb looks like
  - d)  why your premises have become a target.

- Try to keep your cool and do not become agitated.

A bomb scare!

**Task 3 ➤**     The security officer is concerned at the number of recent bomb threats by terrorist and activist groups. There is a general feeling that the majority of employees do not know what action to take in the event of evacuation of the premises or an explosion. You are asked to prepare a notice of procedures which is **clear and concise** to be placed on all departmental notice boards. Use headings where necessary and consider these points:

a)     **Rules** for evacuating the building.

b)     Dealing with **suspicious objects.**

c)     Dealing with **threatening telephone calls.**

d)     **Contacts** to be informed.

e)     Contacting occupiers of **other buildings** in the area to be evacuated.

## Making outgoing telephone calls

It is just as important to follow the correct procedures in **making** external telephone calls as it is in receiving incoming calls. As before **always** consider the person at the receiving end of the call.

When you are making outgoing calls be PREPARED:

• Place yourself in the recipient's shoes.

• Remember to be courteous.

• Enjoy conversing with others.

• Plan and make notes of the main topics you wish to discuss.

• Always have a note pad handy to write down details.

• Remember to **listen** to what is being said.

• End the call politely.

• Decide on any further action to be taken.

Telephone calls can be expensive so try to make non-urgent ones outside peak times.

Try to familiarise yourself with the different telephone tones you will hear. These are:

• **The dialling tone** which is a burring sound and means you can start dialling the required number.

• **The ringing tone** which is like a double pulse being re-run until the telephone is answered. If the telephone goes unanswered after a few minutes, hang up and try again later.

• **The engaged tone** is a short, sharp, single burst repeated regularly; the number you require is engaged or the exchange is being used to capacity. Try again later.

• **Number unobtainable** is a continuous high pitch tone which means that the telephone you wish to connect with is out of order, has been disconnected or is temporarily out of service.

• **Inter-district engaged announcements** such as 'lines from London are engaged, please try later' indicating that lines from one destination to another are fully utilised. Try again later.

● **Changed code or telephone number announcement** which is a recorded message to indicate that district codes or frequently-used telephone numbers have been altered; new details are also announced. You will not be charged for the initial call.

### Regularly used telephone numbers
It would be almost impossible to keep a note of every telephone number used at work. However, to save time every office worker needs to keep a list of numbers which are used on a regular basis. These will include business contacts, service providers, local hospitals, travel services, etc.

**Task 4** ➤     Make out a list of telephone numbers you use on a regular basis – these could include family, friends, dentist, etc.

**TIPS** ➤ ➤     **Preparing and making a call**

■ Check the dialling code and telephone number.

■ Press the numbers carefully and allow time to connect.

■ If you think you have hit the wrong button replace the receiver and start again.

■ **Know in advance** who it is you wish to speak to.

■ Keep **points for discussion** prepared in advance.

■ If **numbers** have to be relayed double-check them and repeat them over to the recipient.

### International dialling
You can dial direct to many international numbers but you must remember the following four steps to successful connection:

1. Dial the international code which is 010.

2. Then dial the country code.

3. Then dial the area code.

4. Finally dial the number you require to connect with.

You will not normally hear the ringing tone immediately so be prepared to wait – do not assume the call has not connected. If you regularly make international telephone calls, list the time differences between the UK and the countries you contact often.

### Log of outgoing calls
Some organisations like to keep records of all outgoing calls made from their offices. It is also useful for the switchboard operator to keep track of calls made and those still to be processed. Sheets of out-call cards are also useful to take details from staff members wishing to be connected to various numbers. Examples are shown overleaf.

```
┌─────────────────────────────────────────────────┐
│              OUT-CALL CARD                       │
│      Time:    11.22    Ext:   351                │
│      Caller:   Peter Gould                       │
│      Number required:  041-226-3791              │
│      Person to contact:  David Murphy            │
│      Message if unavailable:  The new            │
│      leasing figures seem in order.              │
│      Contracts can be processed.                 │
│                                                  │
└─────────────────────────────────────────────────┘
```

## LOG OF OUTGOING TELEPHONE CALLS

| Date | Time | Tel no | Contact | Firm | Action taken |
|------|------|--------|---------|------|--------------|
| 17/8 | 11.22 | 041-226-3791 | D. Murphy | Ingrams | Message left |
|      |      |        |         |      |              |
|      |      |        |         |      |              |
|      |      |        |         |      |              |
|      |      |        |         |      |              |

**Task 5 ➤**

1   Write down details of time difference between the countries below and the UK.

2   Then find the complete number you would dial to connect a call from your area to:

a)  Hobart 771439
b)  Vancouver 209176
c)  Genova 203524
d)  Paris 43570556
e)  Stockholm 2004
f)  Amsterdam 241783

g)  Le Harve 35250003
h)  Toulouse 61627065
i)  Bremen 14161
j)  Antwerp 476532
k)  Buenos Aries 0091876
l)  El Paso 171514

m)  Kusadasi 489532
n)  Geneva 3999367
o)  San Feliu de Llobregat 11112091
p)  Tavira 871652
q)  Sandefjord 5451 432 11112091
r)  Casablanca 131319.

### Emergency calls

You must learn the procedure for making emergency calls as you never know when you will need to use this service. There are three main emergency services which you can connect with by dialling **999**:

• Police

• Fire

• Ambulance.

The procedure is as follows:

- Dial 999 and state which service(s) you need.

- Describe the nature of the emergency and give your name, location you are calling from and telephone number.

- Give clear directions to the scene if asked for (you can use local landmarks such as hotels, industrial sites, banks, churches, etc. for routing).

**Task 6** ➤ What other emergency numbers would you keep a note of? Look up details and take note of local numbers you would use in these emergencies:

a)  a gas leak
b)  burst pipes leading to flooding of the building
c)  a power failure
d)  glass repairs
e)  joinery repairs
f)  accidental spillage of toxic material
g)  telephone out of order.

## Cleaning and maintaining office equipment

Office machinery and equipment is costly to replace. It is essential to carry out routine cleaning of all equipment, especially VDU screens, typewriters and printers. Follow these basic guidelines:

**Warning! Never use ammonia-based cleaners on or around the printer.**

- Use anti-static cleaners, never spirit-based ones, to clean the screen and plastic case of a VDU.

- To maintain print quality, thoroughly clean your typewriter or printer when:
    - you change the toner cartridge or ribbon;
    - after printing about 6000 pages;
    - whenever print quality problems occur.

- Clean the **outside** of the printer or typewriter with a damp cloth.

- Clean the **inside** with a dry lint-free cloth.

## Assessment activity 14.1

**Remember! Keep your work from this activity for reference and assessment.**

This activity will be carried out in the form of a role-play. During the role-play you should keep a log of all situations dealt with and complete the necessary documents. These should be kept in your folder as evidence of completion.

You will require an incoming calls log sheet, an outgoing calls log sheet, telephone message forms and out-call cards. (Take copies of all these forms from the back of this book.)

Situation

Today you are working as a temporary switchboard operator.

It is 9 a.m. on Monday morning and you have just arrived for work.

The Managing Director has called a meeting of all departmental heads. It will commence at 9.15 a.m. and should finish around noon.

## ROLE-PLAY CARDS

**Telephone caller 1**

**Time: 9.05 a.m.**

You are Jacqueline Ross of 24 Chapelhill Mount. You have applied for the position of Word Processor Operator with Microplus.
You have received notification of the interview to be held on Friday at 10.30 a.m. but you are sitting an exam then. You telephone to try to change the time of your interview.

**Telephone caller 3**

**Time: 9.35 a.m.**

You are Mathew McClymont, Purchasing Officer with J & B Williams.
You telephone the Sales Manager at Microplus to obtain a price for some new office furniture.

**Telephone caller 2**

**Time: 9.15 a.m.**

You are Robin Maitland, Chief Accountant with W Priestley & Sons. You have received an invoice from Microplus for £128.78 when the agreed price was £108.72. The invoice number is 0435. This is the third time you have had to query one of Microplus's invoices and you are most displeased.
You telephone, determined to speak to the Managing Director about this inefficiency.

**Telephone caller 4**

**Time: 9.20 a.m.**

You are Dawn Munro. You have just started a tailoring business and are telephoning around to obtain information on local executives. You telephone Microplus for the names and home addresses of all directors.

**Telephone caller 5**

**Time: 10.15 a.m.**

You are Mrs Ruth Barbour, wife of Barry – a Personnel Clerk with Microplus.
Your husband has received an injury while playing football at the weekend. You telephone to let the company know that he will be unable to attend work for a few days.

**Out-call 3**

**Time: 9.30 a.m.**

You are Peter McKenzie, Marketing Assistant. You have just arrived at work and notice a strong smell of gas just outside the building.
You ask the switchboard operator to take appropriate action.

**Out-call 1**

**Time: 9.00 a.m.**

You are Dorothy Goodwin, Sales Manager.
You need to speak to the French Sales Agent, Michel Mercier who is based in Paris, as soon as possible.
You know that Michel will definitely be in his office at 10 a.m. (local time) and you ask the switchboard operator to connect you then.
His number is 182 34667. You cannot remember the code.

**Out-call 4**

**Time: 9.45 a.m.**

You are Fiona Gibb, Personal Assistant. You have been told of an emergency and have to go home immediately.
Your boss, Mr Brown the Managing Director, asked you to order six bottles of wine from the local wine merchant – two each of Muscadet, Frascati and Chablis – to be delivered to his home address at 18 South Crescent.
You ask the switchboard operator if she could deal with this on your behalf.

**Out-call 2**

**Time: 9.10 a.m.**

You are Terence McManus, Personnel Manager.
You have a job advertisement to place in the local paper.
You telephone the switchboard operator to connect you.

**Out-call 5**

**Time: 10.00 a.m.**

You are working at the switchboard when you realise that one of the lines is not functioning properly. You need to report this fault.

# Transmit and transcribe recorded messages

## Telephone answering machines

An answering machine

Telephone answering machines (ansaphones) are a **necessity** for many organisations, large and small. They enable businesses to maintain a 24-hour service to customers and clients. The single person operation, such as a self-employed joiner or carpet fitter, could lose work by not having the telephone answered. Similarly, large organisations may use answering machines to record messages during out-of-office hours.

When an ansaphone is switched on anyone calling the number will hear a taped message similar to this one:

Thank you for calling Microplus. We are sorry there is no one available to take your call. If you would like to leave your name and telephone number someone will ring you back as soon as possible. Alternatively, you may leave a short message. Please speak after the tone.

Telephone answering machines offer these features:

- a dual cassette to provide an outgoing message and record incoming ones;

- tape cut-off facilities allow the incoming messages to be cut off after a certain length of time;

- remote playback facilities allow the user to pick up messages from any telephone using a special remote bleeper.

**Task 7** ➤    Form a group to discuss which type of organisations would benefit most from the installation of a telephone answering machine. List at least ten and discuss the advantages and possible disadvantages.

Many people are wary of leaving messages on an answering machine. It is quite difficult to speak into a telephone when there is no feedback. How do you cope with this one-way communication?

**TIPS** ➤ ➤    **Responding to an answering machine**

■ Speak clearly and slowly.

■ Say who you are, your organisation's name and telephone number (with extension).

■ State the date and time of your call.

■ Spell out difficult or uncommon words.

■ Consult previously planned notes to dictate a message.

■ Repeat important numbers.

■ Use the **telephone alphabet**.

■ Do not panic.

■ Do not replace the receiver on being answered by a machine as this is a wasted call.

■ State whether you want the recipient of the message to call you back or if you will ring again.

■ Leave a short message if necessary but keep it short or you may be cut off.

## The telephone alphabet

When using names, addresses or unusual words it may be necessary to spell these out for the recipient in order to avoid misinterpretation. However, in some cases spelling may not be sufficient as some letters (for example, T,B,P) can sound very similar. Letters can be identified using the standard telephone alphabet:

| | | | | | |
|---|---|---|---|---|---|
| A | ALFRED | J | JACK | S | SAMUEL |
| B | BENJAMIN | K | KING | T | TOMMY |
| C | CHARLIE | L | LONDON | U | UNCLE |
| D | DAVID | M | MARY | V | VICTOR |
| E | EDWARD | N | NELLIE | W | WILLIAM |
| F | FREDERICK | O | OLIVER | X | X-RAY |
| G | GEORGE | P | PETER | Y | YELLOW |
| H | HARRY | Q | QUEEN | Z | ZEBRA |
| I | ISAAC | R | ROBERT | | |

**Task 8 ➤**    Write down the details you will use if the number you call is switched to an answering machine in these situations:

a)   You ring the tax office to enquire about your new tax coding.

b)   You wish to change your hospital appointment.

c)   You wish to cancel a theatre booking.

d)   Your television set has broken down and you need it repaired.

e)   You wish to book tickets for a pop concert.

f)    You need a stationery order filled quickly.

g)   Your budget account statement does not show the last payment.

h)   You are ill and cannot manage in to work today.

i)    You are entering a contest in the local newspaper and you have to provide answers over the telephone.

## Assessment activity 14.2

**Remember! Keep your work from this activity for reference and assessment.**

Have someone record these messages onto an answering machine (an ordinary tape-recorder can be used if necessary). During this role-play keep a log of all situations dealt with and complete the necessary documents. These should be kept in your folder as evidence of completion.

You will require a log of recorded messages and telephone message forms; these can be photocopied from the back of this book (pages 263 and 260).

### ROLE-PLAY CARDS

| |
|---|

**Ansaphone message 1**

**Time recorded: 0815 hrs**

Hello, this is Barry Coleman of Computeraid. Our computer system has just gone down. We need your help urgently.
Please have your Sales Manager telephone me as soon as possible.
The number is 775143.
Thanks.

**Ansaphone message 2**

**Time recorded 0825 hrs**

Hello, this is Julia Walters of the local council. I had booked two of my staff onto the Health and Safety Course next week. I am sorry but I will have to cancel and book them on the next course which starts in four weeks' time.

**Ansaphone message 3**

**Time recorded 0842 hrs**

This is Phil Bryce from Genesis Consultants in the High Street. I have been left high and dry by my Personal Assistant who has decided to up and off on some weird and wonderful travel tour. Some people have no consideration for others. I was a good employer and she never had any complaints about her working conditions. I don't deserve to be treated this way – I am devastated. I need help urgently and was wondering if Theresa McPherson would oblige.

**Ansaphone message 4**

**Time recorded 0854 hrs**

Hello. My name is Tammy George of 69 Honeysuckle View. I would like to apply for the post of Receptionist advertised in this week's Guardian. Could you please send me details. Thanks.

**Ansaphone message 5**
**Time recorded 0858 hrs**

Hello this is Benji Singh from the cash and carry. Our orders have been held up due to the road conditions in this terrible weather. I am very sorry but your catering order will be delayed and I cannot guarantee delivery before noon. Some of the goods can be provided but fresh meats, fish and vegetables cannot. What do you want me to do?

**Ansaphone message 6**
**Time recorded 0900hrs**

This is Grace Wilks speaking. I have an interview with your Mr McManus at 3.15 this afternoon. I know it is short notice but I am afraid I will not be able to make it today. My son has been up all night with some sort of virus and I have had to call the doctor in. I would appreciate it if Mr McManus could arrange to see me at some other time as I would like the job. If he cannot I will understand.

**Ansaphone message 7**
**Time recorded 1310 hrs**

Hello. Spiros Garcia speaking from Rigsby & Co Ltd. Could I book my Personal Assistant on the Time Management Course next week. I would like you to confirm the booking and let me know the days of attendance and cost please. You can reach me on 33891, extension 41.

**Ansaphone message 8**
**Time recorded 1318 hrs**

Jean Smith here. On the way home for lunch Patricia had a slight accident with her car. She is not seriously hurt but I think she has whiplash injuries so I am taking her into the accident department at the local hospital. I will telephone again when I come home.

**Ansaphone message 9**
**Time recorded 1330 hrs**

I need to get a message to Bahir Khan who is attending the Advanced Autocad course. His father has taken ill and he needs to come home straight away.

**Ansaphone message 10**
**Time recorded 1344 hrs**

Hello. My name is Jeremy Tate. I have recently moved back to Britain after working for some time in Germany. My main employment has been in computer programming. I am looking for work and wonder if your organisation has any vacancies at present — either full-time, temporary or permanent. My address is 1211a Pelican Way and my home telephone number is 440092.

# MEMORANDUM

TO:    Switchboard        DATE:  Today's date
FROM:  Rachel Bywaters    REF:   Answering Machine Message

---

The current message being played to callers who connect with the ansaphone is incorrect. The message states that the office is open from 8.30 a.m. till 4.30 p.m. when in fact we are open from 9 till 5.
   I am  also concerned at the tone of voice in the message - it is not very friendly. Please prepare a new message and record it on the outgoing tape. Be welcoming and pleasant and speak a little more slowly this time.

# MEMORANDUM

TO:    Switchboard        DATE:  Today's date
FROM:  Terence McManus    REF:   Telephone Message

---

Please telephone Mr Graham Jones at Jones Brothers to ask for a reference on Eric Windsor who used to work as Accounts Manager for their company. If he wants he can fax it to me on 0294 605154.
   Their offices will be closed today so will you leave this message on the ansaphone.

# MEMORANDUM

TO:     Switchboard       DATE:  Today's date
FROM:   Mr Brown          REF:   Answering Machine Message

---

The new message on the answering machine is still not
right. What about the information on the lunch hour -
this has been missed completely. Restate the hours of
business as 9 a.m. till 1 p.m. and 2 p.m. till 5 p.m.
Also ask callers to leave a **brief message** as we are
losing some communication details.
   Please compose and record a suitable message.

# MEMORANDUM

TO:     Switchboard       DATE:  Today's date
FROM:   Jim Dunlop        REF:   Telephone Message

---

I have to go to a seminar in Paris for a few days. I
need to pass on a message to Bryce Fordyce at Excel,
telephone number 0242 22818. I have been trying to
contact Bryce for a few days now but he seems to have
gone off on holiday.
   If you cannot contact him personally could you leave a
message on his ansaphone. The message is:

   I have set up the meeting for the Round Table to be
   held in the Golden Goose Hotel on Monday evening
   next at 7.30 p.m. sharp. Bryce will need to prepare
   notes on the recent fundraising parachute jump -
   especially the profits for our campaign to keep St
   Barts open.

**Internal caller**

**Time 5 p.m.**

**Angela Greeman**

I know it's late but I forgot to get a
message to Roseanne Grenville of Ace
Management Systems. Could you leave
a message on Ace's answering machine
to tell Roseanne that Monday's
Extending WordPerfect course has
been posponed till the following week
due to the the Bank Holiday.

# Transmit and receive copies of documents electronically

## Facsimile equipment

The modern office would be incomplete without the installation of a facsimile machine (fax for short). Have you used one yet? They are similar to the one shown here:

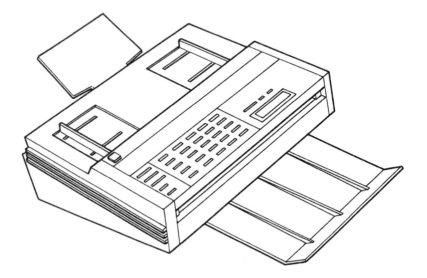

A fax machine

### What can a fax machine do?

Using facsimile equipment we can transfer exact copies of documents from one location to another using the telephone lines almost anywhere in the world. This transmission only takes a few seconds. The following documents can be transmitted by fax:

- typed or handwritten text
- drawings
- diagrams
- photographs
- written records
- advertising literature.

### How does a fax work?

The document to be transmitted is fed into the fax machine where it is read and converted into a language understood by the telephone mechanism. It is then sent to the receiving fax machine and converted back to its original, recognisable form.

### Advantages and disadvantages

Faxes can only be transmitted via **compatible** equipment. This means that the user and recipient's machines must be able to communicate with one another.

| Advantages | Disadvantages |
|---|---|
| Speedy delivery of information | Expensive to use |
| Easy to operate | Requires compatible equipment |
| Very efficient | Faxed copies deteriorate over time |

The major advantage the fax has over telex is that material does not have to be typed and documents can be sent with complete accuracy.

**TIPS ➤ ➤**

### Sending documents by fax

- Decide if it is absolutely necessary to use this facility before transmitting – think of the cost and weigh this up against the urgency of the message.

- Always use a transmission cover sheet indicating the number of pages, similar to the one shown below.

---

**MICROPLUS LIMITED**
**18-23 Long Avenue**
**BRISTOL**
**BB10 7ZL**

Telephone: Bristol (0791) 449214
Fax: (0791) 77081

FACSIMILE TRANSMISSION COVER SHEET

To: *Western Training Services*

Fax no: *0292 - 611675*

From: *Peter McColm*

MICROPLUS LIMITED

No of pages in this transmission (including this sheet): *2*

Our fax no: 0791 77081

Message:

*I confirm the booking for James Dempsey and Neill McPherson on the Autocad Course next week.*

PLEASE CONTACT US IF YOU DO NOT RECEIVE ALL THE PAGES

■ If you send a three-page document then the number of pages indicated would be four (the document plus the cover sheet).

**Task 9 ➤**     Design a transmission cover sheet for your college or place of work. Print out one copy and photocopy it for use in the tasks which follow.

**Task 10 ➤**   1   The management have decided to update the fax machine in the office and replace it with a more intelligent system. You are asked to look through catalogues and choose a new machine. Look for one which provides these features:

a)   **Automatic dialling** – regularly used numbers can be held in the memory. Press a button and the transmission will begin automatically.

b)   **Automatic redialling** – if the number is 'engaged' on the recipient's machine then it is not switched on or is being used by another caller.

c)   **Auto-timer** – transmission can be timed to allow copies to be sent later. Handy if papers have to be sent abroad or if you wish transmission to take place in the evening when the office is closed.

d)   **Reduction/enlargement** – similar to the facilities offered by the photocopier – this allows larger documents to be sent through.

e)   **Automatic feeder** – feeds in multi-page documents.

f)   **Telephone connected** – an indication can be sent to the recipient to pick up the telephone when the transmission is complete, allowing a conversation to take place.

g)   **Printed receipt** – gives a detailed list of transmission details.

h)   **Multiple polling** – network collection of all documents in a specific time span, for example, overnight or at weekends.

i)   **Speedy transmission** – between 15 and 20 seconds per page.

2   Using a fax directory find these organisations' fax numbers:

a)   Infast SRL 1v La Spezia, 20142, Milan.

b)   Facchinetti Teresiano, Casc Cortenuova, Torrion Quartara, 28100 Novara, Italy.

c)   Altairac ETS, 490063 rte Nimes, 30560 St Hilaire Brethmas, France.

d)   Spuittechniek BV, 12 Kipstr, 3011 RT, Rotterdam.

e)  Autovox 981, v Salaria, 00199 Roma, Italy

f)  Bernard Kreif Consultants, 260911, 115 r Bac, 75007 Paris, France.

g)  TW Mail Service Int BV, 154-158 Flevostr, 1442 PZ Purmerend, Netherlands.

h)  Emnid GMBH & Co, 25 A Bodelschwingstr, 4800 Blelefield 1, Germany.

**Task 11 ➤**

1  Prepare a cover sheet, and enter details on an outgoing fax log sheet, for these documents which have to be faxed:

a)  Although you have given the Managing Director all supporting papers required for the Management Committee Meeting at the Red Lion Hotel, you have just received a telephone message to say that he has left the agenda at home. You need to get a copy to him immediately – the fax number is 264734.

b)  While you were out of the office on Wednesday morning a telephone call came through from Miss Clark, Secretary to Mr McGinty of G A Services in Manchester. They have not received your letter confirming flight details, time of arrival/ departure, etc. for the Managing Director's visit. Fax these through to them; the number is 345678.

c)  Embassy Hotel Group have left a message requesting prices for some goods it wishes to order. Rosemary Wishart needs these details for a meeting which she is going into at 1400 hours. It is now 1230 hours so the information needs to be faxed through to (041) 332 4592.
   The goods are:

   | | | |
   |---|---|---|
   | one lockable filing trolley | 083946 | £108.00 |
   | one projector trolley | 057132 | £134.00 |
   | one overhead projector | 109616 | £670.76. |

   All items are subject to VAT at 17.5 per cent.

2  Enter these details on your incoming fax log sheet:

a)  You telephoned Chong Studios two days ago asking them to send through a complete list of new stationery prices. The Training Manager needs the information for this afternoon and the details have still not arrived. Telephone the company and ask them to fax the details.
   At 1200 hours the fax comes through but the cover sheet indicates that three pages were transmitted and you only received two. Contact the company and explain the problem, asking them to re-transmit the missing details. Keep the Training Manager informed of the situation. The completed fax eventually arrives at 1230 hours. Ensure that the fax is delivered to the Training Manager immediately.

b) The Station Hotel accounts department has rung complaining that the bill for a meeting has not been paid. It says the invoice was sent out two weeks ago and requires immediate payment, otherwise it will take legal action. After a detailed search of outstanding invoices, you realise that the invoice has not been received.
Contact the hotel and ask them to send the invoice through by fax and you will deal with the matter promptly. When the fax comes through it is totally illegible. Contact the hotel again and ask them to send the fax through again.

c) Mr M Palmer of Quick Print Limited in Carlisle has sent through a fax confirming the time of the dinner party that the Managing Director and his wife will be attending. Indicate receipt on your log sheet and ensure that the Managing Director is aware of all the arrangements.

# Telex

The telex system is operated by British Telecom using dedicated lines. A teleprinter has a keyboard similar to that of a typewriter with a visual display unit (VDU) attached. Letters are printed in capitals. Modern electronic machines offer these facilities:

- microprocessor control
- message editing
- memory storage to allow later transmission
- rearrangement of text
- short code calling
- multiple copy production
- the same message can be sent simultaneously to more than one destination.

Many large organisations use telex facilities and British Telecom produce a United Kingdom Telex Directory. Telex has earned a good reputation and telex communications can be carried out over most of the world. Telex is like a telephone conversation in written form. Subscribers can communicate with each other quickly and efficiently.

## How does telex work?

- The telex operator dials the correspondent's telex number and waits for the correspondent's **answerback** code to be displayed. This ensures a successful link has been made.

- The telex operator then types in the communicator's own **answerback** code.

- The message can be recalled from memory for transmission or be typed

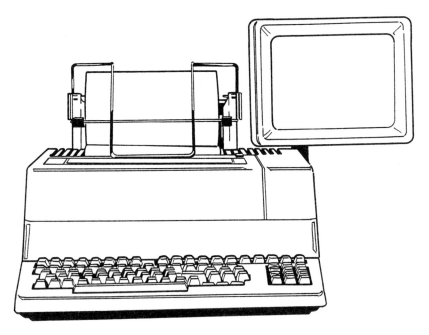

A telex machine

in there and then. On completion, the operator will again type in the answerback code to signal the end of the message.

- The message is received almost immediately, in text form, at the receiving teleprinter.

A series of messages can be sent back and forth between the communicators.

Telex communication is carried out when permanent records need to be held. Like the fax, telex may be used at any time of the day or night provided the recipient has left her/his machine switched on.

| Advantages | Disadvantages |
|---|---|
| Quick and accurate<br>Information can be relayed back and forth<br>Written record obtained<br>Information can be sent at convenient times between two countries with wide time differences<br>Cheaper than fax<br>Messages can still be prepared while machine is receiving incoming data | Slower than teletex (see below)<br>Recipient's machine must be switched on<br>Graphs and artwork cannot be communicated this way<br>Charges are rated by distance, time spent during transmission and according to time of day. |

## Teletex

The newest competitor for telex is the teletex network electronic mail service. Teletex transmits data electronically through the telephone network or PSDN (packet switched data network). Transmission takes place from the memory of the user's computer or word processor to the memory of the recipient's. Transmission of information is similar to that of telex but much faster. Incoming and outgoing data can be sent automatically. Copies can be stored on floppy disk or printed out for paper filing purposes.

### Advantages of teletex

- Top-quality text is produced using upper and lower case letters.
- All symbols of the keyboard can be used.
- An A4 page takes approximately 10 seconds to transmit.

## Electronic mail systems

There are many forms of electronic mail (e-mail) networks available to businesses today. Electronic mail is any system which allows information to be communicated between computers via a central computer. An organisation may have its own internal e-mail system to deal with information being sent throughout its various offices. For external systems, businesses have to subscribe to **electronic mail bureaux**. Customers are then allocated a personal **mail-box number** which has to be used in all communication.

### How does e-mail work?

Your mail-box number is typed in followed by a password, the recipient's mail-box number and the communication to be transmitted. The central computer receives the information and routes it to the recipient's box for storage until it is collected electronically. When the recipient wants to pick up mail a link is made with the central computer and any messages are displayed on screen.

**Task 12 ➤**   Read up any literature you can obtain on electronic communication systems. Write a report which will help the Company Secretary decide on the most suitable system to be installed in the office. The system will need to allow access to various organisations throughout the world and must be speedy and cost-effective.

---

## Assessment activity 14.3

**Remember! Keep your work from this activity for reference and assessment.**

Design a log sheet to record incoming faxes and another to record outgoing faxes. Throughout your course you need to enter details of all faxes you transmit and receive at work or college. You must record these details:

- the date
- the sender
- the recipient

- the organisation

- pages sent/received

- any action taken, for example, asking for re-transmissions or pages which are missing.

Attach copies of original documents sent by fax to the outgoing log.

# UNIT 15 | Reception

## Receive and direct visitors

Unit 8 of Book 1 dealt with receiving and directing visitors. Read that unit for revision on processing incoming and outgoing telephone calls, taking and passing messages, and receiving and assisting callers.

A receptionist is often the first point of contact a visitor has with an organisation so always try to be helpful and polite. Show you are pleased to see the visitor and always look as though you mean it. Prepare yourself for **ACTION!**

**A**      acknowledge the arrival of visitors and stop what you are doing, if possible;

**C**      converse with visitors – do not wait for them to speak to you first;

**T**      take down details from visitors to enable you to assist in meeting their requirements;

**I**      investigate delays in appointment times and keep visitors informed;

**O**      offer assistance when required;

**N**      never leave the reception desk unattended.

**Task 1 ➤**

1   Look up the meaning of the word 'reception' in a good dictionary. List the different meanings given.

2   Look up these meanings and again list them.

3   When you have prepared this list form a group and discuss what you think the duties of a receptionist are.

4   Finally, decide on at least five qualities you would expect to find in a receptionist.

## Reception duties

Contrary to the **glamour** image which often surrounds the role of the Receptionist the job requires hard work and various skills. Receptionists need to show an ability in:

- advance planning

- creating good human relations

- responding to enquiries

- receiving visitors and performing introductions

- conversing pleasantly

- giving information and directions

- making and receiving telephone calls

- taking messages

- asking 'open ended' questions

- explaining policies

- escorting visitors

- using their own initiative.

## Security in reception

You have to be well prepared to receive all types of visitors, follow company procedures and maintain security. **Security** in the 1990s is of major importance. Any member of staff employed in reception has to follow strict procedures which can include any, or all, of these:

- All visitors must report to a central point – either reception or at the security gate where:

    i) a visitor's pass or security badge will be issued;

    ii) visitors should be asked for identification if there is the least possible doubt about the reason for their visit;

iii)    every visitor must give her/his name, the organisation represented, car registration number and name the member of staff or department being visited.

- The visitor must never be allowed to wander about the premises unaccompanied.

- When the visitor's business is complete she/he should be accompanied to the reception/security point and signed out, and the visitor's pass or security badge returned.

A receptionist needs to have numerous pieces of information to hand to carry out the job properly. You not only have to **welcome** visitors to the organisation you also need to be well informed. What kind of information will a receptionist frequently be asked for? Examples could include:

- local taxi telephone numbers;

- various local telephone numbers;

- details of car parking facilities in the area;

- information on train and coach times;

- facilities offered by local hotels and restaurants.

It is best to make up and keep your own personal directory of such details which will save you time in looking up various information sources.

**Task 2 ➤**    Make out a list of telephone numbers and details of local facilities which meet the above criteria and add a few examples of your own.

## The visitor with an appointment

The reception desk is normally notified in advance of any visitors who are expected by staff members. Notification of appointments should be given at least a few hours prior to the arrival of the visitor by means of an internal telephone call, memo or written list to reception. Large organisations usually request that notification is carried out at least **one day** in advance. Why do you think this is necessary?

As soon as the Receptionist receives information about appointments the details should be recorded in an **appointments book** or on the computer if the organisation uses an **electronic diary.** Information has to be entered **line by line** and in **strict sequence**. It should then be double checked to ensure there are no omissions. Overleaf is a completed page of an appointments book.

### Dealing with pre-arranged visits

Visitors who have made appointments will be expected, not only by the intended hosts, but also by the Receptionist. Use your initiative here and let visitors know that they are welcome to your organisation.

You will gain **bonus points** in **customer care** if you can adapt your greeting to suit the occasion, for example, 'Good afternoon, Mrs Bryson –

## APPOINTMENTS BOOK

Day and date: Friday 9th April 199—

| Time | | Name of caller | Company/Address | To see |
|---|---|---|---|---|
| 09.00 | | | | |
| 09.15 | ✓ | Roz Mack | Fast Forward | J. Dunlop |
| | | | | |
| 10.00 | ✓ | Peter Boyle | Bonus Aid | Mr. Brown |
| 10.30 | ✓ | Frank Belt | 12 Manse Road | T. McManus |
| | | | | |
| 11.00 | | | | |
| | | | | |

Mr Dunlop is expecting you, please take a seat and I'll let him know you are here' or 'Jane will show you through to the Business Centre, Mrs Bryson'.

Always be **first** with the greeting.

## Dealing with the unexpected

No matter how organised you are there may be occasions when there are delays in meeting visitors' requirements. For example:

- the member of staff who is to receive the visitor may be delayed;

- the visitor arrives early for an appointment;

- you receive an unexpected visitor.

You will need to use your initiative in dealing with these situations. Always be tactful, be ready with a good excuse, offer refreshments and light reading material but above all keep the visitor informed.

**Never** give the impression that the visitor is a nuisance or unwelcome.

## The visitor without an appointment

There are times when you receive visits from people without appointments. These visitors may be:

- family and friends of staff members;

- postal workers;

- personnel delivering goods;

- sales representatives;

- people looking for information;

- people wishing to speak with members of staff.

The Receptionist should enter details of these visitors in the **visitors' register** which will be similar to this one:

## VISITORS' REGISTER

**Day and date** ....Friday 9th April 199—.................................................

| Time | Name | Company/address | Seen by | Action taken |
|---|---|---|---|---|
| 10.12 | P. Collins | Dual Business | D. Goodwin | Met at Reception |
| 11.14 | A. Davis | Polson & Co. | K. Bywaters | Escorted to Legal Department |
|  |  |  |  |  |
|  |  |  |  |  |

Follow these steps when receiving visitors without an appointment:

- Enter the visitor's details in the visitors' register.
- Ask the caller to give you brief details of the purpose of the visit – and take notes.
- Telephone the department or member of staff concerned and give brief information about the caller and the purpose of the visit:

  a) If the visitor can be seen let her/him know.

  b) If the member of staff cannot receive the visitor today ask her/him to make an appointment for a future date and time. Record the details in the appointments book.

Some visitors (sales representatives, for example) need to be diverted from the contact they ask to see. However, never assume that a caller will not be seen by another member of staff. Always consult the member of staff or department concerned. Invent a plausible excuse if the visitor cannot be seen. Use your initiative to decide the line of action to be taken, but always remember to be tactful and polite. Suggest an alternative or attend to the visitor yourself.

### Business cards
Business people often have **business cards** which they will offer to the Receptionist when they arrive at the desk. These cards show details of the visitor's name, company represented, company address and telephone number and may also include the visitor's home telephone number. This information saves you from asking too many questions and lets you enter details in the appropriate register. It is normal practice to file these cards in alphabetical order in a card index box.

**TIP ➤ ➤**    **Filing business cards**

- File business cards according to the name of the **company** represented.

## Staff in/out book

The Receptionist needs to know which members of staff are in or out of the building at any given time. Visitors may call on the off-chance of speaking to a member of staff and the Receptionist needs to know if the member of staff is indeed available. The **staff in/out book** also assists other employees who may be looking for members of staff who cannot be located in their own departments.  All staff members need to be encouraged to enter details in the staff in/out book when leaving and entering the building. Details should be recorded as shown in the example below.

### STAFF IN/OUT BOOK

Day and date ...... 9th August – Monday ......

| OUT | | | | | IN |
|---|---|---|---|---|---|
| Time | Name | Department | Gone to | Expected | Time |
| 11.06 | Tracy Gillmour | Business Centre | Dual Business | 12.15 | 12.10 |
| 11.45 | Rachel Bywaters | Legal | Four Seasons Hotel | 14.00 | 13.50 |
| 13.45 | L. Pearson | Computing | Circuit board | 15.00 | 15.10 |

## Giving directions

Working as a receptionist you will not only be asked for directions to various departments within the organisation but also to destinations outside.

Have you ever been stopped in the street and asked for directions to a street or building you know well? Did you have to stop and think about it? Were the instructions you gave the enquirer clear and concise?

A receptionist will find it handy to create lists of directions and small maps which can be relayed or given to enquirers.

**Task 3 ➤**    1    Using small pieces of card (roughly 8 x 8 cm) draw up a clear and concise list of directions you would give to people enquiring about the  best route to reach your office or college from each of these:

a) the local bus station

b) the local train station

c) the nearest airport

d) the motorway or link road.

Think carefully about this task and consider the inclusion of various landmarks such as churches, theatres and hotels which may be situated close by.

2 When you have finished drawing up lists get together with others in your group and discuss the routes each of you decided upon.

3 Finalise the lists and use details from them for the later role-play tasks.

**Task 4 ➤** Draw a rough map of your building (college or workplace). Follow the pattern of the map below and indicate, using keys, the various floors of the building and departments within. Keep this map for your own use in the tasks to follow.

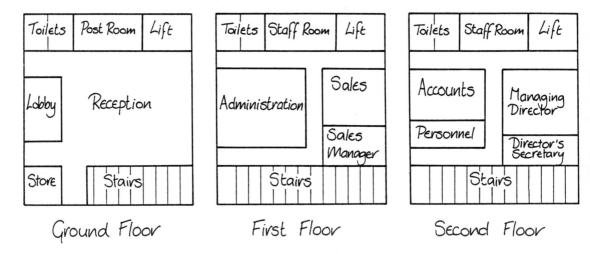

Ground Floor     First Floor     Second Floor

## First aid

While working as a receptionist you may be called upon to deal with people who suddenly feel ill or sustain minor injuries. These visitors or staff will need some form of **first aid** until skilled medical attention can be administered. Every receptionist needs to ensure that a well-equipped first aid box is kept at reception, containing these items:

| | | |
|---|---|---|
| Asprins | Elastoplast | Cotton wool |
| Bandages | Safety pins | Tweezers |
| Thermometer | Paracetamol | Scissors |
| Antiseptic | Antiseptic cream | Lint. |

You also need to be aware of how to deal with fainting, minor burns and nosebleeds.

### Fainting
When a person faints, gently turn them onto one side with one leg forward and arms clear. This is known as the **recovery position** shown below. Loosen any tight clothing like ties and top buttons of shirts. If the person does not come round quickly send for expert medical help.

### Nosebleed
Make sure the person is sitting upright in a chair and place a bowl under the chin, then squeeze the nose. Tell the person not to swallow and to try to breathe through the mouth. If the bleeding does not stop send for medical help.

### Burns and scalds
If possible, place the affected part of the body under cold running water. Remove any clothing which may stick to the skin and cover the burn with a light sterile dressing or clean lint. Finally, bandage gently. If it is a serious burn or scalding send for medical help or have the person taken to the accident and emergency unit immediately.

### Recording accidents at work
An accident book should always be kept at the reception area.

Page of accident book

| Date | Time | Details | Action taken | Reported to | Medical attention/ outcome |
|------|------|---------|--------------|-------------|----------------------------|
| 10/8/93 | 9.05 | L. Pearson fell downstairs | Taken to casualty | P. Gould | Sprained ankle. Off work for 1 week. |
| | | | | | |
| | | | | | |

Details of all incidents and treatments administered need to be recorded fully. You must **always record accidents**, however minor, in case of later claims for compensation against the company. Find out your organisation's procedure for recording accidents. Who would you report incidents to?

## Maintain the reception area

What is the first thing you look for or notice when you enter a doctor's surgery, a government office, council buildings, solicitor's premises, hospital foyer, business premises, etc?

The reception area is the **focal point** of an organisation for four main reasons:

- It is the first part of the premises to be viewed by a visitor.
- It projects the image of an organisation which is all-important to business.
- It is the central point of contact with the organisation.
- It is where enquiries are made and information is provided.

In other words, it creates the initial impression and is often the **first communication link** a visitor has with an organisation.

**Task 5 ➤**    1   Form a group and discuss at least three different organisations' reception areas which you have visited. Think about the impression you gained of the organisation and the staff by the way you were treated. Take a note of plus and minus points from the discussion. Think about the following:

a) Did the reception area have pleasant surroundings? Was it nicely furnished, clean and tidy, bright and comfortable?

b) Did the Receptionist make you feel welcome and at ease?

c) Was the Receptionist helpful?

d) Were you kept informed while waiting to be met by a member of staff?

d) Would you enjoy visiting the premises again? If not, why not?

2  When you have finished discussing this topic write up some guidelines to follow which would assist people in welcoming visitors to their workplace.

3  If you have access to a desk-top publishing package try using this facility to design a completely new layout for the reception area of your workplace or college. If these facilities are not available use colouring pens and paper which can be just as effective. Indicate where you would position coffee table, chairs, magazine racks, plants, couches, etc.

A duty which should never be neglected is keeping the reception area neat, tidy and attractive looking.

**TIPS ➤ ➤**    **Maintaining the reception area**

■ Keep all magazines neat and tidy (usually on the magazine rack beneath a coffee table or in a magazine holder).

■ If the organisation displays its products at reception make sure these are current.

■ Keep plants and flowers fresh looking and dust their leaves regularly.

■ Clear away cups and saucers as soon as visitors have finished with them, but do not make people feel rushed into finishing their refreshments.

■ Keep tables and chairs tidy – reposition them, if necessary, when callers move on.

■ Empty ashtrays and wastepaper bins periodically.

■ Remember the health and safety regulations and check regularly to ensure that there are no potential hazards.

**Task 6 ➤**    Write down any other points you can think of which would help in ensuring the reception area is well maintained.

## Displaying notices in reception

A notice board is often situated on a prominent wall within the reception area. This may be because it is the one place where employees and visitors alike will notice information. It is often the duty of the Receptionist to compose notices to place on the board or wall of the reception area. All notices have a purpose and they must be displayed in a manner which will attract attention.

**Task 7 ➤**     You receive the following memos while working at reception in Microplus. Carry out the requests and remember the content of the notices when you are carrying out your assessment activity at the end of this unit.

---

### MEMORANDUM

TO:      Reception              REF:   No smoking policy
FROM:  Rachel Bywaters    DATE:  16th March 199-

---

As you will be aware this company has adopted a **no smoking** policy throughout the organisation. Draw up a notice to display in reception to inform visitors of the new policy. However, be diplomatic in the use of words - don't sound dictatorial. Try something like 'the management and staff of Microplus thank you for adhering to their newly introduced no smoking policy'. Use visual aids if necessary - the notice must stand out, be attractive enough to draw attention to it and placed in a prominent position.

---

### MEMORANDUM

TO:      Reception          REF:   New security measures
FROM:  Jim Jamieson     DATE:  22nd June 199-

---

Further to the theft of a visitor's handbag from reception last week it is important that people become more vigilant and aware.

For this reason I would like you to design a notice and visual display to be placed on the notice board in reception which will grab people's attention. Something along the lines of the recent police campaign to deter car thefts would be appropriate.

---

## Safety and security at reception

As well as making sure that visitors are looked after the Receptionist is also responsible for preventing accidents from happening in the reception area. Always check that:

• Carpets are not frayed or loose – report any that need repair.

• Loose wires do not trail from electric sockets to appliances.

- Fire exits are not blocked.

- Doorways are kept clear of bags, boxes and briefcases.

- Lighting is adequate.

- All electrical appliances are unplugged at the end of the day.

- There is at least **one fire extinguisher** in the reception area and you know how to use it.

- You know the organisation's fire drill procedures.

- The first aid box is available and stocked with the necessary supplies.

## Assessment activity 15.1

*Remember! Keep your work from this activity for reference and assessment.*

During this role-play you will receive and direct visitors, receive incoming telephone calls, maintain the reception area and follow health and safety procedures.

You must also keep the reception area tidy, ensure all records are up-to-date and accurate, and deal with each situation in a professional manner. Keep a log of all situations dealt with along with support material.

You will need to have handy:

- appointments book

- visitors' register

- staff in/out book

- blank message forms

- internal telephone directory

- map of building

- reference books

- list of frequently-used telephone numbers.

From these memos which have been received at reception this afternoon complete the appointments book for tomorrow.

---

### MEMORANDUM

| | |
|---|---|
| TO: Reception | DATE: 3rd August 199- |
| FROM: Jim Dunlop | REF: Appointments for tomorrow |

Please note the details of visitors expected by my department tomorrow:

| Name | Company | To see | Time |
|------|---------|--------|------|
| Pauline Foulkes | CarpetAll | J Dunlop | 0900 hrs |
| Brenda Reilly | Brenda's Kitchen | P McColm | 1030 hrs |
| John Alderman | 5 Star Taxi Services | J Dunlop | 1430 hrs |
| Peter Bowles | Sports Empire | K Newall | 1545 hrs |
| Jenny Parr | Pavilion Travel | J Dunlop | 1630 hrs |

## MEMORANDUM

TO:     Reception           DATE: 3rd August 199-
FROM:   Karen Shearer       REF:    Appointment for tomorrow

---

Please note that Rachel Bywaters is expecting Brian
Barry from the Planning Department tomorrow at 1500 hrs.
The meeting will last for approximately one hour. Please
inform the switchboard to hold all calls during this
meeting.

## MEMORANDUM

TO:     Reception           DATE: 3rd August 199-
FROM:   Richard Lowe        REF:    Appointment

---

Dorothy Goodwin has an appointment with Henri Rouvier, a
Sales Agent from our French Office, tomorrow morning at
0930 hrs. Please contact me when Henri arrives and I
will meet him personally at reception.

This is an important meeting and means that Dorothy will
be engaged all morning. She will then be taking Henri to
lunch at the Station Hotel where a booking has been made
for 1230 hrs.

Dorothy will not be free again until 1430 hrs. Could you
please inform the switchboard to divert any calls for
her to my extension.

## MEMORANDUM

TO:     Reception           DATE: 3rd August 199-
FROM:   Margaret Murphy -   REF:    Notification of absence
        Marketing

---

Please note that John Allen is attending a marketing
seminar in London tomorrow and will not be back at the·
office until late afternoon the following day.

---

## MEMORANDUM

TO:      Reception          DATE:  3rd August 199-
FROM:  General Office    REF:   Jim Jamieson's
                                         appointment for tomorrow

---

Jim Jamieson has an appointment with Bryan Wendell from
Securicor at 1400 hrs tomorrow.

---

## MEMORANDUM

TO:      Reception          DATE:  3rd August 199-
FROM:  Fiona Gibb        REF:   Mr Brown's appointments
                                         for tomorrow

---

Please note the details of these visitors expected by Mr
Brown tomorrow:
Simon Pettifer of Eurobond at 0900 hours
Janine Tilsley of Business Express at 1000 hours.

---

## MEMORANDUM

TO:      Reception          DATE: 3rd August 199-
FROM: Personnel          REF:   Interview list for tomorrow

---

Please note that Theresa McPherson and Terence McManus
will be interviewing these candidates for the position
of Administrative Assistant tomorrow:

| Name | Address | Time |
|------|---------|------|
| Lawrence Khan | 61 Grosvenor Way | 1130 hours |
| Justin Wills | 12 Citrus Park | 1200 hours |
| Leona Paulin | 3 Amber Square | 1330 hours |
| Madge Griffiths | 9 Pentland Drive | 1400 hours |
| Ken Wong | 133 Maple Grove | 1430 hours |
| Naomi Powell | 48a Sidney Street | 1530 hours |

---

## MEMORANDUM

TO:       Reception          DATE:  3rd August 199-
FROM:   Petra Edmunds      REF:     Appointment

---

Please note that Peter Gauld is expecting Rebecca Ashid
from the Road Transport Association tomorrow at 1300
hours.

---

## MEMORANDUM

TO:       Reception          DATE:  3rd August 199-
FROM:   Angela Freeman      REF:     Appointment

---

Please note that Gavin Todd is expecting Mrs Madgwick
from CADET at 1330 hours tomorrow. Gavin expects the
visit to last one hour.

## ROLE-PLAY CARDS

---

**Visitor 1 Time:  0900 hrs**

You are Pauline Foulkes from
CarpetAll. You are visiting the offices
of Microplus where you have an
appointment to meet Jim Dunlop, the
Business Centre Manager. You have a
very bad cold which is affecting your
hearing. Act this part out as if slightly
deaf when responding to questions by
the Receptionist.

---

**Telephone caller 1 Time: 0909hrs**

You are Henri Rouvier, a sales agent,
visiting from France. You have an
appointment with Dorothy Goodwin in
20 minutes time. You have arrived at
the airport and taken delivery of your
hired car. You have tried,
unsuccessfully, to find a map of the
area. You ring Microplus and ask the
receptionist for directions to the office
from the airport.

**Visitor 2 Time:  0910 hours**

You are Simon Pettifer from Eurobond. You have an appointment with Mr Brown, Managing Director, of Microplus for 0900 hrs. The train was late arriving and you apologise for being late.

**Visitor 3 Time: 0915 hrs**

You are Maria Bonachelli a sales representative from Ace Cleaning Products. You approach the reception desk of Microplus and ask to speak to the person responsible for purchasing the company's cleaning materials. You will be asked to sign the visitors' register and provide your car registration number which is F552 JSD.

**Visitor 4 Time: 0925 hrs**

You are Sheila Cope. On passing the offices of Microplus you notice a strong smell of gas coming from the building. You enter the building and approach the reception area. You let the Receptionist know you think that there may be a gas leak.

**Visitor 5 Time: 0940 hrs**

You are Celia Briggs and you have to deliver a parcel of advertising literature to John Allen the Marketing Manager of Microplus. You require a signature from Mr Allen on receipt of the parcel.

**Visitor 6 Time: 0950 hrs**

You are Janine Tilsley of Business Express. You have an appointment with the Managing Director of Microplus, Mr Brown, at 1000 hrs.

**Visitor 7 Time: 1020 hrs**

You are the driver of the post van delivering a registered letter to Microplus. Obtain a signature from the Receptionist for receipt.

**Visitor 8 Time: 1028 hrs**

You are Brenda Reilly from Brenda's Kitchen in the town. You have an appointment to meet Peter McColm of the Business Centre at 1030 hrs.

**Visitor 9 Time: 1045 hrs**

You are Hugh Rolf from Rank Zerox. You arrive at Microplus in the company van registration number K55 TSD. You have been called there to repair the new colour photocopier in response to a call from Michelle Thomas. Ask for directions to the Reprographics Section.

**Visitor 10 Time: 1115 hrs**

You are Lawrence Khan of 61 Grosvenor Way in the town. You have been called for an interview at Microplus for the post of Administrative Assistant. Your interview is with Mr McManus and Mrs McPherson. You approach the reception desk and announce your arrival. You are very nervous and as a result become very talkative. Ramble on to the Receptionist about everyday things like the weather, the bus journey etc.

**Visitor 11 Time: 1210 hrs**

You are Justin Wills of 12 Citrus Park. You have an interview at Microplus today for the position of Administrative Assistant. You cannot remember the name of the person the interview is with and you have left the letter at home. You are also late for the appointment which should have been at 1200 hrs. You do not offer an apology for this. Ask the Receptionist how long the interview will last as you have arranged to meet your friends for a game of snooker at 1245 hrs. You take a seat in the reception area and light up a cigarette.

**Visitor 12 Time 1255 hrs**

You are Rebecca Ashid from the Road Transport Association. You arrive at the reception of Microplus for an appointment with Peter Gauld the Transport Manager. As you wish to have lunch after the meeting ask the Receptionist to recommend a good hotel in the area which serves home-made bar lunches.

**Telephone caller 2 Time: 1300 hrs**

You are Peter Birt from British Gas. You are telephoning the Receptionist at Microplus to inform the company that the reported gas leak has been attended to and everything is now okay. Thank the Receptionist for reporting the matter promptly.

**Visitor 13 Time: 1322 hrs**

You are Leona Paulin and have come to the offices of Microplus to be interviewed by Mrs McPherson and Mr McManus. The position you are being interviewed for is that of Administrative Assistant. You are very shy and the Receptionist should have to prise information from you. Your address is 3 Amber Square.

**Visitor 14 Time: 1356 hrs**

You are Bryan Wendell from Securicor. You have an appointment with the Head of Security at Microplus for 1400 hrs. You cannot remember the man's name so ask the Receptionist to supply you with the necessary details. Ask the Receptionist if she/he could supply you with the time of trains to London this afternoon.

**Visitor 15 Time: 1358 hrs**

You are Madge Griffiths of 9 Pentland Drive. You are attending the offices of Microplus for an interview by Mr McManus and Mrs McPherson for the post of Administrative Assistant. Ask the Receptionist if she/he can give you any leaflets or information about the company which you could read while waiting.

**Visitor 16 Time: 1420 hrs**

You are John Alderman of 5 Star Taxi Services. You have an appointment with Jim Dunlop of Microplus at 1430 hrs. As you are a little early begin chatting to the Receptionist. You ask if Carol Cummings still works in the Stock Room of the company. Ask if it is true that Carol has left her husband and is living with a man much younger than herself. Start to tell the Receptionist about one night you had Carol and a young man as passengers in your taxi.

**Visitor 17 Time: 1430 hrs**

You are Ken Wong of 14 Maple Grove. You have an interview for the job of Administrative Assistant with Microplus. The interviewers are Mrs McPherson and Mr McManus. Ask the Receptionist what kind of people they are and what the other people are like who have been for the interview. Also ask if she/he thinks you have a chance of getting the job and for the times of the buses back to town.

**Visitor 18 Time: 1445 hrs**

You are Joyce Young of Premier Paper Supplies. You call into the office of Microplus on the off-chance of speaking to the Purchasing Manager. You wish to show samples of some new paper products you are marketing. You have arrived in car registration G326 KLD. The Receptionist should try to make an appointment for you at a later date but be persistent and ask if it is possible to see the Purchasing Manager today. Tell her that it will be weeks before you are back in the area and that this is too good a deal for the company to miss, etc.

**Visitor 19 Time: 1455 hrs**

You are Brian Barry of the Planning Department with the local council. You have an appointment to meet with the Company Secretary of Microplus, Rachel Bywaters, at 1500 hrs.

**Visitor 20 Time: 1525 hrs**

You are Naomi Powell of 48a Sidney Street. You are attending an interview at the offices of Microplus. The interview is with Mr McManus and Mrs McPherson and is scheduled for 1530 hrs.

**Visitor 21 Time: 1540 hrs**

You are Peter Bowles of Sports Empire. You have an appointment with Karine Newall of the Business Centre at Microplus at 1545 hrs. Your leg is in plaster and you are supported by crutches (due to a footballing accident). You struggle to the reception desk.

**Telephone caller 3 Time: 1610 hrs**

You are Jenny Parr of Pavilion Travel. You telephone the Receptionist of Microplus to cancel an appointment you had with Jim Dunlop of the Business Centre at 1630 hrs. Your car has broken down on the motorway and you are waiting for assistance. Ask to make another appointment for the same day and time next week.

# UNIT 16 | Text processing

---

## Produce a variety of business documents from handwritten/ typewritten drafts

Those students wishing to recap on basic letter writing, layout, correction signs, etc. should refer to Book 1. Students will need access to word-processing equipment to carry out the tasks in this unit.

### Producing business documents

What is meant by business documents? How many are you familiar with?

**Task 1 ➤**

1 Form a group and test your understanding by discussing the kind of information which may be communicated by these business documents:

   a) letters

   b) minutes

   c) reports

   d) memoranda

   e) notices

   f) tabulated articles.

2 Can you think of any other business documents which would be produced by text processing?

### Text processing using screen-based equipment

The screen or visual display unit (VDU) shows an electronic page which usually displays about 20 lines of your document and 80 characters across the page. The status line at the bottom of the page displays other information to help guide you, for example, the current drive in use, page number of document, name of document and the position of the cursor on the line.

There are also many function keys (the keys marked F1, F2, etc. at the top or left-hand side of the keyboard). These can save time when creating, editing, saving and retrieving documents.

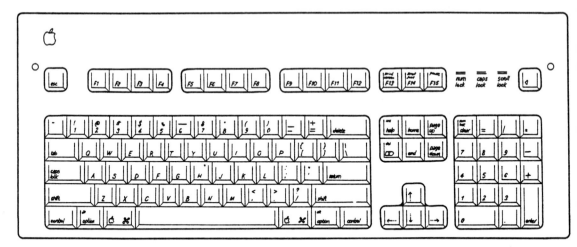

**Task 2 ➤**    1 Ask your tutor or supervisor at work to provide you with an instruction manual for the word-processing package you will be using. Photocopy the operation notes word-processing sheet given on page 266 and enlarge it, if necessary. Here is an example of a completed sheet for use with WordPerfect 5.1.

## OPERATION NOTES WORD PROCESSING

| Function | Procedure |
|---|---|
| TO CHANGE MARGINS | Press Shift + F8 and choose Option 1 from the sub-menu, then choose Option 7 and type over existing margin settings. Press F7 to return to document screen. |
| TO SET TABS | Press Shift + F8 and choose Option 1 from the sub-menu, then choose Option 8. Press Ctrl+End to clear existing tabs and type in numbers for tabs to be set. Press F7 to return document to screen. |
| TO SET TOP AND BOTTOM MARGINS | Press Shift + F8 and choose Option 2 from the sub-menu, then choose Option 5 and type over existing settings. Press F7 to return document to screen. |
| TO EMBOLDEN TEXT | Highlight the text to be emboldened by pressing Alt+F4 and move the cursor along the complete text to be emboldened. Then press F6. |

Look through the manual of the system you use to find the procedures involved in the functions shown above.

2   Fill in your sheet by writing the instructions for your system which enable the following functions to be carried out:

a)  Formatting – changing right- and left-hand margins, line spacing, justification, setting tabs, setting decimal tabs, setting top and bottom margins, page numbering, inserting headers and footers and selecting paper type.

b)  Changing text – inserting and deleting characters, indenting, emboldening, changing to block capitals, inserting and deleting sentences and paragraphs, underscoring, highlighting and underscoring the same piece of text.

c)  Moving and copying text – moving words, sentences and paragraphs from one point to another, copying blocks of text.

3   Can you think of any other useful functions to be included in your own notes?

**Note**: Always make sure you have some blank copies of the operation notes sheets in your folder as these will come in useful later.

## Producing text to mailable copy

When you type a document it is your responsibility to check that your work is accurate. Check your grammar and improve your spelling by:

- reading more carefully

- not skipping words

- paying attention to words and their meanings

- checking words are used in the right context.

Word processors drastically reduce the time and effort involved in preparing business correspondence. Not only is it easier to correct any errors, it is also simple to keep standard letters on disk for instant recall.

The tasks in this unit have been divided between typing from manuscript (handwritten copy) and from typescript.

**TIPS ➤ ➤**

**Typing from manuscript or typescript**

■ Always follow the special instructions for display and note guidelines regarding line spacing.

■ If margins and line spacing are not indicated leave 1 inch right and left margins and use single-line spacing.

■ Read completely through the handwritten work first to become accustomed to the style of writing. This also familiarises you with the content of the document to be typed.

■ If in doubt about a certain word or block of text do not guess – ask the writer to clarify the text or ask another member of staff for help. If you are still not sure try to think what the word or phrase might be and look up a good dictionary to see if the word fits the textual context. As a last resort leave blank spaces in the document where the words will fit when you clarify them.

■ Type abbreviated words – other than the generally accepted ones of Mr, etc – in full (for example, accom – accommodation).

■ Follow the rules for typing amounts and figures unless indicated otherwise.

■ Never assume that the writer has used the correct grammar or spelling – whether the copy document is in typescript or manuscript form.

**Remember!**
It is your responsibility to check that all your work is accurate and is displayed in the appropriate format or housestyle.

## Common word-processing terms

Before you key in any text, there are some additional terms you need to become familiar with:

● **Cursor** – as it is keyed in, text will appear at the point where the cursor is positioned. The cursor is a small, flashing line which appears on the screen.

● **Prompts** – a message may appear in either the upper right-hand corner or the lower left-hand corner of the screen, on the status line.

● **Wordwrap** – as you key in text there is no need to think about line endings as the word-processor software decides when a new line should begin. You can just keep typing to the end of the paragraph and the text will 'wrap round' to a new line as necessary. At the end of the paragraph, however, you should press the **Return** key twice.

● **File names** – every document created must be given a file name. Ideally the name of the file should give a clue as to its contents. The file name must not include spaces or punctuation.

● **The escape key** – the **Esc** key can be used to cancel any function or operation which you do not wish to continue. It is also useful if you get into difficulty and cannot find a way out. Pressing Esc will return the screen to normal.

Students who are proficient typists and are familiar with basic text processing can proceed directly to Assessment activity 16.1. Others should work their way through the practice tasks and take notes of the layouts and displays of the various business documents in use.

**Remember!**
Follow the organisational housestyle in use at your place of work or college when completing these tasks

**Task 3 ➤**   Using 1 inch margins and single-line spacing, type the following paragraph following the correction symbols. Give the document the name **Wordpro**.

#
⌥
⌥

or return
key ∧

∧

⟨9f⟩  only∧

```
        #       In its most basic form wordprocessing can be thought of
        ⌥       as a very efficient method of producing typewritten
                documents. The original text must be entered to the word
        ⌥       processing system via a keyboard. As the text is keyed
                in it is is displayed on a screen.
                   When using a word processor you may find some keys act
   or return    differently from those of the typewriter. When moving
    key ∧       around the screen do not use the space bar as this will
                create gaps in the text. Only use the cursor control
                keys to move around the text. When entering text there
        ∧       is no need to bother about line ending within
                paragraphs. The wordwrap facility enables you to type
  (9f)  only∧   continuously. It is necessary to press return at the end
                of paragraphs.
```

## Proof-reading

Before saving and printing a document it is necessary to **proof-read for errors.**

**TIPS ➤ ➤**

Save a
tree in '93 —
Save some
more in
'94

### Proof-reading

■ Do not print out a document which has not been proof-read as this not only takes more time, it is also a total waste of resources. Be environmentally conscious and save paper.

■ It is simple to proof-read a document on screen by using your cursor keys to move around.

■ If you have made any errors correct them using the insert or delete facilities. Once you are totally sure that your document is correct then save and print.

**Task 4 ➤**   Proof-read Wordpro on screen then print off one copy of the complete text and ask a student or colleague to double-check it for you.

## Keeping a record of files created

Most word-processing packages access the recall document facility straight from the function keys. This saves time searching through the disk directory of files.

To be able to recall a document you must know the name of the file. It is good practice to get into the habit of manually recording details of files you create, whether they are word processing, database or spreadsheet ones. It is also useful to record the contents of files. Try using an index like the one overleaf.

## INDEX OF WORD-PROCESSING FILES

| AUTHOR | FILENAME | CONTENTS | DATE |
|---|---|---|---|
| RM | Wordpro | Task 3 work | 1-03-9- |
|  |  |  |  |
|  |  |  |  |
|  |  |  |  |

Photocopy the blank index of word-processing files on page 267 and start recording details of the documents you create in the tasks and assessment activities which follow.

**TIPS ➤ ➤**   **Allocating document names**

- Give documents names which are relevant to their contents.

- Enter document names on the index whenever the document is complete. Never try to enter names in batches as you will probably forget what some contain.

- Use short names where possible – no more than six characters.

- You cannot use hard spaces in your filenames. However, if you need to split the characters try using the Shift+underline key.

- If you are naming a file which has been copied from a master document it is best to use an extension, for example, Wordpro2 or Let2.

- At the end of the working day always back-up your master documents onto floppy disk.

**Task 5 ➤**   Using 1 inch margins and double-line spacing type the paragraph, opposite, which you should name **Company**.
Then, proof-read and print out one copy of the correct text, and ask another student or colleague to check it for you.

> **NOTE**
> In each of the tasks which follow make sure that you proof-read on screen, print out the correct text and get someone to check it for you.

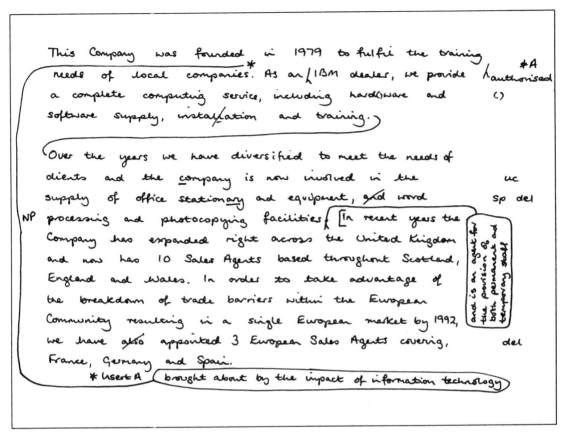

## Headings

In blocked style, headings all begin at the left margin. The most commonly used headings are main, shoulder, paragraph and side.

A **main heading** may be displayed in closed capitals or spaced capitals, with or without emboldening. Two spaces should be left between words in closed capitals and three spaces between words in spaced capitals. The return key is pressed three times after a main heading to begin the first line of text (leaving two clear lines).

**Shoulder, paragraph** and **side headings** may be displayed with initial capitals and emboldened or in closed capitals without emboldening. The return key is pressed twice after the shoulder heading to key in the first line of text.

**Paragraph headings** may be typed in two different ways. The first few words of the first sentence may be underscored or emboldened, or the heading may stand on its own. Two spaces are left between the paragraph heading and the first word of text which follows. The paragraph heading may be followed by punctuation such as a full stop or colon.

**Side** or **marginal headings** are typed to the left of the set left margin. They may be typed in closed capitals or initial capitals with underscore. From the left margin, space in once for each character and space in the longest line of the side headings plus three extra spaces. Set a tab at this point and use your indent key to type in the body of the text.

### Enumerated items

Paragraphs and items are sometimes numbered or lettered for easy reference. The numbers or letters may stand on their own, they may be enclosed in brackets or they may have a single bracket after them. Two spaces follow the last figure, letter or bracket.

### Spacing

One or two spaces may be left between words in closed capitals in a main heading or in subsidiary headings (shoulder, paragraph and side). If words in closed capitals are displayed in the body of the text, one or two spaces must be left between the words in capitals to be consistent with the spacing adopted in earlier headings.

**Task 6 ➤**    Identify as many of the above headings and enumerated items as you can from the text in this book.

**Task 7 ➤**    Using 1 inch margins and single-line spacing, type the following document. Use side headings for searching and sorting. Give the document an appropriate filename.

*a sophisticated*

*(ts)*

DATABASE                                    *means*

A database is ~~an~~ electronic filing system. It is a ~~way~~ of storing information in an organised way. There are two basic functions of a database = sorting and searching.

*by*
*Computerised*
*could (s)*
*you*

SEARCHING refers to the process ~~in~~ which certain items are selected from a larger group. Without the use of a database this task would have to be done manually and ~~would~~ take several ~~more~~ hours to complete. However, the computer can give the relevant information within a few seconds.

*stored or*

SORTING refers to any action that alters the order in which information is presented. A company may require a list of all its customers in alphabetical order. If you were given a list of 1000 names and asked to sort them into alphabetical order how long do you think it would take you? The computer can carry out this function in a few seconds.

**Task 8 ➤**    Using 1.5 inch margins and one and a half spacing, type the following document. Use paragraph headings for **employees** and **visitors**. Allocate a suitable filename.

IDENTIFYING PERSONNEL

*people and*
*stringent*

*(s)*

The increase in terrorist attacks from various factions on property in Britain has led to a call for more security measures to be undertaken by various large organisations which may be viewed as potential targets. Some very basic precautions can ~~easily~~ be taken by any organisation.

**Employees**

*works/*

Many companies now issue/passes to employees. These passes normally have the employee's photograph for identification and are signed by the individual.

*may/*

Employees ~~should~~ be asked to show these passes on entering or leaving their place of work. These passes are renewed each year.

**Visitors**

Many organisations do not allow strangers to walk around the premises unaccompanied. In some, visitors are issued

*or cards/*

with badges /which are handed back to the Receptionist before leaving the building.        (*l.c.*)

## Producing block style business letters and memoranda

If you need to revise on this subject refer to the relevant units in Book 1. The following tasks will enable you to practise your skills; follow closely the instructions given.

**Task 9 ➤**    Using 1 inch margins and single-line spacing, type the following letter on A4 headed paper and prepare an envelope to match.

---

JD/

Today's date

Domino Ltd, 73 Duke Street, LIVERPOOL    LV7 4AE

For the attention of Yvonne Dallas        – embolden & underscore

Dear Yvonne

The /software package we have designed for your personal and office    /accounts

computer is now ready for use. As specified by you the program is user

friendly and I am confident that it will meet all your ~~company's~~

needs The package consists of Nominal Ledger, Purchase Ledger, Sales    / Stock Control

Ledger, /Payroll and Job Costing Units.

Please let me know where and when you would like the package

*NP* demonstrated. [You had also been enquiring about the provision of

short courses on Autocad for your employees. I am pleased to

inform you that these courses begin on Monday next (insert

date) at 0930 hours in our Bristol centre. Each course lasts

for two weeks (Monday – Friday).

Due to the increase in demand I would advise you to complete the

attached enrolment form /by return.

Yours sincerely

*CAPS* James Dunlop

BUSINESS SERVICES MANAGER

Enc

---

**Task 10 ➤**    Using 1 inch margins and single-line spacing, type the following letter on A4 headed paper. Insert the signed letter in a window envelope.

TMcM/

Today's date                CONFIDENTIAL              (Embolden & Caps.)

Mrs Carol Kincaid
41 Bourne Grove
BRISTOL

Dear Mrs Kincaid

DEVELOPMENT OFFICER

above ⌐¶  Many thanks for contacting us regarding the position of
   ⌐¶       ~~Development Officer~~ with our company. I have pleasure in
   ⌐¶ bf⌐  enclosing an Application Form which ~~you~~ should completed
   (sp)     and return to the (Personel) Department before the closing
            date if you wish to be considered for the post.
                To avoid substantial postage costs the receipt of your
            form will not be acknowledged. However, if you require
   ⌐¶       confirmation that your application has been received
            please enclose a stamped ~~stamped~~ addressed envelope.
                You will only hear from us again if you are selected
            for interview which will normally be within four weeks.
on this     If you do not hear from us within that time you may
occasion o⌐ assume that your application has been unsuccessful⌐

            Yours sincerely


            Terence McManus
            PERSONNEL MANAGER

            Enc

## Tab columns

Tabs are used to create text in tabular form. Each column is marked by the tab stop. Tabs are simple to create and text can be easily manipulated to change position, delete, copy or insert another column at any point in a table.

**TIPS ➤ ➤**    **Typing tabbed columns**

- Count the spaces of the longest set of figures or words in the column before setting tabs.

- It is best to insert new positions (tab stops) and widths of tab columns.

- Leave equal spaces between columns using uneven amounts of characters – the most common being three, five or seven spaces.

- Unless instructed otherwise left-align columns under headings.

## Using decimal tabs in columns

Word processors have a facility that aligns numbers on the decimal point. This makes the typing of columns of figures a rapid and easy task.

**Task 11 ➤**    Create this document placing tab stops at the appropriate places.

PRICE LIST
A4 1 Colour Printing (Top Quality Paper)

| Quantity | White ~~Coloured~~ | ~~Coloured~~ White |
|----------|-------|----------|
| 100 | 15.20 | 15.10 |
| 200 | 23.10 | 21.80 |
| 300 | 31.00 | 28.50 |
| 400 | 38.80 | 35.30 |
| 500 | 46.70 | 42.10 |
| 600 | 54.60 | 48.80 |
| 700 | 62.40 | 55.60 |
| 800 | 70.30 | 62.40 |
| 900 | 78.20 | 69.10 |
| 1000 | 86.10 | 76.00 |

All prices quoted are inclusive of VAT. *one*
Delivery times range from one day to ~~two~~ weeks from date of order.

**Task 12 ➤**    Using 1 inch margins and single-line spacing type the following letter and prepare an envelope.

To|
Today's date

Dual Business Systems, Unit 2, Aragon Court, Runcorn  RX2 0JP

Dear Sirs

We have recently received your new catalogue and price list and are attracted to three items in particular. Would you please quote us for the items listed below:

178038        2-Door Cupboard 4036E            1016 x 953 x 489 mm

178 02X        Roller Blind Cupboard 7236RRB      1829 x 953 x 489 mm

178011        2-Door Cupboard 7236E            1829 x 953 x 489 mm

As we require to remain competitive with other companies in our area it is imperative that we can offer realistic | prices. We, therefore, assume ∧ and reasonable that you will be able to offer us trade/discount and reasonable credit ∧# facilities.

In the first instance we | will place an order for |⅓ of each item.        ∧ would
However, should this type of furniture appeal to | customers as we feel ∧ our it will, we | would then be ordering larger quantities." [we look forward to receiving your quote and letter of credit terms etc.

Yours faithfully

June Oliver
PURCHASING MANAGER

**Task 13 ➤**    Use single-line spacing and margins of 1 inch to produce these memoranda.

---

MEMORANDUM

To: John Allen                          Ref: New Catalogue
From: Dorothy Goodwin                    Date: Today's date

I have just looked over the new catalogue which is due for issue in July 199-.

On the whole I like the layout and /congratulate you and [ would] your staff for this. However, may I suggest a little more detail be [to] given /ix the description of the new Personal Computer plus Desk-c? top Laser Printer "Excel" which is being produced /for our company [especially] and is to be marketed /soon. [ quite]    [uc]

[NP] (This computer and printer will retail at a very competative  [sp]
price, which I think our /competitors will find hard to match. [ [ rivals]
feel that a one page illlustration ought to be used to highlight
the launch of our "own make pc and support equipment".    [embolden]

I will let you know / the number of catalogues required by  [ ASAP]
this department for distribution to our customers. It will
probably be almost double the quantity /received last year    [ we]
due to our continued growth/.    at home and abroad

---

**MEMORANDUM**

TO:     All Managers      REF:  Smoking Policy
FROM: Terence McManus      DATE: Today's date

_____

overwhelmingly
The recent vote among employees/came down in favour of a
"No Smoking"policy being adopted by the Company.[The    Ⓝ
Director's and Union Representatives subsequently held a
meeting to discuss staff facilities. The aim was to try
to come to a suitable arrangement for all employees.

We are all in agreement that employees and visitors
should no longer be allowed to smoke in the reception
area or offices or reception area. /The same facilities
However, (l.c.)    for making tea and coffee and the provision of daily
newspapers will be found in both the "Smokers" and "Non
Smokers" Common Rooms. Arrangements have been made for
Room 303 to be designated a "Smoker's Common Room" where
members of staff and visitors can relax in the same
atmosphere to be found in the "No Smoking" Common Room.
Would you convey these details to your departmental
members.

# Letters with tear-off strips

If a letter has to have a tear-off slip to be returned by the recipient, either a continuous series of **hyphens** or **dots** from edge to edge of the paper or margin to margin should indicate the tear-off slip.

The return key is pressed two or three times before and after the line of hyphens or dots.

One or two spaces should be left before the start of a dotted line, as after Name, Contract number and Address in the tear off slip shown in Task 14 below.

The return key is pressed twice between the dotted lines where information is to be filled in to allow for handwriting.

**Task 14 ➤**   Produce the letter on page 166 on A4 letterhead paper and type an envelope to accompany it.

**Task 15 ➤**   Create this form, to be enclosed with the previous tear-off letter, using an appropriate layout.

---

MICROPLUS LIMITED

Form CS199

REVISED PRINTER SERVICE AND MAINTENANCE CHARGES

| Equipment | Model | Cost |
|---|---|---|
| Roland Raven | LP-1170PS | £272.45 |
| Sharp | JX-9500QPS | £189.00 |
| TI OmniLaser | 2115 | £201.20 |
| Unisys | AP9210 | £165.75 |
| Xerox | 4010 XScript | £230.00 |
| Xerox | 4030 XScript | £230.00 |
| QMS | PS2200 | £221.90 |
| QMS ColourScript 100 | 301 | £307.75 |
| Panasonic | KX-P4455 | £213.35 |
| OkiData OkiLaser | 840 | £220.00 |
| New Gen Turbo | PS/300 | £219.45 |
| NEC Silentwriter | 2 290 | £265.00 |
| NEC Colourmate | PS | £386.00 |
| Microtek TrueLaser | MTP-306 | £202.00 |
| Kyocera | P-2000 | £179.50 |
| AGFA Compugraphic | 9400PS | £186.00 |
| Apple Laserwriter | Basic | £198.00 |
| Apple Laserwriter | IIg | £149.00 |
| Apple Laserwriter | Plus | £138.75 |
| Brother | HL-4PS | £202.00 |
| Brother | HL-8PS | £201.00 |
| Dataproducts | LZR-1260 | £177.00 |
| Dataproducts | LZR-960 | £198.00 |
| Fujitsu | RX7100PS | £202.00 |
| HP Laserjet | IID PostScript | £155.50 |
| HP Laserjet | III PostScript | £158.50 |
| IBM LaserPrinter E | 4019 PostScript | £219.50 |
| IBM LaserPrinter 10L | 4029 PostScript | £221.20 |
| IBM Laser Printer | 4019 PostScript | £216.00 |
| Inmac MicroLaser | PostScript | £204.00 |

*Typist   Type list in alphabetical order*

DG/

Today's date

Mr Nigel Lambert
Ashley Leisure
14 St Annes Road
Blackpool   (CAPS)

Dear Nigel

(SERVICING AND MAINTENANCE CONTRACT - PRINTERS)  (embolden)

As you will be aware we have been able to hold our
servicing and maintenance charges at the same rate ~~for~~ *recently*
~~the past 3 years. Since then~~ We have been faced with
rising costs of transport, labour and parts, as a result
of which we have been forced to revise ~~these~~ charges. I
enclose a list of the new charges which come into effect
on 1 ~~August 199 .~~ (next month)

*since 1989*

I trust you wish your contract to remain in operation
and I ~~would appreciate it~~ if you would complete the
tear-off slip below and return it to me as soon as
possible.

*(u.c.) will be glad*

Yours ~~faithfully~~  *sincerely*


Dorothy Goodwin
SALES AND SERVICING MANAGER


Enc

- - - - - - - - - - - - - - - - - - - - - - - - - - - - - - - - - -

Name.......................................................

Contract number............................................

Address ...................................................

...........................................................

...........................................................

I wish/do not wish* the above contract to remain in
operation at the revised scale of charges listed in Form
CS199.

*(u.c.)*

Signed.....................................................

Date ..................................

*   Delete as required

## Letters with continuation sheet/s

When a letter runs to more than one page, subsequent pages are known as **continuation** sheets.

Letterheaded paper should be used for the first sheet only. For continuation sheets, the paper should be plain but of the same size and quality as the headed paper.

In all matters of style and layout, continuation sheets should be consistent with the first page.

Each continuation sheet should include:

• the page number starting with 2 (as the first page is not numbered);

• the date of the letter;

• the name of the addressee.

Leave at least half an inch and no more than 2 inches at the bottom of each page.

If a paragraph has to be divided between two pages, there should be a minimum of two lines on each page.

### Example of continuation sheet layout

|  |  |  |
|---|---|---|
|  | ← Leave 1 inch from the top of the page |  |
| 2 | ← Page number | Press return twice |
| 9 April 1993 | ← Date | Press return twice |
| Mr G Welsh | ← Addressee | Press return three times |

**Task 16 ➤**

Following the rules applying to letters that run over one sheet type the following letter onto A4 headed paper. Use 1 inch margins and single-line spacing. Also provide an envelope.

```
AB/
```

✳ A  *As well as the supply of hardware and software we offer a complete training service to customers. Our latest addition has been the inclusion of a Business Services Centre which provides secretarial & financial services to small businesses and members of the public.*

```
Mr F Diplas
Ministry of Labour
40 Pireos Street
GR-10182 Athens
GREECE

Dear Mr Diplas
```

*operating*    *the UK (in full)*

```
Microplus has been trading in Britain since 1979. The
business began trading in office furnishings and
equipment. By 1989 the Company had grown to such
proportions that it was converted to a PLC with 6      (in full)
Regional Branches throughout the United Kingdom. Since
1990 we have expanded and moved into the highly
competative computer market. ✳ A
```

(sp)

(Initial caps)

```
Since Britain entered the European Economic Community
our Company has benefited from increasing trade links.
```
*/ the*

We have been able to promote expansion in 3 ~~other~~ European countries - France, Spain and Germany, with branches in Paris, Malaga and Bon. (sp)

*Mme* / *stet* Our agent in Greece, /D Michopoulou, has advised us that the time is ripe to expand and open a branch in your country. We have ~~recently~~ carried out a feasibility study and surveyed various organisations within the business community to measure interest ~~in such a project~~. Our findings determine that opening a branch in Athens would be of mutual benefit to both ourselves and the business community.

*in Pieros* / Ideal premises have been negotiated/and we would hope that, subject to Government approval, the business could open in August 199-. *We would propose that, initially, one of the British managers would oversee the start-up and engage 10 staff members.* (Run on) Mme Michopoulou, would be employed as Manager of the Athens Business Centre.

*the* / I have made arrangements to meet with Mme Michopoulou on Monday (typist insert date as 2 weeks on Monday) at 1000 hours in the Atlantis Room of my hotel -/Athens Emporium, 14 Nikoloudi & Papada Street, Athens 115-26.

I would like to take this opportunity to invite you to this informal meeting where we could possibly arrange further talks on the project.

I look forward to your reply.

Yours sincerely


Alan Brown
MANAGING DIRECTOR

# Invitation and agenda for meetings

It is normal practice to send out an **invitation** in the form of a **notice** or **summons**. The notice must be sent out in plenty of time to allow attendees to prepare for the meeting.

The invitation contains:

- **title of meeting –**                        AGM, Committee Meeting, etc.

- **place, date and time –**              venue noted with correct time and date

- **note of response –**                    instructions for indicating whether a person will be attending or not.

The notice may be sent out at any time before the meeting but it is usual to give at least a week's notice. In the case of an annual general meeting (AGM) the notice and accompanying documents should be distributed at least one month in advance.

### Accompanying documents

The notice of meeting and agenda can usually be combined and sent together. Copies of minutes of the previous meeting and papers to be discussed will also normally be sent out prior to or with the invitation.

**TIPS ➤ ➤**    **Typing an agenda and notice of meeting**

- The notice begins with a description of the meeting and place, date and time.

- All lines begin at the left-hand margin.

- The notice of meeting is typed in single-line spacing.

- The agenda is typed in double-line spacing.

- Copies are sent to all committee members for an ordinary meeting.

- Copies are sent to all members of the organisation for an AGM.

### Chairperson's agenda

It is common practice to type a special agenda for the use of the Chairperson, whose function it is to ensure that the meeting proceeds without interruption. The Chairperson's agenda contains more information on important points typed as notes, numbered and detailed on the right-hand side of the original.

### Agenda

An **agenda** is a list of matters to be discussed at a meeting. The usual order of an agenda is:

- apologies for absence – from members unable to attend;

- minutes of the previous meeting – detailing the items discussed, voted on and passed by the committee;

- matters arising out of the minutes – developments on points brought up;

- correspondence – letters sent, the contents of which have to be divulged to members;

- reports – Secretary's report or Treasurer's report;

- special points for discussion – outings, charity involvements, dances, etc.;

- date and time of next meeting – convenient to all;

- any other business (AOB) – sundry items.

**Task 17 ➤**    Using 1 inch margins, type the notice of meeting and agenda shown overleaf.

## Minutes

Minutes are a brief formal record of the contents of the meeting and the outcomes. They are usually produced by the Secretary to provide a record of items discussed, decisions taken and acknowledgements received and have three purposes:

- to record formally the proceedings;

- to provide the basis for any action to be taken;

- to indicate how policies or future plans should be developed.

NOTICE OF MEETING WITH AGENDA

MICROPLUS STAFF SOCIAL CLUB
25 LONG AVENUE
BRISTOL

NOTICE OF MEETING

There will be a meeting of the [Committee of the] Microplus Staff Social Club in the Red Lion Hotel, Prince's Suite, [on] Friday 5 March 199-. [at 1900 hours]

AGENDA
1    Apologies for absence
~~2~~ 3 Matters arising from the Minutes
~~3~~ 2 Minutes of the last meeting
4    Correspondence
~~8~~ 7 ~~Any other business~~    Initial caps
~~6~~ 5 Secretary's report
7 6 Date and time of next meeting

LORRAINE PEARSON
Secretary

Note: Members unable to attend should indicate by ~~letter~~ [before] or telephone Monday 1 March.

Room 36a
Staff Club
Microplus Limited

19 February 199-

**TIPS ➤ ➤**    **Taking and producing minutes**

■ Minutes must be accurate so listen carefully.

■ Minutes must be clear and concise even if the events of the meeting are confusing.

■ Minutes must contain a precise register of all people attending the meeting.

■ Minutes are written in the past tense, for example, the Secretary reported that an estimate had been received....

■ Minutes are produced in the order in which events took place even if the meeting does not follow the order of the agenda.

■ Produce a draft set of minutes as soon as possible after the meeting when points are still fresh in your memory.

■ Let the Chairperson have a copy of the draft before producing the final text to be distributed to members.

■ In your draft raise any queries or points to be clarified for the Chairperson's attention.

### Typing minutes

When typing minutes there is a logical, set pattern which needs to be followed:

- Begin the document by typing a heading in blocked capitals (it can also be emboldened), for example, MICROPLUS STAFF SOCIAL CLUB. The heading can be at the top left-hand corner or centred.

- Give a brief description of the meeting including the place, date and time.

- Then type a detailed list of those present in this order: Chairperson; other officials; members listed alphabetically.

- The numbered points of the agenda are then dealt with in the order events occurred.

- At the end, leave space for the Chairperson's signature together with the date on which the minutes were signed.

**Task 18 ➤**  Type up these minutes and insert numbers as appropriate:

MINUTES OF MEETING of Microplus Staff Social Club held on Friday 5 March 199-. at 1900 hours in the Red Lion Hotel.

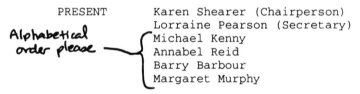

PRESENT        Karen Shearer (Chairperson)
               Lorraine Pearson (Secretary)
*Alphabetical order please* — Michael Kenny
               Annabel Reid
               Barry Barbour
               Margaret Murphy

**1. Apologies**

Apologies were received from Petra Edmunds and Paul Holden.

**2. Minutes**

The Minutes of the meeting held on Friday 2 February were read and signed by the Chairperson as being a true record.

**3 Matters Arising**

There were no matters arising.

**4 Correspondence**

(i)   A letter of thanks was received from Bristol Hospice for the sum of £975.38 which was raised at the recent Dinner Dance.

(ii)  A letter was received from Bristol Sports Club inviting us to take part in ~~the~~ Bungee Jump on the last Sunday in July. It was agreed that we would take up this invitation and a reply ~~will~~ be sent.

*their charity sponsored would*

**5** <u>Secretary's Report</u>

This document has already been circulated to Members and was approved by all present. Adoption was proposed by Annabel Reid and seconded by Michael Kenny.

**7** <u>AOB</u> — (in full)

It was agreed to try to attract new members to the club. Leaflets are being printed and they will be distributed to staff members during the early part of next month.

**6** <u>Date of Next Meeting</u>

hours ↲    It was agreed to meet next on 5 May at 1930/ in the Red
Hotel ↲    Lion↲

Chairperson .........................................

Date        .........................................

## Itinerary

Itineraries act as reminders to people, alerting them of where they should be at any given time. Itineraries can range from small pieces of card (which can be placed in a handbag or pocket) covering one day's appointments (an appointments itinerary) to one or two sheets of A4 paper detailing a travel itinerary for a number of days.

When making travel arrangements and drawing up an itinerary a sensible allowance must be made for travel time between appointments.

**TIPS ➤ ➤**

**Typing an itinerary**

- Appointments or details should be listed sequentially and the 24-hour clock used for times.

- Leave one clear line space between each item on the itinerary.

- Highlight important points by emboldening.

- Separate itineraries should be typed up for each day of a business trip.

**Task 19 ➤**

Type up this itinerary in the correct time order.

ITINERARY — embolden

<u>Mr Alan Brown - 9 April 199-</u>

1430    Ace Management Services, 27 Portland Street, Stephen Gillan, Acting Managing Director.

1000    Pembroke Printing, 4 Avon Road, Pauline Blair, Human Resources Manager.

1300    Astor Hotel - lunch with Mr Jeffries of Executive Travel.

| | |
|---|---|
| 1130 | Tatler Publishing, Belstead Road, Justin Hastings, Managing Director. |
| 1600 | Ashley Leisure, 14 St Anne's Road, Neill Dickson, Training Manager. |

## Financial statements

You may be asked to type up statements which show income and expenditure, profit and loss, or receipts and payments. These are all known as financial statements.

**TIPS ➤ ➤**

### Typing financial statements

■ The spacing between the money columns should be equal and in uneven units, for example, 3, 5, 7 spaces.

■ The spacing between the description column and the first money column should be the same or greater than the money columns.

■ The £ sign in the headings must be in line with the first figure in the column.

■ The £ sign in the totals must appear next to the first figure on the line, for example, £30,000 not £ 30,000.

**Task 20 ➤**   Produce the income and expenditure account shown overleaf on A4 paper following the guidelines above.

MICROPLUS STAFF SOCIAL CLUB

*embolden*

INCOME AND EXPENDITURE ACCOUNT FOR THE YEAR ENDING 30 MARCH 199-

| INCOME   – *embolden & underline* | £ | £ | £ |
|---|---|---|---|
| Members' subscriptions | | | 5,785 |
| Corgi, raffle and bingo profits | | | 560 |
| Fund raising | | | 3,275 |
| Interest received | | | 295 |
| | | | 9,915 |

| EXPENDITURE   – *embolden & underline* | | | |
|---|---|---|---|
| Donations to charities | | 4,695 | |
| Insurance | | 264 | |
| Fees | | 179 | |
| Equipment for Gymnasium | | 320 | |
| Depreciation: | | | |
| Equipment | 175 | 175 | |
| General Expenses | | 148 | |
| | | | 5,821 |

*embolden*

SURPLUS OF INCOME OVER EXPENDITURE                     £ 4,094

# Reports

What is a report? Get together in a group and discuss documents you produce which may come under the title **report**.

A variety of documents may be classified as reports and blocks of text which constitute a report will vary in length from a few paragraphs to a substantial number of pages. The British Association for Commercial and Industrial Education's definition, to be found in Report Writing, states that a report is:

> a document in which a given problem is examined for the purpose of conveying information, reporting findings, putting forward ideas, and, sometimes, making recommendations.

In business and administration the types of reports which you will come across most often are formal reports and informal reports.

**Formal reports** are normally wordy and take up a number of pages. They are most often used for external publications and are circulated outside an organisation, for example, government reports.

**Informal reports** are normally circulated internally within an organisation and are often quite brief. It is likely that most of your work will concentrate on informal rather than formal reports.

When producing reports the **organisational housestyle** must be followed so you need to become familiar with your own workplace styles and layouts.

### Structure of an informal report

A report which considers recommendations or solutions is often structured in this way:

Part 1 – describes the purpose of the report.

Part 2 – relays information on the subject of the report as concisely as possible.

Part 3 – lists possible courses of action or suitable solutions.

Part 4 – gives recommendations of action to be taken or solution chosen with justification of choice.

Part 5 – provides illustrations such as diagrams, charts, pictograms, etc.

Part 6 – provides appendices giving supplementary information.

When the report is solely for information it normally covers only:

- purpose   • information   • conclusion   • appendices.

### Layout of an informal report

Before beginning to type a report think about the contents of the document. All reports must contain:

- a **heading or title** – which summarises the purpose of the report. This must be short and to the point and above all relate to the contents of the report;

- a **brief description** – giving the reason for the report;

- a **method summary** – stating the resources employed in investigating problems;

- the **findings** – giving the results of investigations;

- the **recommendations/conclusion** – summarising the choices or solutions, etc.

**Task 21 ➤**     Produce this report:

REPORT ON SELECTION OF THE MOST SUITABLE INFORMATION
PROCESSING SYSTEM FOR PRIMETIME INSURANCE SERVICES -
MANCHESTER.

1 PURPOSE OF THE REPORT     *embolden*

*information processing*
*(sp.)*

The purpose of the study is to examine and analyse the
current system in use in the client's company and the
manpower needed to to accomodate the work load.

This report provides a summary of the study.

3     AIMS AND OBJECTIVES     *embolden*

The major aims of the study were to reveal advanced
equipment which met the needs of the client, provided the
highest level of capabilities, required little staff
retraining and allowed room for expansion. The objectives of
the new installation would be to:

*(c) provide high quality output*

(a)    eliminate backlogs of work
(b)    simplify input procedures
(d)    automate records processing
(e)    reduce time taken to create and maintain records
(f)    link repetitive procedures

2     BACKGROUND     *embolden*

A study of available equipment was made, which considered
running costs; keying in procedures, input time and quality
of output from the system; production capacity and
flexibility of the system.

4 PROCEDURE     *embolden*

*(sp.)*
*subsequently*

The study was conducted over a ten-day period. Data was
collected on questionaire forms completed during one-to-one
discussions with staff and ~~then~~ analysed by the computer.

5 THE PRESENT POSITION     *embolden*

The limitations of the present system are:
-    backlogs are often created in the typing pool which
     calls for employment of additional temporary staff and
*A →* overtime working - including week-ends.
-    the quality of many documents is below standard due to
     spelling mistakes or grammatical errors. Corrections
     are often unsightly, therefore documents need to be re-
     typed which causes further delays and back-log build-
     up.
-    there is often a lack of sufficient secretarial and
     administrative support to managerial staff.
*organisation* -  there are no standards, layouts or formats used in
     ~~various~~ productions of documents

*A — documents often have to be retyped due to minor errors or amendments being required.*

6 SCOPE OF THE STUDY     *embolden*

The study took into consideration the length of the working

35/ week, which was ~~30~~ hours, and the costs of staff involved. During the study the work of 25 text processing staff was surveyed. The type and length of documents produced, and the extent to which they underwent revision, was also considered, with the following results:

```
Length of Documents    -    1 page         13%
                       -    2+ pages        87%
Document Revision      -    simple          25%
                       -    moderate        28%
                       -    complex         27%
                       -    repetitive      20%
```

### 7 BASIS OF THE REVIEW  — embolden

The review of equipment was conducted using the five basic areas detailed below:

Production capability
Compatibility with other equipment
Training and support required      Operator / (l.c) / operator /
Equipment and software service and support provided
Costs - manpower and equipment.

### 8 CONCLUSION  — embolden

As a result of the study the new EXCEL (Microplus) ELITE system was recommended as the most suitable information processing system to meet the needs of the client.

(Current Date)

---

## Assessment activity 16.1

This assessment will test your ability to produce a variety of business documents of approximately 1200 words in total, in a 2.5 hour working period. The documents to be produced will be from this list:

- letters
- envelopes/labels
- memoranda
- reports
- notices
- tabulated material
- articles for display
- lists comprising alphabetical, numerical, chronological and general information.

## Activity A

Create this **job description** using 1 inch margins and save it as **TRJOB**.

*\*A To assist in the development and delivery of training programmes in word processing, database & spreadsheet, autocad & computerised accounts.*

**MICROPLUS LIMITED**

DEPARTMENT           -    BUSINESS CENTRE

POST TITLE           -    **INFORMATION TECHNOLOGY TRAINING OFFICER**

SALARY               -    £16,765 - £19,530                    *②*

RESPONSIBLE TO  -    Business Centre Manager

LIAISON WITH         -    COMPUTING TRAINING OFFICERS
                          CLERICAL LIAISON OFFICERS
                          BUSINESS CENTRE MANAGER
                          *TRAINING & RECRUITMENT MANAGER*

PRINCIPAL ROLE  -    To teach information technology on
                          courses throughout the organisation. *\*A*

MAIN FUNCTIONS

1.    Lecture in information technology on courses throughout the organisation.

*(in full)*
*u.c.*

2.    Coordinate the teaching on particular courses in IT as identified by the business centre manager and training and recruitment manager.

*4*    ~~2~~.    Take responsibility for a group of students including induction, reviews and enrolment.   *sp*

**Student note: stop typing this document and save to return to it later. Go on to Activity G which is urgent.**

*3*    ~~4~~.    Liase with the Training Manager in the design,       *sp*
              development and application of the syllabus for
              selected Information Technology Courses.

5.    Prepare assignments and carry out any assessment of
              students */ required by any appropriate validating authority.*

6.    Attend departmental meeting when required.

7.    Undertake Company services as follows:
              (a)   Membership of Committees and Development
                          Groups.
              *(b)   Participation in Staff Development.*

8.    Teach any additional subject appropriate to skills and experience.

9.    Perform any other duties as the Business Centre Manager
*reasonably*      may / require and as defined in the Conditions of
              Service.

## Activity B

Create this letter to be sent out to applicants for the position of
**Information Technology Training Officer**. Name the document **TRLETAP**.

Dear Applicant

Thank you for showing an interest in applying for a post with our organisation.

As requested I enclose an Application form which you are encouraged to complete and return as soon as possible / to the following adress:  L*A

    Mr Terence McMenus
    Personnel Manager
    Microplus Limited
    18-23 Long Avenue
    BRISTOL

The organisation's Equal Opportunities Policy requires that all recruitment and selection decisions /are monitored. In order to facilitate this  sp  Lbe, I /enclosed a confidential questionaire which you should complete  L have sp and return with your application for employment. [I have also  NP enclosed a job description outlining the responsibilities which the successful applicant / is expected to have.  L will be

May I thank you for your interest in the post and wish you success in your application.

Yours faithfully

Personnel Manager

    *HA  , but certainly before the closing date shown in the advertisement*

## Activity C

Display the following Application for Employment Guidance Notes in
block style. Use 1 inch margins and single-line spacing. Leave spacing
and a half between the figured paragraphs. Save the document as
**EMPGUIDE** and print out one copy.

2 /  <u>EQUAL OPPORTUNITY</u>

    It is the policy of the Company that:

2 /.1  there shall be equal opportunities in the fields of recruitment, education, training and promotion irrespective of colour, race, nationality, ethnic or national origin, religion, social background, marital status, sex, age or disability of job applicants and existing employees.

U.C.  The policy is aimed particularly at helping groups

*persons* /

of people who may face difficulties in obtaining
employment or in gaining promotion, e.g. women,
disabled ~~people~~ and ethnic minorities.       ③

2         /.2     all employees will be given equal opportunities
and, where appropriate, special training to
progress within the company.       *U.C.*

2         /.3     all employees will be recruited, trained and
promoted on the basis of (fitness and ability) for *trs*
work.

1   /        <u>CONDITIONS OF SERVICE</u>

*on request*     Detailed Conditions of Service are available, if you are
appointed, but the following is a summary of the major
Conditions of Service:

\#            **Salary**
Salaries are paid four weekly into your bank account.
Salaries are normally paid on a increasing scale with
progresssion to the next point of the scale within one
*tl*         year of appoirment or on acquiring qualifications or
experience. *Full details will be given in the event of an
offer of employment being made.*

*25l*        **Holidays**
Holiday entitlement is ~~23~~ days per year and 12 days
public holidays per year.

**Company Pension Scheme**
On appointment you will be invited to join the company
*u.c.*       pension scheme. The current rate for contributions is
5% and full details are available on request.

**Staff Life Assurance**
A non-contributory staff life assurance scheme is in ~~in~~
operation.

**Attendance**                          *a*
All staff are expected to maintain an ~~a~~cceptable level
*sp*         of attendance. ~~Supervisers~~ should be notified of
*sp*         illness before 1000 hours on the first day of <u>absense</u>.

*u.c.*       **Sickness Allowance**
The sickness allowance scheme ensures the make-up of
salaries during sickness. The <u>entitlment</u> periods are
*sp*         related to service and range from 1 month's full pay
and 1 month's half pay during the first year of service
6            to ~~six~~ month's full pay after 5 years of service.

3        <u>MEDICAL FITNESS</u>       (*nominated by the Company*

Entrants are required to satisfy a medical practitioner,
as to their fitness for employment.

**(Note:** Use paragraph headings for sub-headings at Item 1 –
Conditions of Service.)

4    **PROBATION**

*sp.*

The first 6 months of service is regarded as
probationery.

5    **DAY RELEASE**

*u.c.*

Day or block release facilities are available to
entrants under 18 years of age to study examinations
leading to qualifications recognised by the Company.

over 18 /
y o a
*sp*

*u.c.*

Similar facilities may be made available to other
entrants in line with the Company's commitment to TQM.
In particular everyone is asked to try to achieve a
Vocational Qualification either by workplace assessment
or attending night classes, for which the company will
pay costs.

*in full - Total Quality Management*

## Activity D

Prepare envelopes and insert a copy of the Job Description,
Employment Guidance Notes and letter to these applicants:

James O'Hare, 44 Manor Park Drive
Lisa Drummond, 8a Harbour View
Mark Richards, 11 York Place.

## Activity E

Produce the memo shown on the next page and insert the menu as
shown following the instructions. A copy has to be distributed to each
departmental manager. Use single-line spacing and 1 inch margins for
this activity.

## Activity F

Send a memo (in report form) to the Company Secretary listing these
general operating expenses for last year. Title the report, enter the total
in each column and insert monthly totals as appropriate.

| MONTH | HEATING & LIGHTING £ | VEHICLES & HAULAGE £ | TELEPHONE & FAX £ | INSURANCE & LEGAL £ |
|---|---|---|---|---|
| January | 356.54 | 607.77 | 583.63 | 124.95 |
| February | 298.65 | 409.22 | 176.92 | 190.45 |
| March | 321.12 | 756.00 | | 115.22 |
| April | 167.64 | 555.22 | 478.60 | 411.13 |
| May | 319.33 | 200.56 | | 102.77 |
| June | 291.17 | 756.00 | | 99.00 |
| July | 315.22 | 481.55 | 612.31 | |
| August | | 269.90 | 277.57 | |
| September | 408.76 | 115.42 | | 378.40 |
| October | 413.12 | 333.09 | | |
| November | 359.20 | 566.64 | | |
| December | 411.10 | 406.03 | 662.77 | 756.00 |

**(Note:** Save the original using single-line spacing then change the
spacing in rows January – December to spacing and a half.)

MEMORANDUM

TO: All Staff

FROM: Terence McManus

REF: Annual Dinner Dance

DATE: Insert today's date

*A from my office and the Staff Club

Arrangements have been finalised for this year's annual dinner dance. vc
The Dance will be held in the Meteor Hotel on 18 June, at
1900 hours. Tickets will be available /[ *A during the preceding 4
weeks, priced /£10 per couple.        L at

**Student note: save this document and return to it later – go to Activity F and produce the document which is needed for a meeting in 20 minutes' time.**

The cost has been kept low this year due to the contribution made
by the Staff Club through their fund-raising efforts. This contribution has
been /recognised by Mr Brown, who has also offered to pay for    L welcomed
wines and drinks during the meal.)
·I am sure you will have no complaints about the menu which is:

MENU

Prawn Cocktail

Florida Salad

French Onion Soup
     x x x

Sole Mornay

Cod in Butter Sauce
     x x x

L Beef Wellington
  Sirloin Steak              L Duck à l'Orange
Salmon Parcels
Crown of Lamb
Roast and Creamed Potatoes
Broccoli, /and Asparagus      L Cauliflower
     x x x
Sherry Trifle
Hot Chocolate Fudge Cake with Cream
     x x x L Fresh Fruit Salad and Cream
Cheese Platter
Coffee
After Eights

TYPIST
Display menu effectively
in centre of page

## Activity G

Type the following itinerary for Mr Brown's trip to Greece.

---

SUNDAY (insert date)

1210 hrs          Leave London Heathrow for Athens Flight No. BA632 (Club Class)

1750 hrs          Arrive Athens - Pick up car keys from Hertz reception

                  Hotel:  Athens Emporium                    CAPS + EMBOLDEN
                          14 Nikoloudi + Papada Street
                          Athens 115-26

MONDAY (insert date)

1000 hrs          Meeting with Mr Diplas and Mme/Michopoulou in Atlantis      l #
                  Room of Hotel   le
                                              They
1900 hrs          Dinner with Mr/Diplas. He will meet you at the         + Mrs
                  Hotel    le

                  Dinner has been booked for $7^3$ for 1930 hrs and a
                  reservation has been made to attend the floor show at
                  2200 hrs   in the hotel Olympic Suite

TUESDAY (insert date)

1015 hrs          Mme Michopoulou will meet you at the Hotel Reception            le

1045 hrs          Meeting with Mr Nikolas and Mr Christianos at:
                  → # A
                  Pireous Leiswe Centre
                  Pireous SR - 10225
                  (2nd floor)

1500 hrs          Visit to Athens Business Centre with Mme Michopoulou + Mr Nikolas

1600 hrs          Visits to Olympic Stadium and National Museum with
                  Mr Niklas and Mme Michopoulou                    Lo

1900 hrs          Dinner at hotel with Mr and Mrs Nikolas, Mr Christianos
                  and Mme Michopoulou
                                          1900
                  Dinner is booked for 2000 hrs

WEDNESDAY (insert date)
                                                      over breakfast
1030 hrs          Final meeting with Mr Nikolas and Mme Michopoulou∠

1645 hrs          Leave Athens for London - Flight BA7513 (Club Class)

1830 hrs          Arrive London Heathrow - Rachel Bywaters will meet
                  you at airport

        # A   Contracts are in wallet folder -
              marked PIREOUS NEGOTIATIONS

---

## Student questionnaire

Produce draft answers to these questions and then check you have listed the correct details. Produce as text the final copy and have a group discussion on the answers.

1    List at least four important features you would look for in choosing a word-processing system for your office.

2    Can you give two **advantages** a manual typewriter has over an electronic machine?

3    List at least four **advantages** of using a word processor rather than a typewriter.

4    What is meant by these word-processing terms:

   a)   flashing cursor

   b)   status line

   c)   wordwrap?

5    Microplus have acquired a local stationery supplies company. The offices there are using typewriters and manual recording systems. Your boss has asked you to assess the equipment and make out a list of new equipment to be bought which will speed work up and provide greater accuracy. You are asked to type up a report on your findings which must list the pros and cons of:

   a)   electronic equipment

   b)   computers

   c)   new manual equipment.

Which system did you choose? Why?

# UNIT 17 | Audio transcription

## Produce a variety of business documents from recorded speech

**Task 1 ➤** What are the advantages and disadvantages of producing text from recorded dictation? Discuss these with your group.

How many from this list did you come up with?

| Advantages | Disadvantages |
|---|---|
| The typist does not have to be present during dictation. | When text is being produced the dictator may not be available to answer queries. |
| Dictation can be recorded away from the office. | A lot of the personal contact between boss and secretary is lost. |
| Tapes can be sent to the office for text production. | When tapes are re-used there is no copy record of actual text and instructions dictated. |
| Dictation can be recorded as new items arise. | The quality of dictation is often poor and instructions can be unclear. |
| The audio-typist does not need such extensive training as a shorthand-typist. | The typist must have good knowledge of vocabulary, spelling, grammar and punctuation. |
| Typists can often produce text quicker from recorded speech than from shorthand notes. | Recordings can be accidentally erased. |
| The typist can attend to other tasks while dictation is taking place. | Dictators often forget to give basic information to the typist. |

**Task 2 ➤**
Form a group and each member record a different task from Unit 16 onto tape. Swop tapes and produce the text required. Then:

a)   List essential points which the dictator omitted from the instructions.

b)   Have someone else check your hard copy for spelling mistakes.

c)   List layout instructions which you think were unclear.

When you have completed this task you will probably realise how difficult it is to actually dictate adequate instructions for someone else to play back and understand fully.

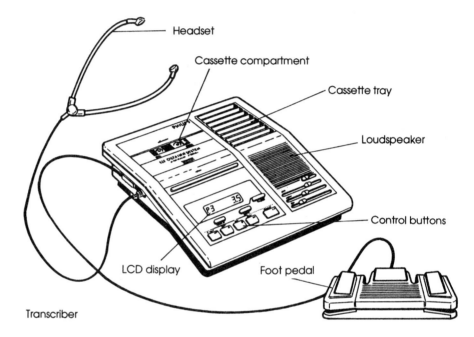

Transcriber

**TIPS ➤➤**

**Audio dictation**

■ Practise using the equipment and become familiar with its operation.

■ Plan the order of the material to be dictated.

■ Make notes to remind you of details and referencing, for example, files to be referred to or previous correspondence.

■ Indicate clearly at the beginning of the dictation the requirements to be fulfilled, for example:
  - margins and line spacing
  - special instructions (confidential, urgent, etc.)
  - stationery type and size to be used
  - refer to length of item by indicating counter mark or index of machine.

■ Indicate the type of document to be produced (letter, memo, report, itinerary, etc.).

■ Adopt a method of distinguishing clearly between instructions and material which has to be produced.

- When dictating the body of the text spell out any unfamiliar words or names.

- Use the **pause** facility when you stop to think as this will avoid gaps in the recording.

- Always check part of the recording for clarity of speech and quality of dictation.

**Task 3 ➤**   Get together with your group again and try dictating another task from Unit 16. Swop tapes and type up the required document. Were the instructions clearer this time?

## Audio conventions

The Royal Society of Arts have laid down these dictating conventions:

1. The start of a new paragraph will be indicated by the word 'paragraph'.

2. Punctuation marks will be dictated, for example, full stop, question mark, colon, semi-colon, dash, exclamation mark and hyphen.

3. Commas and apostrophes are not to be dictated.

4. Brackets (parentheses) will be dictated as 'open brackets ... close brackets' and inverted commas as 'open quotes ... close quotes (also indicate if single or double). Can also be dictated as 'inverts on and inverts off'.

5. When typing double agents such as he/she, the stroke is indicated as 'oblique'.

6. The spelling of unusual words should always be given immediately after the word has been dictated, for example, Mme Michopoulou (M M E  M I C H O P O U L O U) and the telephone alphabet may also be used.

7. Headings – instructions should always be dictated before the words of the heading, for example, centre heading, embolden.

8. Numbers are typed according to organisational housestyle conventions. However, where numbers have be in a specific form this should be indicated by stating either figures or words.

9. The use of initial and blocked capitals is indicated prior to the word(s).

10. Use the 24-hour clock when typing times, for example, 9 p.m. is typed as 2100 hours.

**Task 4 ➤**   Form a group and again dictate different tasks from Unit 16 onto a recorder. Swop tapes and type up from the dictated material.

## Other formalities

As you know, most organisations have their own housestyle for producing business documents. You must always follow your particular organisation's guidelines when producing text from manuscript, typescript, audio and shorthand material.

**TIPS ➤ ➤**

**Typing text**

- Adopt the **normal layout** according to documents being produced.

- Use **open punctuation.**

- Consult a **good dictionary.**

- Always **check grammar.**

- Take care when typing **plurals.**

- Pay particular attention to **instructions.**

## Methods of indexing

The person dictating the material to be processed can mark the beginning of each passage on an index. This will let the typist know how long each dictated passage lasts. In the past, indexing was prepared manually by the dictator who would write down on a piece of paper the start and stop numbers of each document.

Modern indexing is carried out within the equipment itself and can be demonstrated by your supervisor or tutor. Some machines display the actual time of the dictation and special messages or instructions to the typist. When indexing is correctly carried out it helps the typist to:

- estimate the length of the material as accurately as possible;

- decide size and type of stationery needed;

- note any instructions before starting.

Some organisations do not rely on indexing and prefer the dictator to instruct the typist as follows:

- prepare a short letter to ...

- produce a lengthy memo

- type up this lengthy report

- this letter is rather long and will require a continuation sheet, and so on.

Find out the conventions of your own organisation and practise as much as you can. Above all follow these **golden rules:**

- **familiarise** yourself with the equipment used and learn how to **operate it properly;**

- always use a **headset** or **earpiece** which is comfortable to wear for long periods;

- arrange your **work area** in such a way that you have immediate access to electrical sockets, the word processor, stationery supplies, files and reference material;

- always **check the finished document** before forwarding to the dictator.

**Task 5** ➤  Draft answers to these questions and then discuss them with others in your group.

1   The management of Microplus have decided to open sub-offices in regional areas. These offices will be manned by an agent and secretary. The Agent will be kept extremely busy and will rarely be available at the office. Look up various catalogues on audio equipment and decide which system you would suggest for optimum efficiency. Type up a report on this and remember to justify your recommendation.

2  What would you list as essential requirements for efficient transcription of audio dictation?

3  What other uses might an audio system be put to in the office?

4  List the major advantages and disadvantages of audio transcription against shorthand transcription.

---

# Assessment 17.1

**Remember! Keep your work from this activity for reference and assessment.**

Ask your lecturer at college or supervisor at work to provide you with taped material for this assessment.

# Shorthand transcription

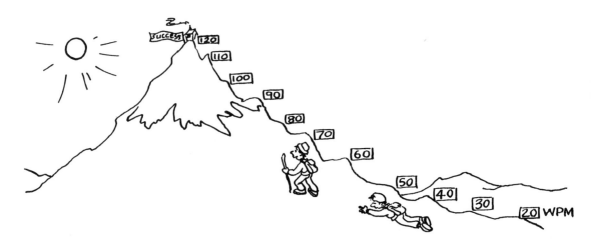

---

## Produce a variety of business documents from dictated material

**Task 1 ➤**   What are the advantages and disadvantages of producing text from shorthand dictation? Do you think shorthand dictation is preferable to audio dictation? Discuss this with your group. How many from this list did you come up with?

| Advantages | Disadvantages |
|---|---|
| The dictator is available to answer any questions or clear up queries. | The shorthand typist must be available to take shorthand dictation. |
| Personal contact between boss and secretary is maintained. | In-depth, lengthy training is necessary. |
| Instructions and special items can be double checked. | Dictation periods are often interrupted by telephone calls, visitors, etc. |
| The typist does not need such a good knowledge of vocabulary or spelling skills. | |
| There is hard copy of the material dictated. | |
| Shorthand typists can achieve great speeds; therefore, this method can be very fast. | |

## Shorthand systems

Some shorthand systems are based on symbols while others are based on the letters of the alphabet. The most widely used systems for business are:

Teeline — based on the alphabet; has less theory to learn; is capable of producing very high speeds; is widely used by journalists.

Pitman New Era — uses symbols as the base and has a lot of theory attached; is time consuming to learn; not as easy as Teeline.

Pitman 2000 — modernised, user-friendly version of New Era with a lot less theory; the outlines are longer which does not produce as high speeds as the original system.

Speedwriting — another which is based on the alphabet and has less theory to learn; less chance of achieving high speeds with this system.

Gregg — much used system in USA; uses symbols; can produce very high speeds.

During the late 1980s office workers were warned to watch out for the demise of shorthand due to the increasing use of new technology. However, the 1990s has witnessed an increase in popularity of shorthand with executive staff favouring this method of dictation. Ask any busy executive who has had a secretary with shorthand skills if she/he would settle for anything less. The answer is likely to be 'NO'!

Whatever the system used the most important aspects of shorthand writing are that:

- It can be written at high speeds.

- It has a greater degree of accuracy than longhand.

- It can be read back to the dictator.

## Learning shorthand

Why do you want to learn shorthand? Ask yourself these questions:

- Am I prepared to work hard?

- Do I like a challenge?

- Will I enjoy learning shorthand?

- Am I prepared to give up at least one hour a day to practise and increase my speed?

You must be prepared to work hard right from the start and try not to miss any lessons. To become a good shorthand writer and achieve high speeds you will need to have answered 'Yes' to all the above questions.

**TIPS ➤ ➤**     **Learning shorthand**

■ Use an **alphabetically indexed book** for jotting down important vocabulary, special outlines and word groupings. This lets you identify items which require practise.

- Use the **appropriate textbook** which will explain the theory of the system you are learning.

- Use a **fine point pen** for writing.

- Use a **spiral shorthand notebook** for writing as the pages are easily flicked over.

- Write **from the front page to the back** and then turn the book over to re-use the pages.

- Before you use the book **rule a left-hand margin** of 1 inch throughout. Use this space for inserting instructions, alterations and corrections.

- Practise regularly, at least for **an hour a day.**

- **Read back** your shorthand notes as soon as possible and make your own notes in the margin to speed up transcription.

- Do not make your outlines any larger than necessary – the **smaller** the outline the **quicker** you will be able to write.

- **Say the word** to yourself as you draw the outline – this will help you to remember it.

- Aim to **develop light, sweeping strokes** which flow and allow you to achieve high speeds.

- **Draw a line** through your notes once they have been transcribed.

**Task 2 ➤**

Remember! Shorthand is all about writing quickly and accurately.

Form a group of at least four and record tapes of tasks in Unit 16. This time speak slightly slower than your normal rate and use a stop-watch with a second hand to count the dictation time. Count the words in the tasks used and find out your speed in words per minute (w.p.m.). Swop the tapes and transcribe from the other three.

**Task 3 ➤**

Continue the process as in Task 2 using documents from textbooks found in the college or workplace. Alternatively, ask your lecturer or supervisor to provide you with material for transcription. Check each other's transcribed material and keep practising.

**TIPS ➤ ➤**

**Practising shorthand**

- **Do not** overdo things and repeatedly draw the same outline for hours on end in the hope that you will remember it. This is not effective – the maximum number of times in any session for one outline should be ten.

- Tape simple business material passages of one to two minutes duration at various speeds. Try taping them at your current speed then up the speed by 20 w.p.m. each time. **Challenge** yourself to reach higher and higher speeds each time.

- At least once a week return to previous passages you have transcribed and find out how much your speed has improved.

- Work in pairs and take turns to read material to be transcribed.

- Practise for only **30 minutes at any one session** – no longer. If you carry on for lengthy periods you will run out of energy and your speed will fall.

## Getting down to business

Once you have become proficient as a shorthand typist your boss will expect you to look and play the part of an executive's personal assistant. Prepare yourself for a long dictating session by:

- adopting the correct         –        sit with your feet flat on the floor;
  **posture**

- putting your book on the    –        then it will not slither about;
  **desk**

WRONG                                    RIGHT

- keeping your book **straight** –      do not write at an angle;
- holding your pen **lightly**    –      keep your fingers straight;
- using a **right-hand margin**   –      for the dictator's comments – keep the left-hand margin for your own notes;
- **dating** each page            –      at the bottom of the page for quick reference;
- reading through **your notes** –      as soon as possible after the dictation has finished;
- using a **new page**            –      for special documents or text to be produced;

- crossing out **old work** — as soon as you have finished transcribing it;

- remembering **punctuation** — devise an easy method of indicting the beginning and end of sentences and paragraphs (remember the full stop).

> **Note**
> Try to obtain a copy of the 700 COMMON WORD LIST and practise outlines of words from this for a few minutes each day.

## Assessment activity 18.1

> **Remember!** Keep your work from this activity for reference and assessment.

The activities below can be read out by another student in your group. Alternatively, each member of the group could record one on tape. These activities are for shorthand transcription at 70 words per minute.

**Activity A**

Letter to Mrs A Jones, Chief Buyer, Sema Design, 18 John Street, Surrey with a copy to Sales Agent, John Hughes, replying to an enquiry about office equipment.

Dear Mrs Jones   Thank you for your enquiry of 16 June. Please find enclosed our catalogue and price / list of typewriters and word processors we are able to provide.

As you will see from our / brochure we supply mainly the Apple range of typewriters and word processors. On special offer this month are / the Apple 4 at £800 and the Apple 6 at £1200. These prices include free printer and // free software pack. We will be happy, of course, to quote on request for other ranges of machines. /

All models can be given for a trial period of 14 days. Should you require to take / advantage of this service, please contact our representative, Mr John Hughes, who will make all the arrangements. / I enclose his business card for your information.

Delivery will depend on the make and model chosen but, // in general, will be no more than two weeks from the date ordered.

Customers ordering in excess of / 5 machines will be entitled to an extra discount of 10%.

Our representative, John Hughes, will / be in your area within the next week and will be in touch with you to arrange / an appointment so that he may answer any queries you may have on our ranges. Yours sincerely //

## Activity B

**Memo to John Hughes from Dorothy Goodwin regarding a quotation issued.**

I have today received an enquiry from a new company in your patch who are planning to purchase / some typewriters or word processors. They are Sema Design, 18 John Street, Surrey. I would like you / to call on their Chief Buyer, Mrs Jones, some time next week as she hopes to be placing / an order very soon.

I am attaching the quotation I have issued. You will notice that I // have granted an extra discount of 10% if more than 5 machines are ordered. This discount is, / of course, open to negotiation.

I would like to draw your attention to the fact that I am / not receiving the monthly reports promptly. It is essential that each report is completed and forwarded to / me within two days of the end of each month. These reports are very important as it // is company policy to make a careful study of trends throughout the country.

I would also remind you / that, due to our holiday shutdown, expense claims should be sent in one week early this month./

## Activity C

**This is a letter from T McManus, Personnel Manager, inviting a job applicant for an interview.**

Dear Miss Smith  With reference to your recent letter of application for the post of Chief Buyer with / our company, we are happy to inform you that you have been placed on the short-list / of candidates. We shall be glad if you will attend for interview on Tuesday, 18 July at 10/ hundred hours.

As you require to travel a long distance, we have booked accommodation for you at the // Grand Hotel for Monday. This hotel is only 50 metres from our offices. If you decide to come / by car, we will pay expenses at the rate of 45 pence per mile and we will, / of course, pay all your hotel expenses in full.

The day will commence with a tour of our / offices followed by a medical test. Lunch will follow at 1230 hours, after which the formal interview will take place. You will be interviewed by a panel of four of our executives including the present / Chief Buyer. Our company has just recently begun to offer job sharing for all posts and a / leaflet explaining this policy is enclosed along with a current job description.

Please let us know, by return, if you will be able to attend this interview. We look forward to meeting you. Yours sincerely //

### Activity D

This is a memo from the Personnel Manager to all staff about a car leasing scheme with Hertz Car Hire.

The Board of Directors has given its approval for a new car leasing scheme for staff. The company / will lease cars to employees who do a lot of business mileage each year.

The cars will / be supplied to begin with by Hertz Car Hire who offer almost any make or model. Each employee / will be entitled to full use of the car as if it belonged to him/her personally. All / vehicles will be withdrawn and replaced after the initial year.

Employees travelling more than one hundred miles per / week on business may apply to take part in the scheme. The starting date for the scheme/ is first September. Staff may, however, join at any later date.

Anyone taking part in the scheme must / pay 40 per cent of the hire costs and the company will pay the remaining amount. A / petrol allowance will be paid for business journeys but employees must, of course, pay for the petrol used / on private journeys.

Any member of staff interested in this scheme may obtain details from the Finance Department. //

# UNIT 19 | Arranging travel and meetings

## Make travel arrangements and book accommodation

European trading, networks of UK offices, improvements in transport and quicker access to most countries have led to a growth in business travel.

There are many reasons for business travel. People may need to:

- attend conferences, training courses, exhibitions and trade fairs;

- meet with customers and clients;

- meet with organisational counterparts in other countries;

- meet with business associates throughout the UK and world-wide;

- attend to business at other branches of the company;

- meet with government officials in the UK and abroad.

**Task 1 ➤**  Can you think of any reasons to add to the above list?

Your main duty as a Personal Assistant is to make sure that any business trip is **well organised** and **runs smoothly**. To make sure that a trip is successful you must know the correct procedures for planning and making travel arrangements.

**TIPS ➤ ➤**  **Planning and making travel arrangements**

- Discuss the visit with the person travelling.

- Ascertain the purpose of the visit.

- Find out the immediate destination and details of further locations to be visited.

- Discuss the duration of the trip.

■ Find out what aids and documents will be needed, what reservations are required and details of individual meetings which will take place.

Once you have this information you need to know:

- which information sources to use for assistance;
- which agencies may help and the services they provide;
- modes of travel and the alternatives available;
- how to make and confirm bookings;
- what documentation is necessary;
- the approximate cost of the trip.

As an aid to assist you in receiving all the information needed to plan trips it is a good idea to make up a **check-list**. This can then be run off from the word processor each time you have to make travel arrangements and plan itineraries.

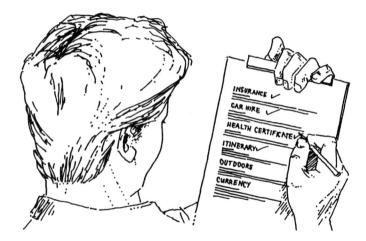

**Task 2 ➤**    Devise a **travel, accommodation and itinerary check-list** for your own use. Type up the document when you are sure the list is complete. Think about:

**The items you have to check:**

- arrange travel
- arrange vaccinations if necessary
- arrange insurance
- book hotel
- check passport and visa
- confirm travel and accommodation details
- documents to copy
- obtain travellers' cheques and currency
- prepare an itinerary (plus a copy for your own reference)

- prepare a list of telephone numbers, fax numbers, etc. for use in case of emergency.

**The person travelling should check:**

- credit cards
- driving licence and international driving permit
- emergency telephone numbers in case of insurance claim, lost travellers' cheques, etc.
- foreign currency
- insurance certificate
- itinerary
- medicines
- passport
- special documents or files
- sterling
- tickets
- travellers' cheques
- vaccination certificate.

# Choosing the best mode of transport

In most cases you will not have much choice over the mode of transport – this will be determined by the nature and location of the visit and organisational guidelines. When there is a choice try not to be tempted into making false economies. You have to take into account:

- the time which may be wasted in travelling by road or rail;
- the distance involved;
- the costs involved – money spent unnecessarily on hotel accommodation, meals, etc. when an overnight stay may not be necessary;
- the class of travel required and the various advantages relating to cost;
- that where a lengthy journey is involved and there is not much time between arrival and a meeting the traveller should arrive refreshed and alert;
- whether work has to be done en route – if the traveller needs to work on papers, etc. then first-class air or rail travel is a must.

Overleaf is a table detailing modes of transport, services and information sources you may need to use when arranging road, sea, and rail travel.

| METHOD OF TRAVEL AND SERVICES PROVIDED | DETAILS REQUIRED | INFORMATION SOURCES |
|---|---|---|
| BY ROAD – CAR – UNITED KINGDOM (Useful for short journeys) | Driver needs current driving licence and insurance documents. For cars over 3 years old an MOT is also necessary. | Yellow Pages, AA and RAC handbooks, Coach guides, Road Maps, A–Z town maps, Local Directories, Hertz, Avis, etc. |
| BY ROAD – CAR– ABROAD (Hired or private) | Driver needs current, clean driving licence and insurance documents. A Green Card and International Driving Permit may also be required. European passport. | Hertz, Europcar and Avis Yellow Pages Travel Agents RAC and AA |
| BY SEA – CAR – ABROAD Ferry, Hovercraft, Jetfoil | Give details of car and passengers. Also state if cabin is to be booked. Check in 1 hour prior to sailing. | Ferry operators (Sealink, P&O, Caledonian MacBrayne), British Rail Timetables, Travel Agents, Prestel, ABC Rail Guide |
| BY TRAIN – CAR – UNITED KINGDOM Motorail | Give car and passenger details and state if accommodation is to be booked. | British Rail ABC Rail Guide |
| BY TRAIN – PASSENGER ONLY – UK Sleeper tickets – for overnight journeys. Intercity Executive – includes 1st class return travel, 24 hrs free parking at certain stations and reservation. Pullman Travel – luxury service on certain routes Short Breaks – includes hotel accommodation for 1 or more nights | Give name of station travelling to. | British Rail Timetables British Rail Direct ABC Rail Guide Travel Agent |
| BY TRAIN – EUROPE Various services | Current European 10 year Passport or Visitor's Passport. Give name of station, town or city travelling to. | Cook's Continental Individual Country's Railway Organisation Travel Agents |
| BY TRAIN – OUTSIDE EUROPE Various services | Current European 10 year Passport although Visitor's Passport will be accepted in some countries – check details. Give name of station, town or city travelling to. | ABC Air/Rail Europe and Middle East Guide Individual country's railway organization Travel Agents |

**Task 3 ➤**

1 Your boss has been in Cardiff on business. She will be travelling back from there on Thursday morning to arrive in time, at the office, for an early meeting at 1000 hours. She has telephoned to ask you to book rail travel with InterCity which will allow her to be back in the office for 0930 hours. Breakfast will be required on the train. You also have to arrange for a taxi to be waiting at the station.

   a) Which train would you make a reservation on?

   b) What method of booking would you use?

   c) Which taxi service did you choose and why?

2 Mr Brown has a meeting this Thursday in Calais, France. As it is the holiday weekend he has decided to take his own car with him and travel by ferry. His wife will accompany him on the trip and he wishes to book a cabin for them both. They can leave Dover about 1100 hours on Wednesday but will travel later if necessary. There is no need to book accommodation as they will be visiting friends based in France. They wish to make the return trip on Monday any time after 1200 hours. Mr Brown's new car is an estate, registration number K496 RDT.

   a) Which ferry will you book for the outward and inward journey?

   b) What documents will you advise Mr Brown to take with him?

   c) What is the total cost of the ferry and cabin accommodation?

   d) Which ferry company did you choose? Why?

   e) What sources did you use to find the information required?

   f) Did you encounter any problems with this task? If so, what were they? How did you resolve them?

3 Theresa McPherson is attending a conference In Manchester at the end of this month. She has not decided whether to travel by rail or air. The conference is to be held on a Thursday, commencing at mid-day and she will be able to travel back that evening.

   To help her decide on mode of transport she has asked you to draw up a list of suitable trains and flights she might use. List times of departure and arrival leaving 45 minutes each way to allow for travel from airport/station to city centre.

   Present this information in an appropriate format, for example, memo, table or report, using word-processing facilities.

## Air travel

### Domestic

Business people based in the UK often have to travel within the country by air and these routes are known as **domestic flights**. Although air is more expensive than travel by road or rail it can often work out more economical in the long run.

Why do you think this is? Could it be because:

• executives have busy work schedules and it is uneconomical for them to waste time on making lengthy journeys which may only take an hour by air;

• overnight accommodation, meals and entertainment costs, added to petrol, car hire or rail prices can make road and rail more expensive overall?

British Airways and British Midland both operate a **shuttle service** for people travelling between the major UK cities and London. An advantage for travellers using this service is that they do not have to book in advance. Flights leave airports at regular intervals (usually hourly or more frequently during peak times) and the airlines often have a second plane standing by at busy periods. Savings can also be made if seats are booked 14 days in advance.

Regular flights have to be booked direct with an airline or through a reputable travel agent. **Increased security measures** taken by airport staff have led to check-in times being advanced. Always find out the minimum check-in time at each airport. Do **not** take it for granted that they will all be the same.

### Abroad
Business travellers taking flights abroad are most likely to book seats on **scheduled flights** which are detailed in airline timetables and ABC guides. **Charter flights** are those used by holiday companies. Scheduled flights differ from charter flights as they are generally more expensive and offer different **classes** of travel.

## Baggage allowances

A certain amount of **hand-luggage** (up to 5 kilograms) may be carried onto the plane; this is not included in the weight of luggage to be placed in the hold. Check details of allowances with the airline or travel agent when bookings are being made. Allowances vary according to:

- the class of travel
- the country of destination.

The table below gives information relating to air travel:

| Type of flight | Documents required | Information sources |
|---|---|---|
| **Domestic** | None except tickets. | Airline timetables, travel agents, Oracle, Ceefax, Prestel, British Telecom Traveline. |
| **European** | Passport – either full ten-year (for Cyprus) or visitor's passport (rest of Europe), insurance documents, visa (not required for trips of less than three months). | Airline timetables, ABC Guides, travel agents, Oracle, Ceefax, Prestel, British Telecom Traveline. |
| **World-wide** | Full, ten year passport or visitor's passport (check this), insurance and health certificates, visa (if required). | Airline timetables, ABC Guides, travel agents, Prestel, Oracle, Ceefax, British Telecom Traveline. |

## Booking flights

Flights can be booked direct with the airline or through a reputable travel agent. Before making reservations check:

- if the traveller has a preferred airline;
- the class of travel required;
- the airport and terminals of departure and arrival;
- if the flight is direct or connecting;
- that you have at least two or three choices of flights/airlines to pick from in case flights are unavailable;
- you have noted the correct departure and arrival times of the flights;
- the checking-in time;
- the flight numbers.

### Flight timetables

Practise using airline timetables and become familiar with the various symbols and what they mean.

**Task 4 ➤**    If you have access to a current British Airways timetable or ABC Guide find the answers to the following:

a)  Which airline has daily flights from London Gatwick to Baltimore Washington?

b)  What is the time of flight BA35 on Wednesdays from London Gatwick to Delhi?

c)  What is the flight number of the British Airways flight departing from Manchester at 1910 hours on a Monday and arriving in Paris at 1930 hours?

d)  What days and times can you depart from Belfast to Kuala Lumpur?

e)  What airports in Cyprus can you travel to from Glasgow, Manchester, Newcastle and London?

### Time zones

The table opposite shows the different time zones in operation in various countries. **Summer** for this purpose means late March/early April to late September/October. If in doubt **consult a travel agent!**

Have you ever suffered from **jet lag?** If you have visited countries with time differences it can take a while to adjust. Say you arranged to travel on British Airways Concorde Flight BA001 which leaves London Heathrow Terminal 4 at 1030 hours. You would arrive at John F Kennedy Airport, New York at 0920 hours on the same day arriving **earlier** than you left although the flight takes nearly four hours. However, by 1800 hours that evening your body thinks it is 2300 hours – and time for some sleep. This is **jet lag.**

The same effects happen when you travel to a country which is seven or eight hours ahead of British time. If your flight leaves in the morning it will be late at night or early morning when you arrive at your destination. It will take a few days to adjust. Because of these time differences, airline timetables can show a different day of arrival to the day of departure.

HAVE I REALLY BEEN TRAVELLING FOR 23 HOURS? IS THIS MONDAY OR TUESDAY?

| Country | Winter | Summer | Country | Winter | Summer |
|---|---|---|---|---|---|
| Algeria | +1 | 0 | South Korea | +9 | +8 |
| Australia | | | Kuwait | +3 | +2 |
| Perth | +8 | +7 | Luxembourg | +1 | +1 |
| Adelaide | +9.5 | +8.5 | Malaysia | +8 | +7 |
| Melbourne & Sidney | +10 | +9 | Mexico | −6 | −7 |
| Austria | +1 | +1 | Netherlands | +1 | +1 |
| Belgium | +1 | +1 | New Zealand | +12 | +11 |
| Brazil | −3 | −4 | Nigeria | +1 | 0 |
| Canada | | | Norway | +1 | +1 |
| Montreal & Toronto | −5 | −5 | Pakistan | +5 | +4 |
| Calgary & Edmonton | −7 | −7 | Poland | +1 | +1 |
| Vancouver | −8 | −8 | Portugal | 0 | 0 |
| China | +8 | +8 | Saudi Arabia | +3 | +2 |
| Czechoslovakia | +1 | +1 | Singapore | +8 | +7 |
| Denmark | +1 | +1 | South Africa | +2 | +1 |
| Egypt | +2 | +2 | Spain | +1 | +1 |
| Finland | +2 | +2 | Sweden | +1 | +1 |
| France | +1 | +1 | Switzerland | +1 | +1 |
| Germany | +1 | +1 | Turkey | +2 | +2 |
| Greece | +2 | +2 | USA | | |
| Hong Kong | +8 | +7 | New York & Philiadelphia | −5 | −5 |
| Iceland | 0 | −1 | Chicago & Houston | −6 | −6 |
| India | +5.5 | +4.5 | Los Angeles & San Diego | −8 | −8 |
| Israel | +2 | +2 | USSR | | |
| Italy | +1 | +1 | Moscow & St Petersburg | +3 | +3 |
| Japan | +9 | +8 | Vladivostok | +10 | +10 |
| Kenya | +3 | +2 | Venezuela | −4 | −5 |

**Task 5 ➤**   Find the actual length of time of the flight from London to these countries, taking into account the time differences. Use the summer timetable for this task.

| Depart London | Arrive |
|---|---|
| 1025 hours | Calgary 1625 hours |
| 1300 hours | Delhi 0215 hours |
| 1255 hours | Hong Kong 0910 the next day |
| 1425 hours | Jeddah 2245 hours |
| 2000 hours | Johannesburg 0820 the next day |
| 1130 hours | Kuwait 1925 hours |
| 1215 hours | Los Angeles 1515 hours |
| 1530 hours | Malaga 1920 hours |
| 1415 hours | Mexico City 2230 hours |
| 0920 hours | Moscow 1605 hours |

# Making reservations

The procedures to follow in making travel arrangements will vary from organisation to organisation. You may be required to:

- use a travel department within the company;
- use the services of travel agents.

### Travel departments within an organisation

Large companies whose employees are involved in frequent travel at home and abroad may have their own travel departments that:

- employ staff who are travel specialists;
- have established links with airlines, car-hire companies, hotels, accommodation agencies, specialist travel agencies, consulates, etc;
- provide all necessary travel information on currency, passports, visa applications, vaccinations required, motoring regulations, places to visit and **more importantly** areas to be avoided;
- negotiate special rates with airlines, car rental firms, hotels, etc. which they can demand due to volume of business.

### Travel agents

Smaller organisations find it useful to establish links with a reputable travel agent. A good travel agent will be a member of the Association of British Travel Agents (ABTA) and will offer an extensive range of services to business travellers.

**Task 6 ➤**

List at least ten services which you would expect a travel agent to provide to business travellers. When you have finished get together with your group and find out how many in total you come up with.

How many of these did you have on your list:

- providing rail, air and sea travel information and bookings;
- confirming reservations;
- booking and confirmation of hotel accommodation;
- obtaining special benefits and rates on business travel insurance;
- providing representatives to meet travellers at airports;
- booking car hire and executive chauffeur driven cars;
- providing or recommending interpreters and guides;
- providing travel newsletters to keep business clients informed of special offers and new services being introduced;
- arranging ticket delivery or collection at airports;
- arranging visa and passport applications at short notice;
- arranging the best travel options at low cost;

- arranging foreign currency and travellers' cheques;

- providing itemised itineraries with travel documents;

- providing information on country being visited, for example, a list of 'do's and don'ts', what not to eat, areas to visit and those to avoid, best value for money buys, local customs, motoring tips, etc.

From this list you will see that the role of the travel agent is to **provide, arrange and book** travel. However, all arrangements should **always** be checked thoroughly no matter who does the organising. It is up to you finally to check:

- flight numbers, check-in times, airports and terminals, and times of departures and arrivals;

- that ticket details correspond with booking details;

- the hotel details – dates accommodation is booked for, checking-out times, meals supplied, type of accommodation, etc.;

- that visas and passports are in order;

- that car hire has been confirmed and arrangements are clear for pick up and return of vehicles.

## Booking accommodation

Employees involved in business travel will have their own personal preferences for types of accommodation to be booked but organisational guidelines will have to be followed to ensure that costs are kept to a minimum. Organisations may also use certain hotel groups, have special arrangements and negotiate special rates with them. The type of accommodation booked will also depend upon the seniority of the employee concerned.

When booking accommodation check these details:

| Check | Choices |
|---|---|
| Room type | Single, twin, double |
| Facilities | Tea/coffee-making equipment, drinks dispenser, television, telephone, room service, laundry service, hairdresser, sport and recreation |
| Bathroom | En-suite, shared, bath/shower |
| Business services | Secretarial, facsimile, telex, conferencing, interpreting |
| Location | Near airport, railway station, town centre |
| Parking | Private, hotel grounds, street parking |
| Entertainment | Facilities for entertaining important guests, light entertainment provided |
| Meals | A la carte menu, set menu, bed and breakfast only, light snacks |

## Information sources

There are numerous published sources which can be used. Your college library or a good public library will have a selection of these. Look out in particular for:

Egon Ronay Guide      Good Hotel Guide
ABC Hotel Guide      Financial Times World Hotel Directory
Arthur Eperon's Guide.

## Reservations

Reservation can be made by telephone, fax or telex. However, you must always confirm the booking in writing and ask for an acknowledgment.

When confirming the booking always check that you have given these details:

- the name and contact of your company;

- the name(s) of the visitor(s);

- day, date and approximate time of arrival;

- day, date and approximate time of departure;

- number of days or weeks of visit;

- type of room and facilities required;

- what meals are required, for example, breakfast only, breakfast and dinner, etc., and special dietary requirements;

- agreed costs and method of payment.

**Task 7 ➤**

1 Roger Taylor is visiting Preston on business and will require accommodation for two nights next week – Tuesday and Wednesday. He hopes to arrive at his hotel at approximately 1900 hours (but may be later) on Tuesday and expects to check out at 0800 hours on Thursday. Meals required are breakfast and dinner.

     a) Use a suitable reference book to give him a choice of three hotels and list the facilities of each in a memo.

b) Select a hotel on your list and assume you have reserved a single room with private bath in his name. Write a letter of confirmation mentioning that Mr Taylor may not arrive until about 2000 hours.

2 Dorothy Goodwin has arranged a business meeting with an important client in Newcastle next weekend. If Dorothy can obtain this international contract it will be a tremendous boost to the company. You have been asked to draw up a list of four and five star hotels and the facilities each has to offer.

a) From the list select the one you think is most likely to impress.

b) Assume bookings have been made for two double rooms with en-suite bathrooms for:

i) Mr and Mrs Gericas

ii) Mr and Mrs Goodwin.

c) Confirm the bookings and check you list these details:

i) Mr and Mrs Gericas will arrive at the hotel around 1200 hours on the Friday;

ii) Mr and Mrs Goodwin will arrive at approximately 1030 hours on the Friday;

iii) dinner is required on Friday at 1930 hours and on the Sunday at 2000 hours;

iv) breakfast will be provided by room service on Saturday and Sunday at 0900 hours and in the hotel restaurant on Monday at 0730 hours;

v) both couples will check out around 0900 hours on Monday;

vi) a local taxi has been ordered for 0910 hours to take both couples to the airport.

### Recording details of recommended hotels

It is a good idea to ask employees for comments on accommodation and facilities on their return from business trips. From this information you will be able to build up useful reference lists containing extensive details which will help you plan future trips. You might use a list like the one overleaf.

**Task 8 ➤**  Using the appropriate information sources and a copy of the **recommended hotels** form on page 268, make out your own hotel guides as above listing hotels you would recommend for business use which are:

a) Three or four star, situated close to Newcastle Airport and offer business services.

b) Four or five star, situated close to Manchester Airport and offer business services and sports facilities.

# RECOMMENDED HOTELS

| Name/Address | Rating | Tel. no. | Bedrooms | Bath/Shower | Parking | Meals | Facilities |
|---|---|---|---|---|---|---|---|
| Tower Thistle St Katherine's Wharf | **** | (071) 488 4134 | 826 | Both | Private – 200 spaces | Full range | Sports Centre Conferencing Entertainment |
| Le Meridien Piccadilly | ***** | (071) 734 8000 | 284 | Both | Private | Full range AA Rosette award for Oak Room | Entertainment Room service Conferencing Sports facilities Secretarial and Business services |
| Inter Continental 1 Hamilton Place Hyde Park Corner | ***** | (071) 409 3131 | 490 | Both | Private – 100 spaces | Full range AA Rosette award for Le Souffle Restaurant | Secretarial and business services Translation services Sports facilities Health spa Conferencing Entertainment |
|  |  |  |  |  |  |  |  |

Example of a list of recommended hotels

c) Three star, situated close to Birmingham Airport and offer rooms with en-suite bathroom/shower. The hotels must also offer a full range of meals and room service.

d) Four or five star, situated close to Edinburgh Airport which offer a full range of facilities including secretarial and business services, room service, full range of meals, late drinks licence, full entertainment programme and private parking.

e) Four or five star, situated within 50 miles of Glasgow Airport and offer full secretarial and business services. A full range of other services must also be provided and hotels must be close to excellent golf courses and within driving distance of race courses.

### Booking accommodation abroad

You can make up your own useful reference file to hold details of hotels and accommodation abroad just as you would do for UK information. It is easier to book accommodation abroad using the services of a reputable travel agent. However, you can reserve rooms, etc.:

- by booking through the head office (usually located in London) of an international hotel chain;

- through British Airways hotel booking service (in conjunction with their flights);

- via Prestel;

- by telex.

**Note:** A list of international hotel chains can be found in the *Travel Trade Gazette.* This resource is also excellent for providing further travel information.

### Problems with booking direct

When you book accommodation abroad by a direct method you may encounter some problems. Check:

- **the written confirmation of booking** that must be received from the hotel where accommodation has been booked. The traveller must take this documentation to produce on arrival at the hotel;

- **the method of payment acceptable** – make sure the hotel will either bill the organisation direct or allow the traveller to pay by credit/charge card and check which ones are accepted.

## Travel documents

Always check carefully that the traveller has the correct documents needed for travel within each individual country.

### Passport

Those travellers who stop over in many countries in the course of their business will use a **full ten-year European passport** which is valid for

visits to all countries. If you arrange frequent travel for a number of executives it is a good idea to keep a record of passport renewal dates and numbers. A **British visitor's passport** can be used for short visits to most European countries.

> **Remember!**
> **Lost or stolen passports must be reported immediately to the local police and nearest British consulate in the country where the theft occurred.**

## Visa

Visas are not required for trips of less than three months' duration within EC countries if the traveller has a British/European passport. However, entry to certain countries outside the EC may require the visitor to obtain a visa. Information on this can be obtained from embassies, consulates and travel agencies.

> **Remember!**
> **Visa applications can take some time to be processed so apply as soon as possible to avoid delay or cancellation of trips.**

Travel agents will be able to help with visa applications – ask their advice on current procedures and formalities.

## Vaccinations and health certificates

Travel to some countries may also require the traveller obtaining vaccinations against diseases such as typhoid, cholera, polio and yellow fever. Areas of high risk from one or all of these diseases are:

- Africa
- Asia
- Middle East
- South America.

When visiting these areas it is also wise to take medical precautions against:

- Tetanus
- Rabies
- Malaria
- Hepatitis.

For more information on the vaccinations and certification required write to the British Airways Passenger Immunisation and Medical Centre or obtain leaflet SA35 from the Department of Health.

**Task 9 ➤**

1 Using the appropriate information sources list the vaccinations, certificates and medical precautions necessary for travellers visiting:

| | | |
|---|---|---|
| a) Argentina | f) Guyana | k) South Africa |
| b) Australia | g) Indonesia | l) Trinidad |
| c) Botswana | h) Morocco | m) Zaire |
| d) China | i) Norway | n) Zimbabwe. |
| e) Egypt | j) Phillippines | |

2 If travellers to the above countries had previously visited in the last three months would they require boosters or further medication?

3 Name at least five countries where a traveller is required to have a visa.

4 Which Western European country still insists that all travellers possess a full ten-year European passport?
Can you think of any reason for this requirement to still be in force in the 1990s?

5 Are there any countries outside Western Europe where a British visitor's passport is sufficient?

6 What advice would you give to travellers visiting countries which have high incidences of AIDS infection?

7 What other health advice would you give to travellers visiting any country abroad?

## Taking money abroad

The amount of sterling the traveller takes abroad needs to be kept to a minimum, especially with the increase in theft and muggings in many countries.

It is advisable for the traveller to carry sufficient amounts of foreign currency accepted in each country being visited. This will provide ready cash to meet general expenses until travellers' cheques can be cashed.

Foreign currency and travellers' cheques are normally ordered in advance and can be obtained from banks, building societies, travel agents and bureaux de change points at airports.

### Safest forms of carrying money abroad

Although commission is charged on purchasing and cashing travellers' cheques it is a price worth paying. If they are lost or stolen they will be replaced quickly and free of charge.

The four safest forms in which to carry money equivalents are:

- travellers' cheques • credit cards • charge cards • Eurocard and Eurocheques.

Banks will normally accept any of these forms to issue currency. Large hotels, restaurants, travel agents and some shops will accept these payment methods and are often prepared to provide cash in exchange for a small commission.

**Task 10 ➤** Using appropriate information sources find the answers to these questions:

a) What are the five important features of travellers' cheques which make them a safe way to carry money abroad?

b) What is a Eurocheque and a Eurocard? How would you use a Eurocard to obtain cash from a bank abroad?

c) What is the difference between a credit card such as Visa and a charge card like American Express?

d) Find out what charges are made for changing currency at your:

i) bank

ii) building society

iii) travel agent.

e) Why should you carry some foreign currency with you when travelling abroad?

f) What would you class as general expenses on arrival at the destination country?

g) Using the database which you set up in Task 6 of Unit 13 insert the exchange rate for today's date.

## Preparing itineraries

Refer to Unit 16 for information on preparing itineraries for business trips.

**TIPS ➤ ➤** **Making a final check on travel arrangements and documentation**

Check that both you and the traveller have:

■ a complete itinerary;

■ a list of addresses and telephone numbers of hotels and companies where visits have been arranged;

■ emergency telephone numbers for insurance claims, medical necessities and bank reports;

■ defined contact times for passing on messages on matters of urgency or exchanging information.

Using your prepared check-list, tick off each of these as they are being packed:

- flight tickets, note of flight numbers, time of departures and check-in times;

- passport and visas (if required);

- insurance and vaccination certificates;

- travellers' cheques, credit cards, foreign currency and Eurocard, plus cheque book;

- driving licence, international driving permit and green card;

- detailed maps and other useful information;

- hotel booking confirmations;

- files and papers required for meetings;

- luggage;

- a separate note of passport number, serial numbers of travellers' cheques, credit card numbers, etc.

## Assessment activity 19.1

Remember! Keep your work from this activity for reference and assessment.

1    Roger Taylor has left this memo for you to deal with.

---

### MEMORANDUM

TO:     Office Assistant      DATE: 16 March 199-
FROM:   Roger Taylor

---

I have been invited to a conference in Hetland Hall in Dumfries on the 14th and 15th of next month. The conference runs from 1400 hours to 1630 hours on the 14th and from 0900 hours until 1500 hours on the 15th. Would you please:
a) Book me into a suitable hotel on the 14th.
b) Obtain the full address and telephone number of Hetland Hall.
c) Obtain a map showing where Hetland Hall is.
d) Print me out a route of how to get there from here.
e) Prepare an itinerary for the trip.

---

2    Terence McManus has left this task for you to carry out.

---

### MEMORANDUM

TO:     Office Assistant    DATE: 11th May 199-
FROM: Terence McManus

---

I am attending a seminar in Eastbourne College of Arts and Technology next Thursday and Friday. The address is St Anne's Road, Eastbourne, East Sussex. The seminar

runs from 1100 hours to 1500 hours both days. I intend
to travel by train. Would you please:
a) Book me into a suitable hotel for the Thursday night.
b) Find out train times to get to Eastbourne for 1030
hours and for the return journey.
c) Obtain directions from Eastbourne Railway Station to
the College.
d) Prepare an itinerary.

3 Terence McManus and Jim Dunlop have been asked to present a
paper to a group of employees at James Mackie & Sons Ltd in
Belfast. The presentation is to be held at the Belfast Europa Hotel,
Union Street, Belfast, next Wednesday. The presentation commences
at 0930 hours and finishes at 1400 hours. The two men plan to travel
on the Tuesday and stay overnight at the Belfast Europa.

   In a bid to cut down on travel costs, the two managers have been
asked to travel by train to the nearest ferry terminal (with crossings to
Larne) and then take the ferry to Larne. They wish to collect a hire
car at Larne Harbour and drive to Belfast. Mr McManus will drive and
prefers a Ford Sierra with automatic transmission. Linda Santos has
asked you to carry out the following:

a) Type a letter to the Belfast Europa confirming the telephone
   booking.

b) Select an appropriate car hire firm and confirm the booking by
   letter.

c) Draw up an itinerary and attach a road map from Larne to Belfast
   and any other supporting documents.

d) Send a memo to Mr McManus detailing the approximate costs of
   the trip.

e) Complete your check-list and send a memo to her detailing all
   action taken by you.

4 Alan Brown and his wife have been invited to attend the launch
of a new service at Executive Press, Pedmore House, Dudley. The
ceremony takes place next Tuesday, commencing at 1430 hours
and finishing at 1600 hours.

   A small dinner party is being held for valued customers on the
Tuesday evening and Mr and Mrs Brown have been invited. It is
being held at the home of the Chief Executive of Executive Press
– Gillian Sommerby. Mr and Mrs Brown will, therefore, have to stay
overnight at a local hotel. Complete the following:

a) Work out a suitable route from here to Dudley and give an
   alternative route in case of road works.

b) Select an appropriate hotel and send a letter of
   confirmation.

c) Draw up an itinerary for the trip and make sure to include the christian names of the host and her husband – Gillian and Michael Sommerby. Attach any supporting documents.

d) As Mr Brown has been having trouble with his car recently, look up train and connection times from here to Dudley and vice versa and attach these to the itinerary.

e) Complete your check-list of items. Type a memo to Fiona Gibb detailing all action taken by you and giving the approximate cost of the trip.

5 Thomas McClune and Theresa McPherson have been invited to a seminar regarding student exchanges, entitled 'Petra Project', in Holland next week. They have been invited by a college lecturer, Mr Friddi de Nooijer. The seminar is to take place in Zeeland College, Instituut voor Middelbaar en Cursorisch, Beroepsonderwijs, Molenwater 8, Postbus 279, 4330 AG Middelburg. It will begin on Tuesday at 1000 hours and will finish around 1600 hours. Travel has to be arranged for Monday with British Airways being the preferred airline. Return reservations have to be made for the first possible flight on Wednesday and accommodation booked for two nights at Hotel Arneville, Buitenruststraat 22, Middelburg. Book a hired car from Monday until they leave on the Wednesday. The car will be collected at the airport and Theresa will drive. They wish a dinner reservation to be made at the hotel at 2030 hours on the Monday. On the Tuesday evening they have been invited to dinner at Friddi's house at 1930 hours. You have been asked to carry out the following:

a) Select suitable flights to and from Holland.

b) Type confirmation details to the hotel.

c) Type confirmation details of the car hire.

d) Type a letter to Zeeland College confirming the arrival as a representative is meeting them at their hotel and giving them directions to the college.

e) Provide a road map to Middelburg from the airport.

f) Obtain suitable currency for £300 sterling.

g) Find out a few useful Dutch phrases.

h) Draw up an itinerary and attach any supporting documents.

i) Calculate the approximate cost of the trip.

j) Type a memo to Mr McManus detailing all action taken and giving the approximate cost.

k) Complete a check-list.

**Note:** It takes approximately two hours to travel from the airport to Middelburg.

# Arrange meetings involving three or more people

Meetings constitute a major part of business life for executives and managers. Almost 50 per cent of senior staff time is taken up in activities involving meetings. Why are they so important?

**Task 11** ➤    Are you a member of a club or social organisation? Do you attend meetings? Write down a list of items which may be discussed and decided at these meetings. Then form a group and prepare a final list which details all the activities you have decided on.

## The purpose of meetings

Meetings are planned events which are called to achieve a number of purposes which may include one or more of the following:

- **planning** – looking ahead to new ideas and policies, discussing implementation and forming policy outlines for future development;

- **liaison** – group discussion and debate to reach agreement;

- **assessment** – evaluation of current procedures, profits made and range of products or services;

- **negotiation** – bargaining, arranging contracts, reaching agreement;

- **problems** – identifying, discussing and looking at solutions;

- **briefing** – summarising plans, projects or procedures.

No two meetings will be alike and all will vary in the degree of formality adopted. Much will depend on the purpose of the meeting and the organisational procedures which have to be followed.

## Types of meeting and protocol

Meetings fall into two categories – **formal** and **informal**. You will have to make arrangements for both types and become familiar with the formalities and conventions of these different meetings.

### Formal meetings

- **Annual general meetings (AGMs)** – Public limited companies (PLCs) must hold these **formal** meetings once a year; an AGM is optional for private companies. All shareholders are invited to attend and topics discussed include profit or loss accounts, future investment, new ideas and withdrawal of products and services which are no longer profitable. At the AGM, officers will also be elected.

- **Board meetings** – Regular meetings held involving the Board of Directors of an organisation. These meetings are headed by a chairperson.

- **Committee meetings** – Meetings of elected committee members who generally run a particular group or association, for example, Microplus's Staff Club.

- **Extraordinary general meetings** – These are called when unexpected important items need to be discussed urgently by all members or shareholders of a PLC. These meetings deal with matters which cannot wait until the next AGM, for example, fraud or corruption charges against a senior company official.

### Informal meetings

- **Departmental meetings** – Held to discuss departmental policies, exchange ideas, debate changes and provide company information to staff.

- **Management meetings** – Meetings of managers to discuss company organisation, issues such as TQM (total quality management), inter-departmental links and co-ordination.

- **Staff meetings** – Held to discuss particular items and issues.

- **Working parties** – Composed of a small number of people, usually appointed by a committee, to study, organise and report on a specific subject. May be set up to use the expertise of various employees to implement new routines and guidelines.

## Meetings documentation

Formal meetings are called by issuing a written **notice of meeting and agenda** to delegates. Refer to Unit 16 to recap on this subject.

Informal meetings can be arranged by memo, telephone call or orally. You should also confirm the arrangements in writing or place a notice on the staff notice board. A summary of an informal meeting may be handed out with notes on decisions taken.

**Task 12 ➤**

1 Draw up a list of guidelines you would give to a new employee to assist in planning and organising a **formal meeting.**

2 Write a brief note explaining how a formal meeting differs from an informal one.

3 Describe how a **chairperson's agenda** differs from the ordinary agenda issued to members.

## Arranging meetings

Find out from the member of staff who is organising the meeting:

- the purpose and type of the meeting;

- where and when the meeting will be held;

- who will be attending the meeting;

- which topics will be discussed;

- the plan of the meeting;

- the documentation required.

Most meetings will be planned well in advance but occasionally a meeting will be called quickly to deal with emergencies or disputes.

### Your role in organising a meeting

When you have all the details needed to plan the meeting you will have to make all necessary arrangements to ensure the meeting runs smoothly and according to schedule.

Make up your own check-list for this purpose which will identify the procedures you have to follow and the order in which the following tasks have to be done:

1. If the meeting is being held internally book an appropriate board room, committee room or office for the estimated length of time (allow more time than necessary in case the meeting runs on). Arrange refreshment facilities if required.

2. For an external meeting book appropriate facilities at a conference centre or hotel and arrange catering or refreshments. Also ensure secretarial, translation and office facilities are available if required.

3. Distribute the notice of meeting and agenda, copies of minutes of previous meetings and other supporting documentation

4. Book any equipment – audio-visual aids, flip charts, etc. required for an internal meeting. Check with the external venue to ensure such equipment is available and if not arrange for the supply.

It is your responsibility to note carefully any apologies for absence received and list comments. You may also have to prepare reports and find any information required for the meeting, for example, sales or marketing statistics.

DIVERT CALLS OR TAKE MESSAGES FOR THESE NUMBERS FOR THE NEXT TWO HOURS. DO NOT INTERRUPT THE MEETING UNLESS IT IS AN EMERGENCY.

Prepare a list of delegates attending the meeting. Give a copy of this to the switchboard operator to ensure the meeting is not interrupted by telephone calls. The Receptionist will also be given a copy of this list detailing who is expected and instructions for directing attendees or having them escorted.

Finally, those attending the meeting may require maps indicating the meeting venue and location, car parking facilities and lists of recommended accommodation in the area. Be prepared to send out these details.

**Task 13 ➤**

1 Using various reference sources draw up a list of caterers in your area whose services you could use when organising large meetings.

2 Draw up a further list detailing these caterers' charges for:

a) a buffet lunch for 20 people

b) a sit-down, two-course meal for 30 people

c) providing light refreshments and snacks.

3 Make up another list of companies you could use to hire equipment, including camcorders, videos, OHPs, etc. Detail the charges for each item of equipment for daily and weekly hire.

4 Car parking facilities can be a problem in cities. At Microplus the car parking facilities are sufficient to accommodate the staff and a few extra visitors. However, when there are large meetings scheduled the company has to arrange parking facilities for delegates. List organisations in your area which can rent the company private parking facilities which are secure and within walking distance of the offices. Also list the hourly, daily and weekly charges.

## Final preparations for internal meetings

On the day of the meeting you have to check the following:

| Catering | The room |
|---|---|
| Catering arrangements have been confirmed✔<br>Special dietary requirements have been catered for✔<br>Refreshments have been organised✔<br>Times for refreshment breaks have been confirmed✔ | There is enough seating✔<br>Tables are arranged correctly✔<br>Equipment is in place✔<br>Nameplates are correct✔<br>There is an ample supply of stationery✔ |
| **Environment** | Glasses have been provided and water jugs are full✔<br>Enough ashtrays are in place if smoking is allowed✔ |
| The venue is adequately ventilated✔<br>The temperature is comfortable and can be controlled✔<br>The lighting is suitable✔ | No smoking notices are displayed if smoking is prohibited✔<br>The room is tidy and waste bins are empty✔ |
| **Equipment** | |
| All electrical items are operating efficiently✔<br>Telephones have been switched to divert✔<br>A notice is available to place outside to avoid interruption✔ | |

When the meeting has ended you must return the room to its normal state by:

- clearing away cups, plates, glasses, water jugs
- emptying waste bins and ashtrays
- arranging for equipment to be returned to store
- collecting documents left around
- locking windows and switching off fans.

*Remember! Keep your work from this activity for reference and assessment.*

Read over your notes, minutes, etc. and type them up as soon as possible while details are still fresh in your mind. (Refer to Unit 16 to recap on this procedure.)

If the meeting is an informal one there is no need to keep a record of items discussed, etc.

## Assessment activity 19.2

*Remember! Keep your work from this activity for reference and assessment.*

This activity involves arranging two meetings. Additional evidence is required from the student giving an explanation of the types of meeting and the protocol involved.

Evidence of achievement should be recorded in an appropriate check-list which, along with diaried notes of arrangements, bookings and confirmations, and a copy of the papers for one meeting, should be retained for assessment purposes.

### Activity A (informal meeting)

Terence McManus and Thomas McClune are having a meeting at the beginning of next month with four members of the Bristol Group Training Association. They are Mr Hugh Dickson of Olympia Metals, Mr Gordon Poole of Preston Products, Mrs Jean Mackie of W J Knox and Miss Christine Cochrane of Smithkline Beecham.

The meeting is to discuss new National Vocational Qualifications (NVQs) and is to be held in Committee Room 2 at Microplus's offices in Bristol. It will last for approximately two hours. During the course of the meeting a video on NVQs will be shown. An overhead projector, screen, nobo-board and flipchart will be required. Light refreshments will be made available.

Linda Santos has already telephoned round and the first Tuesday of next month (at 1000 hours) suits the four external delegates.

Two of the delegates, Mrs Mackie and Miss Cochrane, have never attended the premises in Bristol.

Complete the following:

a)   Confirm the arrangements to all participants.

b)   Draw up a brief agenda.  Topics to be discussed are: Background to NVQ, Training Qualifications, Staff Assessor's Award, Video, Discussion, Any Other Business.

c)   Book and prepare the room for this meeting (a **committee room booking form** can be copied from page 269).

d)    Complete your check-list and type a memo to Linda Santos detailing all action taken by you.

## Activity B (formal meeting)

A meeting of the Group Training Committee is held on the last Thursday of every month and Fiona Gibb has asked you to help with the arrangements. Mr Brown chairs the meeting and other committee members are:

| | |
|---|---|
| Mr H Lobban | – Bristol Paper Products |
| Mr J Wilson | – Barr Construction |
| Mrs G Windsor | – Pembroke Printing |
| Mr N Patna | – Club Class Ltd |
| Miss J Lord | – Caledonian Pharmaceuticals |
| Mrs G Sommerby | – Executive Press |
| | Pedmore House, Dudley |
| Mr A White | – Cumbria Classics |
| | 23 Scotland St, Carlisle |

Mr Paul Gould of the local Enterprise Council will be attending the meeting to speak about training grants available.

The meeting will be held at the Dragonara Hotel, Redcliffe Way, Bristol, commencing at 0930 hours and finishing at 1300 hours. Fiona has already made the telephone booking.

The main points for discussion at the meeting are: Treasurer's Report, Minutes of Last Meeting, Chairman's Report, Correspondence.

The members from Carlisle and Dudley will be travelling by car on the Wednesday evening and will stay overnight at the hotel.

You are asked to complete the following:

a)    Send out the notice of meeting, agenda and minutes of the last meeting to all committee members. Include a map of how to get to the Dragonara for the members with accommodation booked at the hotel.

b)    Confirm arrangements to the Dragonara Hotel and let the staff there know that an overhead projector and screen, and light refreshments, will be required.

c)    Type a letter to Mr Gould, confirming his invitation to attend the meeting and advising him of the relevant details.

d)    Complete your check-list and type a memo to Fiona detailing all action taken by you.

# Processing payments

## Make and record petty cash statements

Unit 4 of Book 1 dealt with processing petty cash transactions. Refer to Unit 4 to recap then complete Task 1.

**Task 1 ➤**

1 What three items do you need to operate an efficient petty cash system?

2 What is meant by the **imprest system**?

3 What are analysis columns?

4 If the amount of money in the petty cash was £22.83 how much cash would you need to restore the **imprest** to its original £120 float?

5 Where would you keep the petty cash box during the day? Why?

6 Where would you keep the petty cash box at night? Why?

7 List the seven features of a petty cash voucher which must be completed before handing out cash.

8 List five items which would normally be paid for through petty cash.

## Recording value added tax (VAT)

VAT is the tax added to the value of goods or services at a rate determined by the Government. This rate is currently 17.5 per cent on most goods and services but can change in the Budget each year.

It is now common practice to record VAT on both the **petty cash voucher** and in the **petty cash book**. However, some receipts for goods do not show the VAT content so you must know:

- which goods are subject to VAT;

- the calculation routine to extract VAT from a gross amount.

The most common petty cash purchases subject to VAT are:

- cleaning materials

- stationery purchases

- petrol

- biscuits and luxuries.

### Goods which are not subject to VAT

It is easier to remember goods which do not have VAT added as there are very few of these. The items you will be most concerned with for business use are:

- books, magazines and newspapers;

- travel – train fares, coach fares, taxis, etc.;

- food items (except meals which are **eaten on the restaurant or cafe premises** as opposed to take-away).

**Task 2 ➤**    State whether or not these items will be subject to VAT:

a)    a hamburger bought and eaten at McDonalds;

b)    sandwiches purchased from a take-away;

c)    notepads and pencils;

d)    bus fares;

e)    cleaning materials for the office;

f)    chocolate buscuits for the MD's office;

g)    waste paper bins;

h)    tea, coffee and sugar;

i)    the ABC Guides;

j)    computer disks and paper;

k)    postage stamps.

### Extracting the VAT amount from the gross amount

Suppose an employee gave you a receipt for petrol which shows the total amount paid as £20. However, the receipt does not show how much of the £20 is allocated to VAT. **You** will have to work this out!

An easy way to do this, assuming the current rate of VAT at 17.5 per cent, is to **multiply** the total by 7 and then **divide** by 47 (or multiply the total by 7/47). This gives the VAT amount as £2.98. Thus the net amount is £17.02 (£20.00 – £2.98) and the VAT content £2.98. Try it the other way as a double check – multiply £17.02 by 17.5 per cent.

**Task 3 ➤**    Work out the VAT content of these petty cash purchases:

a) notepad @ £1

b) petrol @ £12

c) ream of copier paper @ £5.95

d) cakes and biscuits @ £3.42

e) taxi fare to airport @ £8.65

f) cleaning cloths @ £2.20

g) interviewee's bus fare 48p.

---

## Assessment activity 20.1

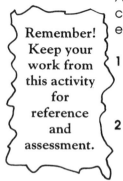

Remember! Keep your work from this activity for reference and assessment.

At the end of this chapter (pages 252-5) you will find completed petty cash vouchers for the month of July, which cover a wide range of expenses.

1    Check all the details and ensure that each voucher has been signed by the person receiving the cash and authorised by a senior member of staff.

2    Then enter the details from each voucher, in strict date order, on a blank **petty cash book** sheet (photocopy one from page 270). At the end of the month the cash sheet has to be balanced and a cheque drawn to restore the float to the original amount of £120.

---

# Receive and record payments and issue receipts

In the modern office it is not only cashiers who must know how to receive payments and issue receipts to customers and clients. All administrative staff are expected to become efficient in handling financial transactions.

When you go shopping do you check your receipt? Most receipts obtained for payment are now till receipts. However, some organisations issue **sales receipts** like the one opposite.

On a sales receipt you have to be careful to fill in the correct details of:

• the customer's name and address;

• the date;

• the number of each item bought, for example, four pens at 25p and the **extension of this** which would be £1.00 in this case;

• the sub-total of the goods;

• the VAT amount;

• the gross amount.

| MICROPLUS LTD | | | |
|---|---|---|---|
| SALES RECEIPT | | 00231764 | |
| CUSTOMER NAME *BOWMAN ELECTRIC* | | ACCOUNT NUMBER | |
| ADDRESS *163 HARBOUR VIEW* | | *013647×S* | |
| DATE *12/10/9–*   ASSISTANT *TK* | | CASH/~~CHEQUE~~/~~CREDIT CARD~~ | |
| Number | Goods description | Unit price | Total |
| *1* | *A4 RINGBINDER* | *£2.99* | *£2.99* |
| *6* | *STAEDLER PENS* | *18p.* | *£1.08* |
| | | | *£4.07* |
| | *Less 10% trade disc.* | | *41p* |
| | | | *£3.66* |
| Comments *NEW BUSINESS CUSTOMER DISCOUNT AUTHORISED BY J. DUNLOP* | | SUB TOTAL *£3.66* | |
| | | VAT *17½%*   *63p* | |
| | | TOTAL *£4.29* | |

**Task 4 ➤**   What would you use the comments box for? Discuss this with others in your group.

## Calculating and recording sales

When working in the stationery shop attached to Microplus's Business Centre there are a few basic procedures to be carried out in calculating and recording sales.

At the beginning of the working day, before the shop opens for business, the Sales Assistant must check the float in the till – this is normally £20.

All purchases are recorded using the sales receipt, commonly called the **scribe**, as shown before. All of the goods and services offered by Microplus are subject to VAT at 17.5 per cent.

### Discounts on sales

Discounts allowed must be deducted before calculating the VAT on the total purchases. Discount categories are listed in the Business Centre Services and Price Guide on pages 37–43.

### Receiving payments in cash

**TIPS ➤ ➤**    **Handling cash payments**

- **Do not put the customer's money straight into the till** – place it on the ledge or clip of the till as an immediate check of how much money the customer has given you. This could save any argument if the customer insists that she/he has been given the wrong change.

- **Count** the change out of the till and into the customer's hand.

- Place the customer's money in the till and close the drawer. **Never leave a till drawer open or walk away from an unlocked till.**

- **Always** take the money from the customer for the goods she/he has bought before wrapping the purchases. This is a security measure which will stop a customer from walking away with goods without paying for them.

If you make a mistake in ringing up the amount of the purchase on the till do not worry as this can be rectified. Try to ensure that you are entering the correct amounts in the first place but if you have made an error cancel the original receipt and issue a new one.

### Security of cash

**TIPS ➤ ➤**    **Keeping cash on the premises secure**

- Do not allow large amounts of cash to gather in the tills. **Transfer** notes to the safe regularly.

- **Bank** all cash at the end of the working day.

- Use **night-safe** facilities if necessary.

- **Two members of staff** must escort money to the bank or safe – never take money to the bank on your own.

- For the safety of staff, daily trips to the bank should be carried out at random times. **Never get into the habit of going to the bank at the same time each day or week.**

- If you have any doubts about cash handling do not hesitate to ask the advice of a senior colleague.

### Payments by cheque

Be extra vigilant when accepting cheque payments. Check the following details.

### Cheque guarantee card

- Does the customer have a guarantee card?

- What is the date of expiry?

- Is the bank code number on the card the same as that on the cheque?

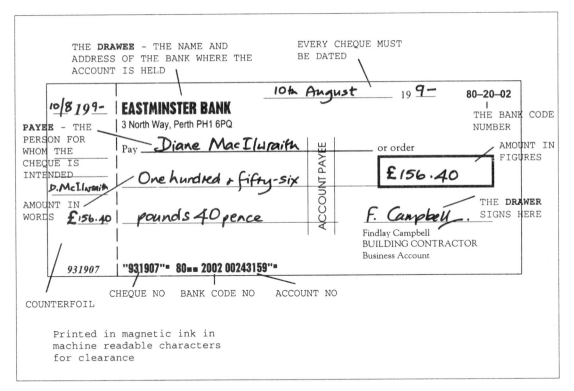

### Cheque

- Has the cheque been dated properly? Check the day, month and year.

- Has the customer entered the amount exactly **in both figures and words** (the two amounts must never differ)?

- Is the cheque crossed and correctly made payable to the company?

- Has the customer signed the cheque in your presence? Never accept a cheque which has been signed prior to purchase.

- Does the signature on the cheque match that on the cheque guarantee card?

- Have errors been initialled by the customer?

- Has the cheque been written in ink? Never accept one written in pencil.

- Is the cheque payment for more than the amount on the guarantee card? The total transaction must be less than or equal to the guarantee figure.

Never accept more than one cheque per transaction guaranteed by a cheque card.

> **Remember!**
> **Always**
> **write the**
> **number of**
> **the cheque**
> **guarantee**
> **card on the**
> **back of the**
> **cheque.**

### Payments by credit card

Many customers now pay for transactions by credit card. The most commonly-used cards are Access, Barclaycard and American Express. Special credit slips and a machine are required to accept payment by these card companies.

As with cheque guarantee cards there are several steps which have to be taken to ensure the validity of a credit card transaction.

> **Remember!**
> **Write all**
> **details in**
> **ink and lean**
> **hard on the**
> **pen to**
> **ensure that**
> **the carbon**
> **copies are**
> **clear.**

- Check that the card has not expired.

- Fill in the credit slip by inserting:

  i)     the correct date

  ii)    itemised details of the goods purchased

  iii)   the correct cost figure for each item purchased

  iv)    the total value of purchases (always double check this).

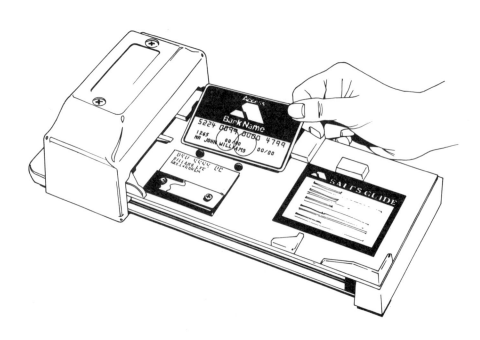

## Procedure for using the credit card imprinter

- Place the customer's card, face upwards, in the space provided in the machine.

- Place the completed slip in the correct position on the top of the card.

- Draw the handle smartly forward and back over the payment slip. Details of Microplus and the customer card must now be entered on the payment slip.

- Ask the customer to sign the top slip in ink.

- Check that details have appeared clearly on **all copies of the credit slip** by looking at the bottom copy.

- Check that the signature on the payment slip is the same as that on the credit card.

- Give the top copy with the receipt to the customer and place the remaining copies in the till.

- As with cheque payments, endorse the customer's receipt with the method of payment, for example, Access.

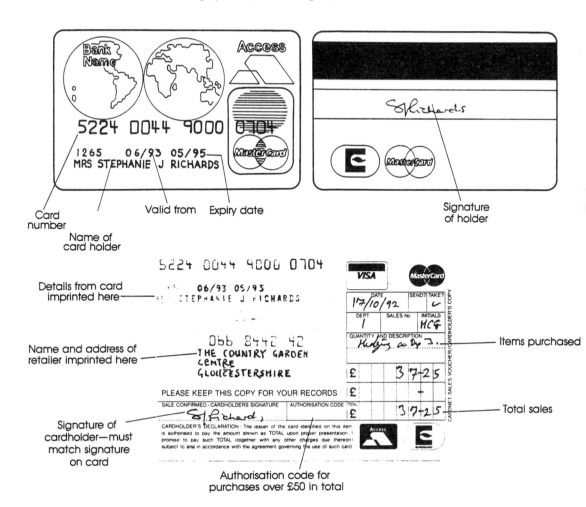

### Warning lists

From time to time the credit card companies send out a list of **void** cards which have either expired, been lost or stolen. It is of great importance that you check this list of void numbers against the card number of the customer.

If you are presented with an unsigned credit card for payment you must **contact the credit card company immediately**. It may have been an error but it could also be a stolen card.

### Correcting errors

Errors in credit card purchase documents can be rectified in the same way as for cheques. Any purchases over the value of £50 must be agreed through a telephone call to the customer's credit card company. If the purchase is authorised you must **write the authorisation number** the credit company gives you on the credit slip.

## Customers buying on account

The majority of customers who buy on account phone their orders into the stores or give details to sales representatives. However, customers may decide to come into the shop to purchase goods if they are required urgently and they cannot wait until the next delivery date. When this happens and the customers request that the goods be put on their monthly accounts follow this procedure:

- Ensure that the company has not overspent its credit limit.

- Deduct the correct discount from the sales voucher.

- Have the company representative who is taking the goods sign the sales voucher in the comments box, verifying that she/he has taken the goods.

- If at any stage of the process you are in doubt, for example, regarding credit limits, ask your Supervisor for assistance.

Make sure you never speak about a customer as if she/he were not there. Be polite and courteous at all times.

**Task 5 ➤**

All calculations for this task must be detailed – extensions, sub-totals, discounts, VAT, carriage charged and change given must be calculated.

You will need to refer to your copy of the Business Centre Services Price Guide (pages 37–43).

### Customer 1

A young student enters the shop and asks your advice about producing a curriculum vitae (CV) on her behalf. She is enquiring about prices for originals and copies. Having quoted the prices to her she orders a three-page master CV and ten copies of the same. Calculate the total of this transaction and the change she will receive from £30.00.

### Customer 2
The Office Junior from Findlay Campbell, Builders, has arrived to purchase some stationery. She buys:

6 HB Pencils @ 12p each;

2 Olympia Carrera Correctable Carbon Ribbons @ £4.45 each;

1 Box Croxley Script A4 White @ £9.30 per box.

Findlay Campbell is one of our small business purchasers who is entitled to a cash discount of 10 per cent. Calculate the change from £20.00.

### Customer 3
Two young schoolboys are in the shop to buy:

2 A4 Refill Pads @ 99p each

4 Staedtler Black Fine Point Pens @ 18p each

2 HB Pencils @ 12p each.

What change would they receive from £5.00?

### Customer 4
A man enters the shop and informs you that he has recently set up in business for himself and is new to the area. You let him know he would be entitled to a 10 per cent discount for cash and he purchases:

2 Boxes A4 Croxley Script White @ £9.30 per box

1 Petty Cash Box @ £15.45

1 Casio Calculator @ £19.29

1 Box Bic Pens, Blue @ 20p per pen (25 in box)

1 Box Verbatim Floppy Disks @ £9.90.

What change would he receive from £80.00?

## Cashing up records

At the end of the working day the member of staff on duty in the stationery shop is required to fill in the following records:

- a cashing up sumary form, and
- a daily cash receipt list.

### Cashing up summary form
The purpose of a cashing up summary form is to simplify procedures and streamline the paperwork within the company. The details of cash, cheques, credit card purchases, etc. are taken from this form and transferred to the paying-in slip for the bank. It acts as a double-check that the cash is correct. Shortages or money over should be recorded on the bottom of the form.

Date: _12/6/9—_

Assistant: _Maureen Harvey_

| | | | | £ | p |
|---|---|---|---|---|---|
| 6 | x £50 | Notes | | £ 300·00 | |
| 11 | x £20 | Notes | | £ 220·00 | |
| 33 | x £10 | Notes | | £ 330·00 | |
| 19 | x £5 | Notes | | £ 95·00 | |
| 4 | x £1 | Notes | | £ 4·00 | |
| 67 | x £1 | Coin | | £ 67·00 | |
| 8 | x 50p | Coin | | £ 4·00 | |
| 32 | x 20p | Coin | | £ 6·40 | |
| 18 | x 10p | Coin | | £ 1·80 | |
| 21 | x 5p | Coin | | £ 1·05 | |
| 15 | x 2p | Coin | | | 30p |
| 13 | x 1p | Coin | | | 13p |

SUB TOTAL   £ 1029·68
ACCESS      £ 153·47
CHEQUES     £ 461·19
VOUCHERS    £ 5·00
TOTAL       £ 1649·34

Cashing up summary form

| CASH RECEIPT LIST | | | DATE _13th August 199—_ | |
|---|---|---|---|---|
| Received from | Cash | Cheque | Credit Card | Other |
| B. Harris | 16·00 | | | |
| P. James | | 122·06 | | |
| Denmap | | | 10·16 | |
| Porter | | 84·00 | | |
| David's | | | 33·03 | |
| | | | | |
| | | | | |
| | | | | |
| TOTAL | 16·00 | 206·06 | 43·19 | |

Daily cash receipt list

**Daily cash receipt list**
The purpose of the daily cash receipt list is to ensure that the Cashier has a list of payments which have been credited to the company bank account. From this list the Cashier is able to credit accounts of customers who have paid their accounts at the shop.

**Task 6 ➤**

It is a local holiday and the offices are closed. The stationery shop remains open and you receive payments of accounts which must be recorded. From the cheques and postal orders that have been received on pages 236 and 237 enter all of the correct payments on the daily **cash receipt list** (to be found on page 274) in the appropriate places and total the sheet before giving it to the Cashier. Note that the postal orders are from these companies:

1.  Vootrobell Limited

2.  Lavery Smith & Co

3.  McIlwaine & Ewart

4.  Jim's Carpet Bazaar

5.  Alan Shoe Supplies.

**Task 7 ➤**

Carry out this task as a role-play exercise with one student acting as the Shop Assistant and other students playing the role of customers. Today the Shop Assistant is working in the stationery store of Microplus. Each day starts off with a £20 float which consists of:

| | | |
|---|---|---|
| 2 x £5 | = | £10.00 |
| 8 x £1 | = | £ 8.00 |
| 2 x 50p | = | £ 1.00 |
| 7 x 10p | = | 70p |
| 3 x  5p | = | 15p |
| 5 x  2p | = | 10p |
| 5 x  1p | = | 05p |
| | | ———— |
| Total | | £20.00. |

*Transaction 1*
1 Casio Calculator @ £27.95; paid by Access.

*Transaction 2*
1 Box A4 Copy Paper @ £6.95; paid by cash.

*Transaction 3*
1 Parker Pen @ £5.99, 1 Box Verbatim Floppy Disks @ £9.95, 2 Foolscap Ringbinders @ £2.25 each; paid by cheque.

*Transaction 4*
1 Secretarial Swivel Chair @ £47.99; paid by cash.

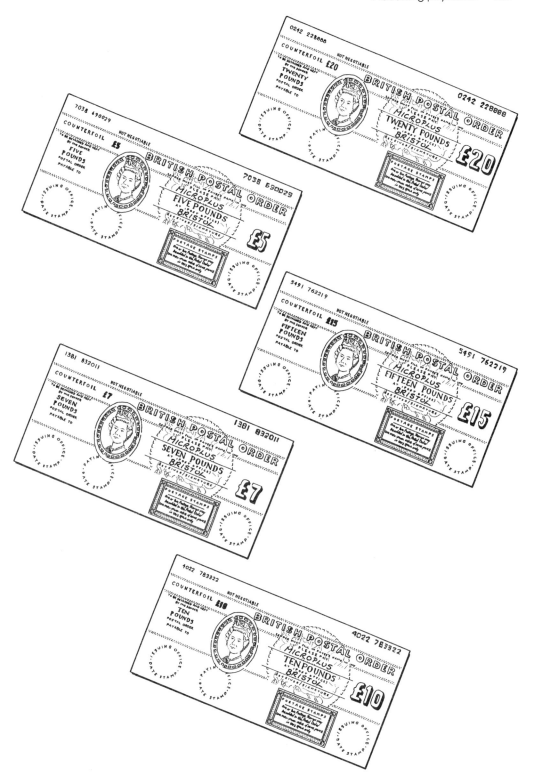

*Transaction 5*

1 Box Brown Envelopes 6" x 3" @ £7.89, 1 Packet Variform 8 Column Cash Ledger Refills @ £5.10, 1 Six Tier Paper Stack @ £20.20; paid by Access.

*Transaction 6*

1 Casio Calculator @ £9.99; paid by gift voucher.

Once all the transactions are completed you are required to total all cash and cash up. Enter details on a copy of the **cashing-up summary** form on page 273. Verify your total by taking an X reading on the till.

**Task 8 ➤**

1   List the correct procedures that you would undertake when accepting:

a)   a payment by cash

b)   a payment by credit card.

2   How would you ensure the validity of a cheque.

---

## Assessment activity 20.1

**Remember! Keep your work from this activity for reference and assessment.**

This activity is carried out in the form of a role-play exercise with the student being assessed acting as the Shop Assistant for the day. Other students will perform the roles of customers with the tutor acting as the Shop Supervisor.During this activity the student is required to process 30 transactions, recording and receiving payments from customers. These transactions will be by a variety of methods.

   The student will start the day with a float of £20 (as listed below) and at the end of the activity will balance the till and complete the cashing up summary form and daily cash receipt list.

**Float**

| | | |
|---|---|---|
| 2 x £5 | = | £10.00 |
| 8 x £1 | = | £ 8.00 |
| 2 x 50p | = | £ 1.00 |
| 7 x 10p | = | 70p |
| 3 x 5p | = | 15p |
| 5 x 2p | = | 10p |
| 5 x 1p | = | 05p |
| Total | | £20.00 |

Use the price list for details of stationery purchases and remember **to add VAT to all transactions.**

**Price list**
Scribe Refills @ £1.95 each
Price Tickets 2" x 2" @ £4.36
Stick-on Labels (small size) @
£12.27
Bic Pens @ 20p each
Olympia Carrera Portable Typewriter
@ £199.99
Olympia Carrera Correctable Carbon
Ribbons @ £4.45
Casio Calculator @ £6.23
A4 Refill Pad @ 99p
HB Pencil @ 12p
Paper Clips @ £1.25
Rubber Bands @ 66p
Rexel Staples No. 6 @ £1.22
Acco Lockable Floppy Disk Storage
Unit @ £17.95
Croxley Script @ £9.30
Staedtler Pens Fine Point Black @
£5.20 per box
Foolscap Ringbinder @ £2.25
Pentel Pen @ 99p
Rexel Meteor Stapler @ £8.25
Rexel Staples No 16 @ £2.30
Eastlight Classic Box File @ £4.53
Derby Bookcase @ £289.00
Post It Notepads (Pack of 10 pads)
@ £3.60
Petty Cash Voucher (Pack of 10
pads) @ £4.35
Nobo Pens @ £7.60 per pack

**WARNING LIST**
**FOR CARDS NO LONGER VALID**
If a card listed below is presented, please retain it and telephone the Authorisation Centre, Southend (0702) 352222 immediately for further instructions.
A reward of £50 will be paid for each of the undermentioned cards retained and returned to the Authorisation Centre.

**NOTE: ALL CARDS ARE PREFIXED WITH NUMBER 5224 UNLESS SHOWN OTHERWISE**

| | | Card expiry date |
|---|---|---|
| GREEN MR | 0092 8122 4680 | 11/94 |
| HILL MRS | 0099 7189 2336 | 09/93 |
| WHITE MRS | 0099 3145 6245 | 08/93 |
| WILLIAMS MRS | 0099 9132 6611 | 07/93 |

## Transaction 1
You require 20 copies of an original A3 document and pay by cash.

## Transaction 2
You are a young German student wishing to send a fax of one page plus cover sheet to Germany. You will wait for the reply to the fax which is also one page plus cover sheet. You pay by Access Eurocard.

## Transaction 3
You require a six page report to be word processed. You want to know the price and pay by cheque. You will call back this afternoon to pick it up.

## Transaction 4
You are Anne Jones from Alan Shoes. You need some office supplies. You are a regular customer of Microplus but do not have an account with them. You pay by cheque for these goods:

10 Scribe Refills
1 Box of Price Tickets 2" x 2"
1 Roll Stick on Labels (small size).

### Transaction 5
You wish to purchase 2 Bic Pens. You pay cash.

### Transaction 6
You are Gordon Reynolds from the local Community Association and you wish to pick up goods you ordered last week. The parcel is made up waiting for you and the bill is £50.90 – you pay by cheque.

### Transaction 7
You are Mrs Wilkinson from the local Neighbourhood Watch Scheme. You wish the regular newsletter to be set up. This month there are eight A4 pages to the newsletter. You wish 500 copies printed and you will pay by cheque.

### Transaction 8
You wish to purchase these goods and pay by Access:

> 1 Olympia Carrera Portable Typewriter and 3 Olympia Carrera Correctable Carbon Ribbons.

### Transaction 9
You purchase these goods and pay by cash:

> 1 Casio Calculator
> 1 A4 Refill Pad
> 1 HB Pencil.

### Transaction 10
You are Rebecca White from A C White Accountants. You need to purchase these small items for the office – remind the Assistant that you receive a 15% trade discount. You pay cash.

> 1 Box Paper Clips
> 1 Packet of Rubber Bands
> 1 Box Rexel Staples No 6.

### Transaction 11
You are a Samantha Powell of Corsa Builders in town. You are a regular customer of Microplus and you wish to send a five-page fax to Bruce Wyllie, Broad Street, Halifax. Pay by cheque.

### Transaction 12
You are Peter Muir from Atco Engineers. You company operates an account with Microplus. You wish to purchase 1 Acco Lockable Floppy Disk Storage Unit at £17.95. Tell the Assistant to charge the purchase.

### Transaction 13
You require these photocopying services and pay cash:

> 100 A4 copies of an original
> 10 enlargements of an original A4
> 5 A3 copies of an original.

### Transaction 14
You are Marty Black from James B Black Accountants – a regular

customer. You need some word processing carried out urgently and delivered to the office by 2 p.m. this afternoon. The address is 9 Orr Square, in town, for which there will be a £5 delivery charge added. You have seven letters to go out: three of which are one-page, one which is two-page; and three which are four-page. You wish to pay now – by cheque.

## Transaction 15
You are a student at the local college. You purchase these items and pay by cash:

> 1 Box Croxley Script
> 5 HB Pencils
> 1 Box Staedtler Pens Fine Point Black.

(When the Assistant asks tell her you have forgotten your student card.)

## Transaction 16
You are the Receptionist at the local doctors' practice. You need to send a fax to the hospital for Dr James. The fax is three pages plus the cover sheet. You pay by cash.

## Transaction 17
You are Mrs Hill from 11 Quarry Street. You wish to order invitations for your daughter's wedding. You have already received a quote from Microplus for 100 invitations at £90 plus VAT. You have made a mistake as there are only 100 guests going to the wedding and these are couples. You only need 50 invitations. You pay by Access. (Card is out-of-date.)

## Transaction 18
You are Cathy Coleman of Polson and Coleman Solicitors. Your firm has an account with Microplus and you receive a trade discount of 15 per cent. Last week you ordered new business cards on behalf of your husband who is self-employed – 300 black and white. You wish to collect the order and pay by cheque.

## Transaction 19
You wish to purchase these goods and pay by cash:

> 1 Foolscap Ringbinder
> 1 Pentel Pen.

## Transaction 20
You are Christine Emery and you wish to pay your account with Microplus. The cashier has gone to lunch so you pay at the shop by cheque. The account is for £720.29p (Write this amount correctly in words and insert £721.29p in figures.)

## Transaction 21
You are the junior hairdresser with Cathy's Salon. The Salon regularly uses Microplus to produce leaflets indicating special offers, etc. You are paying £304.26 by cheque for this month's account. (Cathy has forgotten to sign the cheque.)

### Transaction 22

You are Bryce Robson's secretary. You call at Microplus to collect the order of 500 compliment slips. You have to pay by cheque. You have to fill in the details on the cheque which has already been signed by Bryce. (Cheque crossing indicates that the amount should not exceed £10.)

### Transaction 23

You are Marie Clark of ACE Secretarial Services which has recently set up business. You have placed an order for 500 business cards (black and white) to be printed. You also purchase these goods:

      1 Rexel Meteor Stapler
      1 Box Rexel Staples No 16
      1 Eastlight Classic Box File.

Ask the Assistant about a discount as you will be a regular customer from now on. You pay by cash.

### Transaction 24

You wish to purchase 1 Derby Bookcase. You will pay by Access.

### Transaction 25

You are Cathy Coleman of Polson and Coleman and you wish to pay the company's monthly account for £422.99 by cheque. You forgot to pay it earlier. (Cheque dated 1999.)

### Transaction 26

You are Jim Thompson from Jim's Carpet Bazaar and you are calling to pick up goods you have ordered. The bill is for £48.42 and you pay by cheque.

### Transaction 27

You purchase these goods and pay by cash:

      1 Pack of 10 Post-It Notepads
      1 Pack of 10 Petty Cash Voucher Pads.

### Transaction 28

You are Miles Allison of Branson Industrial Supplies. You call at the office of Microplus to pay your account. The office is closed so you give the cheque for £2000.86 to the Assistant. (No day inserted at date.)

### Transaction 29

You purchase a pack of Nobo Pens. You pay by cheque. (Cheque guarantee card is out-of-date – so pay by cash when this is pointed out.)

### Transaction 30

You are Mrs Williams and are calling at Microplus to collect birthday party invitations you ordered. You will pay by Access and the bill is for £40.00.

# Prepare for routine banking transactions

Do you have an account with a bank or building society? If so, how many of the following services does it provide for you as a personal customer:

- salary paid directly into account;
- cash and cheque payments into account;
- cash withdrawals from account;
- payments for goods and services made by cheque;
- payments for goods and services made by standing order;
- payments for goods and services made by direct debit;
- changing sterling for foreign currency and vice versa;
- issuing travellers' cheques;
- providing a monthly or quarterly statement;
- providing overdraft facilities;
- providing mortgage facilities;
- providing loans;
- issuing credit cards and charge cards;
- out-of-hours services, for example, a cashpoint machine.

What type of account do you operate? Is it a:

- current account
- deposit account
- savings account
- high-interest account?

## Types of bank account

There are various types of account that can be opened by business and personal clients.

### Current accounts

Business customers need to use the facilities associated with operating a current account as certain types of financial services are only available to current account customers. These are:

- cheque book and cheque guarantee card
- overdraft facilities
- night safe facilities
- business loans.

Some banks offer interest on current accounts which remain in credit; others waive certain bank charges for various services, again if the account remains in credit.

### Deposit accounts

Most deposit accounts offer the facilities of instant withdrawal of cash, payment of standing orders and direct debits, use of cashpoint machines, and services such as the provision of travellers'cheques and foreign currency. Deposit accounts usually attract higher interest rates than current accounts. However, you will not normally be offered cheque book facilities with this type of account.

### Savings accounts

Most savings accounts are intended for people who wish to deposit money for a longer term. These accounts offer high interest rates to savers. However, a drawback to this is the fact that banks and building societies usually require a few weeks' notice for withdrawals.

## Cheques

A cheque contains the following information:

- the name and account number of the person or organisation issuing the cheque in payment for goods or services;
- the name of the recipient of the cheque;
- the amount **(in both words and figures)** which is to be paid to the recipient from the sender's bank account;
- the name and the address of the banker along with the bank sort code.

Cheques must be paid into a bank account and normally take **three full working days to clear.**

### Clearing process

What is the clearing process for a cheque? Discuss this with your group and then look at the flow chart below.

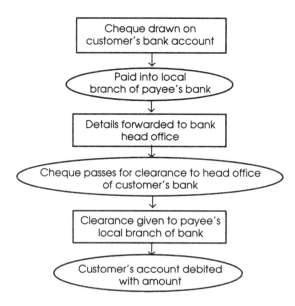

The journey of a cheque from signature to clearing

## Paying into a bank account

Business users have special pre-printed **pay-in books** to detail monies paid into their accounts. On the completed pay-in slip overleaf note the details as shown.

**TIPS ➤ ➤**    **Completing a pay-in slip**

- Insert the correct **date** on the counterfoil and bank record.

- **Sign** the slip at the point **'paid in by'**.

- Use the space provided at the front of the slip to carry out a **cash analysis** as shown above.

- If the **account holder name** is not pre-printed on the slip then enter this in the box provided.

- Detail the cheques and postal orders at the back of the slip as shown above.

- Always **complete the counterfoil** with the exact details as listed on the front page.

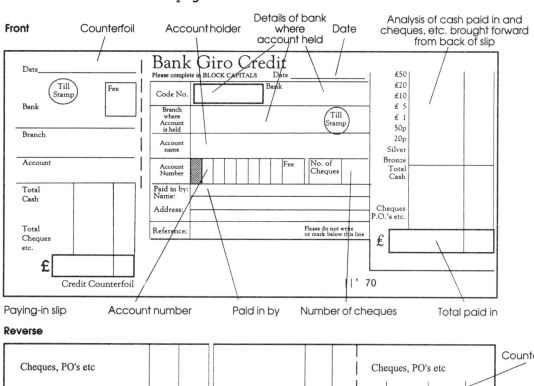

Front — Counterfoil — Account holder — Details of bank where account held — Date — Analysis of cash paid in and cheques, etc. brought forward from back of slip

Paying-in slip — Account number — Paid in by — Number of cheques — Total paid in

**Reverse**

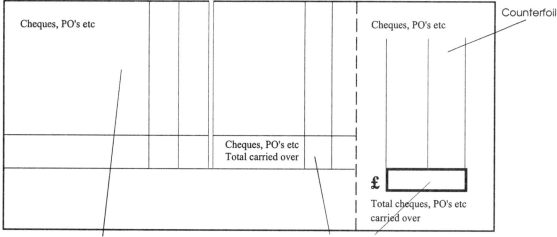

Details of cheques and postal orders listed — Total cheques, PO's carried over to front of slip — Counterfoil

**Task 9 ➤**    Complete a pay-slip for Microplus which details the payments made in Task 7.

## Preparing cash for banking

Would you arrive at the bank with money, cheques, etc. which had all been just thrown into a bag in any order? Discuss this with your group.

### Bagging up

**Bagging up** is the term given to the preparation of cash to be taken to the bank. By carefully preparing cash to be banked you can save a great deal of time and frustration, not only for yourself but also the bank teller. Follow these procedures:

- **coinage** is placed in the special plastic coin bags provided by the banks in the denomination listed at the front of the bag, for example, £5 of 10p pieces, £10 of 50p pieces, £2 of 2p pieces, 50p of 1p pieces, etc.;

- **notes** are usually sorted by:

    a) denomination – £50, £20, £10, £5, and

    b) according to the bank of origin, for example, Bank of England, Clydesdale Bank, Bank of Scotland;

and secured by a rubber band in packs of £100, £200, etc.;

- **cheques** are held together by a paper or bulldog clip;

- **credit card counterfoils** are sorted into type, for example, Access, Visa, Barclaycard, and then held together by a paper clip.

## Withdrawing money from a bank account

Businesses need to draw cash from their bank accounts for petty cash and wages. Although most wages and salaries are now paid directly into the employees' bank accounts by BACS (Bankers Automated Clearing System), some small firms pay wages in cash.

How do you let the bank know the number of £20 notes, £10 notes and coins you will need? You have to provide a breakdown as shown below. Follow this procedure when drawing cash from a business account:

1.    Calculate the **total** amount of money required.

2.    Write out a cheque made payable to **CASH** or **WAGES** or **PETTY CASH**.

3.    **Detail** the **breakdown** of cash required on the back of the cheque, for example:

£50 x 13 =  £650;    £20 x  5 = £100;    £10 x 2 = £ 20;

then **total** this amount. The amount of this total must be the **same** as that written on the front of the cheque.

**Task 10 ➤**

You are working in the wages department and you are asked to prepare a cheque for the cash to be inserted into the pay-packets of weekly-paid employees. Show the breakdown of cash required and write a cheque from these details:

**Week 1**

| | | | | | |
|---|---|---|---|---|---|
| Black, D | 176.35 | Burton, M | 169.42 | Watson, J | 172.11 |
| Bell, P | 183.17 | Brown, J | 194.66 | Fisher, J | 202.31 |

Look at the following tips to help you with this task.

**TIPS ➤ ➤**

**Analysing cash required**

■ Break down the notes and coinage required for each pay packet, for example, £192.36 would be:

| | | |
|---|---|---|
| 3 x £50 | = | £150.00 |
| 2 x £20 | = | £ 40.00 |
| 2 x £ 1 | = | £  2.00 |
| 1 x 20p | = | 20p |
| 1 x 10p | = | 10p |
| 1 x  5p | = | 5p |
| 1 x  1p | = | 1p |
| | | ———— |
| TOTAL | | £192.36 |

■ Detail the total breakdown of **all** pay packets together at the back of the cheque, for example, if you need three £50 notes for one packet, five for another and two for another the total would read 10 x £50.

■ Check that the total amount of all wages agrees with the total of the cheque drawn.

---

## Assessment activity 20.3

> **Remember!**
> **Keep the material from this activity for reference and assessment.**

**Activity A**
Using the cash, cheque and credit card details from the previous role-play (Assessment activity 20.2) prepare a paying-in slip to deposit the monies in the company bank account.(Use a copy of the paying-in slip on page 274.)

**Activity B**
Carry out a cash analysis of the weekly wages for these employees and then draw a cheque for cash from the bank to process the payroll from the details:

| | | | |
|---|---|---|---|
| David Black | £177.27 | Helen Black | £192.07 |
| Michael Burton | £168.49 | James Watson | £181.32 |
| Patricia Smith | £210.08 | Pauline Bell | £177.63 |
| Joyce Brown | £181.11 | James Fisher | £211.85 |
| Rita Anderson | £202.02 | John Armour | £152.13 |

# Make payments to suppliers and others

## Checking and passing invoices for payment

Refer to Unit 4 of Book 1 to recap on this area.

An **invoice** is the document sent to the customer by the supplier when the goods ordered have been despatched, the work carried out has been completed or services have been provided. When you are working in the accounts department it is your job to process incoming invoices for payment and to check thoroughly that the invoices are correct.

Although the amounts being charged to the company may seem to be the most important to check there are many other invoice details which must also be verified as follows:

- the invoice carries the correct name of the company and that the correct department has been charged;

- the invoice ties up with the details on the delivery/advice note which came with the goods;

- the terms of payment are those previously arranged between the company and the supplier;

- the gross price of the goods is correct;

- the number of items received are the correct number invoiced for;

- the VAT rate of 17.5 per cent on goods subject ot VAT is correct and the amount of VAT is calculated properly;

- packing and delivery charges are as pre-arranged;

- the extensions are correct, for example, 5 Packets of Cash Ledger Sheets @ £3.95 = £19.75;

- the correct discount has been deducted;

- the final total of the invoice has been calculated correctly.

## Processing cheques for authorised signature

Having checked invoices, statements and expenses claims, and then passed them for payment, you now have to write the cheques which will be sent to the suppliers or others owed money.

Care has to be taken when making payments by cheque. Certain details have to be entered correctly as follows:

- date the cheque with the correct day, month and year;

- write the money to be paid in **both** words and figures – check that you do not transpose the figures;

- use the area between the crossed lines to add special instructions **(special crossings)** to the bank and to detail that the amount on the cheque should not exceed a certain limit. (For example, if you were sending a cheque to Pitney Bowes plc for £199.00 you would write in the space that the amount does not exceed £200.);

- when drawing cash insert CASH where you would normally write the name of the person or company to whom the cheque is to be paid. It is normal practice also to bracket the word (Wages) or (Petty cash) after this;

- always fill in the counterfoil to the cheque. If paying an invoice or statement insert the invoice/statement number;

- **never** make a payment to a person or company without the authority to do so. Always ensure that you have supporting documentation for a payment when issuing cheques.

**Task 11 ➤**     Issue the following cheques to suppliers and others. Date the cheques as at today's date and sign them on behalf of Microplus:

a)  to Lloyds Bowmaker Limited
per lease agreement 167928
amount £1201.58;

b)  to Prime Business Services
per invoice no. 0028649
amount £663.33;

c)  to Telefusion Communications
per invoice no. 09094
amount £64.39;

d)  to The Sage Group
per statement no. 39
amount £122.67;

e)  to Intel Office Supplies Limited
per invoice no. 308221
amount £3851.60;

f)  to Dual Business Systems
per maintenance contract
amount £303.54;

g)  to Smart Cars
per invoice no: 66354
amount £200.02.

h)  to Theresa McPherson
per expenses claim for (month)
amount £122.34;

i)  to wages for (week ending)
per wages records
amount £3764.09.

## Assessment activity 20.4

> **Remember!**
> **Keep your**
> **work from**
> **this activity**
> **for**
> **reference**
> **and**
> **assessment.**

1  Draw a cheque for £89.75 to E H Barclay and mark the cheque with a special crossing to ensure that it can only be cashed at the Midland Bank in town.

2  After you have completed the above cheque you realise that the amount should have been for £98.75. Rectify this.

3  Complete a cheque for £145.95 to the local electricity supplier. Use today's date and a special crossing to ensure that the cheque may be paid only into the company's account.

4  You have to prepare a wages cheque for today's date and the Wages Clerk has given you the breakdown of cash required in the following denominations:

| | | |
|---|---|---|
| 30 x £50 | 69 x £20 | 48 x £10 |
| 96 x £5 | 108 x £1 | 62 x 50p |
| 38 x 20p | 55 x 10p | 30 x 5p |
| 16 x 2p | 4 x 1p. | |

5  Mr McManus has given you the authority to prepare a cheque for funds for the office party. Fiona Gibbs is collecting all the orders and as there are a few shops she has to visit it is best to give her a cheque for cash. Below is the breakdown of the purchases required:

| | | |
|---|---|---|
| napkins, paper plates, etc. | = | £ 8.42 |
| wines and spirits | = | £106.23 |
| goods from delicatessan | = | £ 69.57 |
| prizes for the raffle | = | £ 33.02 |

6  The milkman has come in to the office to ask for payment of the month's account. He is going on holiday tonight and would appreciate it if you could settle up with him now. There are no departmental heads in the office as it is lunch time. How would you deal with this situation as you do have the authority to sign cheques on behalf of the firm?

7  Hans Khol has been entertaining prospective clients for the company in Germany. He has sent in his expenses claim form and is awaiting a cheque for £298.00 to be sent to him. Although the expense claims are normally dealt with at the end of the month the Sales Manager feels that this is too long for Hans to wait for his money. You have therefore been aurthorised to send him a cheque for this amount bearing in mind that it will have to be in German Deutschmarks.

8  Send Michel Mercier his salary cheque of £1659 plus £222.50 commission in French francs.

| PETTY CASH VOUCHER | No: 001 Date: 1/7/9- | | |
|---|---|---|---|
| FOR WHAT REQUIRED | | £ | p |
| Stamps | | 24 | 00 |
| vat @ 17.5% | | | |
| TOTAL | | 24 | 00 |
| Signature | R. Kennedy | | |
| Passed by | J. Wells. | | |

| PETTY CASH VOUCHER | No: 002 Date: 1/7/9- | | |
|---|---|---|---|
| FOR WHAT REQUIRED | | £ | p |
| Tea & Coffee | | 4 | 80 |
| Biscuits | | 1 | 50 |
| vat @ 17.5% | | | 25 |
| TOTAL | | 6 | 55 |
| Signature | F. Gibb. | | |
| Passed by | M. Thomas. | | |

| PETTY CASH VOUCHER | No: 003 Date: 2/7/9- | | |
|---|---|---|---|
| FOR WHAT REQUIRED | | £ | p |
| Faxes for interviewees | | 16 | 40 |
| vat @ 17½% | | | |
| TOTAL | | 16 | 40 |
| Signature | Y. Gilmour | | |
| Passed by | T. McManus | | |

| PETTY CASH VOUCHER | No: 004 Date: 4/7/9- | | |
|---|---|---|---|
| FOR WHAT REQUIRED | | £ | p |
| Envelopes | | 6 | 95 |
| Polish & Jiff | | 2 | 25 |
| vat @ 17½% | | 1 | 61 |
| TOTAL | | 10 | 81 |
| Signature | J. Brown | | |
| Passed by | M. Thomas. | | |

| PETTY CASH VOUCHER | No: 005 Date: 5/7/9- | | |
|---|---|---|---|
| FOR WHAT REQUIRED | | £ | p |
| Petrol for return journey Bristol to Glasgow. Company Vehicle Reg: K6AA EUW. | | 34 | 00 |
| vat @ 17.5% | | 5 | 95 |
| TOTAL | | 39 | 95 |
| Signature | J. Dunlop | | |
| Passed by | J. Dunlop. | | |

| PETTY CASH VOUCHER | No: 006 Date: 7/7/9- | | |
|---|---|---|---|
| FOR WHAT REQUIRED | | £ | p |
| Flowers for Reception | | 5 | 20 |
| vat @ | | | |
| TOTAL | | 5 | 20 |
| Signature | J. Brown. | | |
| Passed by | J. Brown. | | |

| PETTY CASH VOUCHER | No: 007 Date: 9/7/9- | |
|---|---|---|
| FOR WHAT REQUIRED | £ | p |
| Window Cleaner VAT inclusive | 10 | 00 |
| vat @ 17½% | | |
| TOTAL | 10 | 00 |
| Signature Don French | | |
| Passed by M. Thomas | | |

| PETTY CASH VOUCHER | No: 008 Date: 11/7/9- | |
|---|---|---|
| FOR WHAT REQUIRED | £ | p |
| MILKMAN | 4 | 80 |
| vat @ | | |
| TOTAL | 4 | 80 |
| Signature P. Boyle | | |
| Passed by M. Thomas. | | |

| PETTY CASH VOUCHER | No: 009 Date: 12/7/9- | |
|---|---|---|
| FOR WHAT REQUIRED | £ | p |
| Magazines for Reception | 2 | 12 |
| Biscuits for M.D. Room | 2 | 65 |
| vat @ 17½% | | 46 |
| TOTAL | 5 | 23 |
| Signature F. Gibb. | | |
| Passed by F. Gibb. | | |

| PETTY CASH VOUCHER | No: 010 Date: 15/7/9- | |
|---|---|---|
| FOR WHAT REQUIRED | £ | p |
| 4 Bottles of Wine for Customer Reception on 18/7/9- | 19 | 80 |
| vat @ 17½% | 3 | 46 |
| TOTAL | 23 | 26 |
| Signature B Pearson | | |
| Passed by M. Thomas | | |

| PETTY CASH VOUCHER | No: 011 Date: 15/7/9- | |
|---|---|---|
| FOR WHAT REQUIRED | £ | p |
| Napkins ⎫ For | 5 | 20 |
| Paper plates ⎬ Customer | 2 | 30 |
| Cheese ⎪ Reception | 4 | 84 |
| Biscuits ⎭ | 2 | 09 |
| vat @ 17½% | 2 | 11 |
| TOTAL | 16 | 54 |
| Signature B Pearson. | | |
| Passed by M. Thomas. | | |

| PETTY CASH VOUCHER | No: 012 Date: 16/7/9- | |
|---|---|---|
| FOR WHAT REQUIRED | £ | p |
| Guaranteed Delivery parcel to J. Hughes in Birmingham. | 4 | 25 |
| vat @ 17½% | | |
| TOTAL | 4 | 25 |
| Signature R. Kennedy | | |
| Passed by J Wells | | |

| PETTY CASH VOUCHER | No: 013 Date: 18/7/9- | |
|---|---|---|
| FOR WHAT REQUIRED | £ | p |
| Window Cleaner VAT inclusive | 10 | 00 |
| vat @ 17½% | | |
| TOTAL | 10 | 00 |
| Signature    Don French | | |
| Passed by    R. Bywaters | | |

| PETTY CASH VOUCHER | No: 014 Date: 19/7/9- | |
|---|---|---|
| FOR WHAT REQUIRED | £ | p |
| Taxi fare for Mr. Brown to Heathrow | 17 | 50 |
| vat @ | | |
| TOTAL | 17 | 50 |
| Signature    F. Gibb. | | |
| Passed by    A. Brown | | |

| PETTY CASH VOUCHER | No: 015 Date: 21/7/9 | |
|---|---|---|
| FOR WHAT REQUIRED | £ | p |
| PETROL FOR TRIP FROM BRISTOL TO CHELTENHAM COLLEGE | 6 | 00 |
| vat @ 17½% | | |
| TOTAL | | |
| Signature    R. Bywaters. | | |
| Passed by    R. Bywaters | | |

| PETTY CASH VOUCHER | No: 016 Date: 22/7/9- | |
|---|---|---|
| FOR WHAT REQUIRED | £ | p |
| Flowers for Reception | 8 | 50 |
| vat @ 17½% | | |
| TOTAL | 8 | 50 |
| Signature    F. Gibb. | | |
| Passed by    M. Thomas. | | |

| PETTY CASH VOUCHER | No: 017 Date: 23/7/9- | |
|---|---|---|
| FOR WHAT REQUIRED | £ | p |
| Coffee, Tea, Sugar, Sweeteners for staff room | 8 | 20 |
| Biscuits | 3 | 06 |
| vat @ 17.5% | | 62 |
| TOTAL | 11 | 88 |
| Signature    J. Brown | | |
| Passed by    M. Thomas. | | |

| PETTY CASH VOUCHER | No: 018 Date: 23/7/9- | |
|---|---|---|
| FOR WHAT REQUIRED | £ | p |
| Course fees for attendance at night class - R. Cook | 50 | 00 |
| vat @ 17½% | | |
| TOTAL | 50 | 00 |
| Signature    R. Cook | | |
| Passed by    M. Thomas. | | |

| PETTY CASH VOUCHER | No: 019 Date: 25/7/9- | |
|---|---|---|
| FOR WHAT REQUIRED | £ | p |
| MOT for Company Van H 421 PSD | 21 | 95 |
| vat @ 17½% | | |
| TOTAL | 21 | 95 |
| Signature  D. Logan | | |
| Passed by  D. Logan | | |

| PETTY CASH VOUCHER | No: 020 Date: 26/7/9- | |
|---|---|---|
| FOR WHAT REQUIRED | £ | p |
| Dry cleaning cost for customer jacket (printer ink to be removed) | 5 | 65 |
| vat @ 17½% | | |
| TOTAL | 5 | 65 |
| Signature  L. Pearson. | | |
| Passed by  M. Thomas. | | |

| PETTY CASH VOUCHER | No: 021 Date: 27/7/9- | |
|---|---|---|
| FOR WHAT REQUIRED | £ | p |
| MILKMAN | 9 | 60 |
| vat @ | | |
| TOTAL | 9 | 60 |
| Signature  f. Boyle | | |
| Passed by  M. Thomas. | | |

| PETTY CASH VOUCHER | No: 022 Date: 28/7/9- | |
|---|---|---|
| FOR WHAT REQUIRED | £ | p |
| Window Cleaner | 10 | 00 |
| vat @ 17½% | | |
| TOTAL | 10 | 00 |
| Signature  Don French | | |
| Passed by  M. Thomas. | | |

| PETTY CASH VOUCHER | No: 023 Date: 29/7/7- | |
|---|---|---|
| FOR WHAT REQUIRED | £ | p |
| Postage costs for parcel to Glasgow Office (Datapost) | 8 | 26 |
| vat @ | | |
| TOTAL | 8 | 26 |
| Signature  R. Kennedy | | |
| Passed by  f. Wells. | | |

| PETTY CASH VOUCHER | No: 024 Date: 30/7/9- | |
|---|---|---|
| FOR WHAT REQUIRED | £ | p |
| Cleaning materials | 8 | 25 |
| vat @ 17½% | | |
| TOTAL | 8 | 25 |
| Signature  Don Mack | | |
| Passed by  M. Thomas. | | |

# Stationery

This stationery may be photocopied for use in the classroom.

| Date: | DAY PLAN |
| --- | --- |

**APPOINTMENTS**

| 9.00 | 2.00 |
| --- | --- |
| 9.30 | 2.30 |
| 10.00 | 3.00 |
| 10.30 | 3.30 |
| 11.00 | 4.00 |
| 11.30 | 4.30 |
| 12.00 | 5.00 |
| 1.00 | EVENING |

**THINGS TO DO**

1.

2.

3.

4.

5.

6.

7.

8.

**NOTES**

# APPOINTMENTS BOOK

Day and date: ..........................................................................................................................

| Time | | Name of caller | Company/Address | To see |
|------|---|----------------|-----------------|--------|
| 09.00 | | | | |
| | | | | |
| | | | | |
| 10.00 | | | | |
| | | | | |
| | | | | |
| 11.00 | | | | |
| | | | | |
| | | | | |
| 12.00 | | | | |
| | | | | |
| | | | | |
| 13.00 | | | | |
| | | | | |
| | | | | |
| 14.00 | | | | |
| | | | | |
| | | | | |
| 15.00 | | | | |
| | | | | |
| | | | | |
| 16.00 | | | | |
| | | | | |
| | | | | |
| 17.00 | | | | |
| | | | | |
| | | | | |
| 18.00 | | | | |
| | | | | |

# VISITORS' REGISTER

**Day and date** .................................................................................................

| Time | Name | Company/address | Seen by | Action taken |
|---|---|---|---|---|
| | | | | |
| | | | | |
| | | | | |
| | | | | |
| | | | | |
| | | | | |
| | | | | |
| | | | | |
| | | | | |
| | | | | |
| | | | | |
| | | | | |

# STAFF IN/OUT BOOK

Day and date   .................................................................................................................

| OUT | | | | | IN |
|---|---|---|---|---|---|
| Time | Name | Department | Gone to | Expected back | Time |
| | | | | | |
| | | | | | |
| | | | | | |
| | | | | | |
| | | | | | |
| | | | | | |
| | | | | | |
| | | | | | |
| | | | | | |
| | | | | | |
| | | | | | |
| | | | | | |

## MESSAGE FORM

Message for _____

Taken by _____

Date _____

Time _____

## WHILE YOU WERE OUT

Name _____

Organisation _____

Tel. no. _____  Ext _____

Telephoned          Please ring          URGENT

Returned your call          Called in person

MESSAGE



Signed _____

## STATIONERY STOCK REQUISITION

DEPARTMENT:

| Date | Details | Quantity required |
|------|---------|-------------------|
|      |         |                   |
|      |         |                   |
|      |         |                   |
|      |         |                   |
|      |         |                   |

RECEIVED BY: ....................................................................

FOR OFFICE USE ONLY:

STOCK CARD UPDATED ...................... (PLEASE TICK)    DATE: ...................................

ENTERED ON STOCK CARD BY:    ............................... SIGNATURE: ...........................................

# STOCK CARD

ITEM:
UNIT:
RE-ORDER:

STORES REF:
MAXIMUM:
MINIMUM:

| Date | Received | | Issued | | Balance in stock | On Order | |
|------|----------|----------|------------|----------|--------|------|----------|
| | Inv No | Quantity | Department | Quantity | | Date | Quantity |
| | | | | | | | |
| | | | | | | | |
| | | | | | | | |
| | | | | | | | |
| | | | | | | | |
| | | | | | | | |
| | | | | | | | |
| | | | | | | | |

# CROSS REFERENCE CARD

For correspondence for:

_____

See:

_____

|  |  |  | OUT |
|---|---|---|---|
| Date taken | Folder no. or name | Taken by | Date returned |
|  |  |  |  |
|  |  |  |  |
|  |  |  |  |
|  |  |  |  |
|  |  |  |  |
|  |  |  |  |
|  |  |  |  |
|  |  |  |  |

## CIRCULATION SLIP

**Please read and pass on within 24 hours in order shown below**

| NAME | DEPARTMENT | DATE/INITIAL |
|---|---|---|
|  |  |  |

**Please return to:**

**By:**

# LOG OF INCOMING/OUTGOING* TELEPHONE CALLS

| Date | Time | Caller | Firm | Contact | Action taken |
|------|------|--------|------|---------|--------------|
|      |      |        |      |         |              |
|      |      |        |      |         |              |
|      |      |        |      |         |              |
|      |      |        |      |         |              |
|      |      |        |      |         |              |
|      |      |        |      |         |              |
|      |      |        |      |         |              |
|      |      |        |      |         |              |
|      |      |        |      |         |              |
|      |      |        |      |         |              |
|      |      |        |      |         |              |
|      |      |        |      |         |              |
|      |      |        |      |         |              |
|      |      |        |      |         |              |
|      |      |        |      |         |              |

*Delete as appropriate

| OUT-CALL CARD | | OUT-CALL CARD | |
|---|---|---|---|

**OUT-CALL CARD**

Time: _____ Ext: _____

Caller: _____

Number required: _____

Person to contact: _____

Message if unavailable:

_____

_____

_____

_____

_____

**OUT-CALL CARD**

Time: _____ Ext: _____

Caller: _____

Number required: _____

Person to contact: _____

Message if unavailable:

_____

_____

_____

_____

_____

**PETTY CASH VOUCHER**

No:
Date:

| FOR WHAT REQUIRED | £ | p |
|---|---|---|
| | | |
| **TOTAL** | | |

Signature _____

Passed By _____

**MICROPLUS LIMITED**
**18-23 Long Avenue**
**BRISTOL**
**BB10 7ZL**

Telephone: Bristol (0791) 449214
Fax: (0791) 77081

## FACSIMILE TRANSMISSION COVER SHEET

To: _____

_____

Fax No: _____

From: _____

MICROPLUS LIMITED

_____

No of pages in this transmission: _____

Our fax no: 0791 77081

Message

PLEASE CONTACT US IF YOU DO NOT RECEIVE ALL THE PAGES

# OPERATION NOTES WORD PROCESSING

| FUNCTION | PROCEDURE |
|---|---|
|  |  |
|  |  |
|  |  |
|  |  |
|  |  |
|  |  |
|  |  |
|  |  |
|  |  |
|  |  |
|  |  |
|  |  |
|  |  |
|  |  |
|  |  |
|  |  |
|  |  |
|  |  |
|  |  |
|  |  |

# INDEX OF WORD-PROCESSING/COMPUTER* FILES

| AUTHOR | FILE NAME | CONTENTS | DATE |
|---|---|---|---|
| | | | |
| | | | |
| | | | |
| | | | |
| | | | |
| | | | |
| | | | |
| | | | |
| | | | |
| | | | |
| | | | |
| | | | |
| | | | |
| | | | |
| | | | |
| | | | |
| | | | |
| | | | |
| | | | |
| | | | |

* Delete as appropriate

# RECOMMENDED HOTELS

| Name/Address | Rating | Tel. no. | Bedrooms | Bath/Shower | Parking | Meals | Facilities |
|---|---|---|---|---|---|---|---|
| | | | | | | | |
| | | | | | | | |
| | | | | | | | |
| | | | | | | | |
| | | | | | | | |
| | | | | | | | |
| | | | | | | | |
| | | | | | | | |
| | | | | | | | |
| | | | | | | | |
| | | | | | | | |
| | | | | | | | |
| | | | | | | | |
| | | | | | | | |
| | | | | | | | |
| | | | | | | | |
| | | | | | | | |

# COMMITTEE ROOM BOOKING

| Date | Day | Room No | Time | Name | Purpose |
|------|-----|---------|------|------|---------|
|      |     |         |      |      |         |
|      |     |         |      |      |         |
|      |     |         |      |      |         |
|      |     |         |      |      |         |
|      |     |         |      |      |         |
|      |     |         |      |      |         |
|      |     |         |      |      |         |
|      |     |         |      |      |         |
|      |     |         |      |      |         |
|      |     |         |      |      |         |
|      |     |         |      |      |         |
|      |     |         |      |      |         |
|      |     |         |      |      |         |
|      |     |         |      |      |         |
|      |     |         |      |      |         |
|      |     |         |      |      |         |
|      |     |         |      |      |         |
|      |     |         |      |      |         |
|      |     |         |      |      |         |
|      |     |         |      |      |         |
|      |     |         |      |      |         |

## PETTY CASH BOOK

| Dr | | | | | | | | | | Cr |
|---|---|---|---|---|---|---|---|---|---|---|
| Received | Date | Details | Vo no. | Total paid out | Fares | Cleaning | Postage | Sundries | | |
| | | | | | | | | | | |
| | | | | | | | | | | |
| | | | | | | | | | | |
| | | | | | | | | | | |
| | | | | | | | | | | |
| | | | | | | | | | | |
| | | | | | | | | | | |
| | | | | | | | | | | |
| | | | | | | | | | | |
| | | | | | | | | | | |
| | | | | | | | | | | |
| | | | | | | | | | | |
| | | | | | | | | | | |

# REMITTANCE BOOK

| Date | Received from | Payment | Amount | Signature |
|------|---------------|---------|--------|-----------|
|      |               |         |        |           |

# SALES RECEIPT

| MICROPLUS LTD | | | |
|---|---|---|---|
| SALES RECEIPT | | 00231764 | |
| CUSTOMER NAME | | ACCOUNT NUMBER | |
| ADDRESS | | | |
| DATE          ASSISTANT | | CASH/CHEQUE/CREDIT CARD | |
| Number | Good Description | Unit Price | Total |
|  |  |  |  |
|  |  |  |  |
|  |  |  |  |
|  |  |  |  |
|  |  |  |  |
|  |  |  |  |
|  |  |  |  |
|  |  |  |  |
|  |  |  |  |
|  |  |  |  |
|  |  |  |  |
| Comments | | SUB TOTAL _____ | |
|  |  | VAT _____ | |
|  |  | TOTAL _____ | |

## CASHING-UP SUMMARY FORM

Date: _____

Assistant: _____

| | £ | P |

_____ x £50 Notes _____

_____ x £20 Notes _____

_____ x £10 Notes _____

_____ x £5 Notes _____

_____ x £1 Notes _____

_____ x £1 Coin _____

_____ x 50p Coin _____

_____ x 20p Coin _____

_____ x 10p Coin _____

_____ x 5p Coin _____

_____ x 2p Coin _____

_____ x 1p Coin _____

SUB TOTAL _____

ACCESS _____

CHEQUES _____

VOUCHERS _____

TOTAL _____

## Bank Giro Credit

Please complete in BLOCK CAPITALS      Date _____

| | |
|---|---|
| Date_____ | |
| (Till Stamp)   Fee | |
| Bank | |
| Branch | |
| Account | |
| Total Cash | |
| Total Cheques etc. | |
| £ | |
| Credit Counterfoil | |

Bank _____

Code No. [        ]

Branch where Account is held

Account name

Account Number [shaded][ ][ ][ ][ ][ ]    Fee    No. of Cheques

Paid in by: Name:

Address:

Reference:                    Please do not write or mark below this line

(Till Stamp)

£50
£20
£10
£ 5
£ 1
50p
20p
Silver
Bronze
Total Cash

Cheques P.O.'s etc.

£ [        ]

| | 70

---

| Cheques, PO's etc | | | | Cheques, PO's etc |
|---|---|---|---|---|
| | | | | |
| | | Cheques, PO's etc Total carried over | | |
| | | | | £ [        ] |

Total cheques, PO's etc carried over

---

| CASH RECEIPT LIST | | DATE .............................. | | |
|---|---|---|---|---|
| Received from | Cash | Cheque | Credit Card | Other |
| | | | | |
| | | | | |
| | | | | |
| | | | | |
| | | | | |
| | | | | |
| | | | | |
| TOTAL | | | | |

# Index